For Leah

About the Author

Bradford Tuckfield is a data scientist, consultant, and writer. He received a PhD in operations and information management from the Wharton School of the University of Pennsylvania and a BS in mathematics from Brigham Young University. He is the author of *Dive Into Algorithms* (No Starch Press, 2021) and co-author of *Applied Unsupervised Learning with R* (Packt, 2019). In addition to working as a data scientist and tech manager for top finance firms and startups, he has published his research in academic journals spanning math, business management, and medicine.

About the Technical Reviewer

As lead data scientist at Statistics Canada, Christian Ritter provided critical support to build the agency's data science division from the ground up, including the development of its data analytics platform. He has led projects leveraging natural language processing, computer vision, and recommender systems to serve a variety of clients. Christian is currently leading the agency's integration of MLOps. He is also the founder of OptimizeAI Consulting and works part-time as an independent data science consultant. When not taking on data science projects, he mentors students as part of postgraduate data science programs. Christian holds a PhD in computational astrophysics.

BRIEF CONTENTS

CONTENTS IN DETAIL

INDEX   249

ACKNOWLEDGMENTS

Many people made valuable contributions to this book. Professional mentors and colleagues helped me learn Python and data science and business and how all three can be put together. Included among these mentors are Seshu Edala and Dr. Sundaram Narayanan. Friends, including Sheng Lee, Ben Brown, Ee Chien Chua, and Drew Durtschi, have given valuable advice and encouragement that helped me during the writing process. Alex Freed at No Starch Press was unbelievably helpful throughout the process. Christian Ritter provided excellent suggestions and corrections as the technical reviewer. Emma Tuckfield provided excellent help in the editing process. Jayesh Thorat helped prepare much of the code and data in Chapter 8. My dear grandma Dr. Virgie Day provided lifelong encouragement to my intellectual development, and also inspiration for some of the ideas in Chapter 4; that chapter is dedicated to her. This book is dedicated to Leah, who has been my most important source of support and motivation.

INTRODUCTION

 Some years ago, Hal Varian, the chief economist at Google, confidently claimed that "the sexy job in the next 10 years will be statisticians." In the years since he made that claim, two things have happened: we've started calling statisticians *data scientists,* and the profession has seen enormous growth, both in demand for skilled practitioners and in salaries.

The supply of skilled data scientists has not kept up with the demand. Part of the aim of this book is to help solve that problem by introducing you to all of the main data science techniques being used at today's top firms. Explanations come with working, thoroughly explained code for every example, and we also provide ideas about how various data science methods are applied and how to find creative solutions to challenges. The book is meant to give anyone who reads it the skills to become a data scientist and take on the toughest and most exciting challenges being faced by businesses today.

But data science is more than just a career opportunity. It's a broad field combining elements of statistics, software development, math, economics, and computer science. It allows you to analyze data, detect differences between groups, investigate causes of mysterious phenomena, classify species, and perform experiments—in other words, to do science. Anyone who gets excited about discovering the truth about something hard to understand, or who wants to understand the world better, should feel excited about this aspect of data science.

In short, data science can offer something to nearly everyone. It can help you solve business problems and make your business more successful. It can make you more of a scientist, better able to observe and clearly understand the world around you. It can sharpen your analytical abilities and your coding skills. What's more, it can be fun. Becoming a data scientist means joining a field that's constantly growing and expanding, and this will mean that you need to expand your own knowledge and skills every day. If you feel up to the challenge of learning a wide range of difficult new skills that will help you work better, think better, and get a "sexy" job, read on.

Who Is This Book For?

While we explain each code snippet in everyday language to make the book digestible for someone with no Python experience and not much programming experience, someone who has at least some basic understanding of the fundamentals of programming—things like variable assignment, for loops, if...then statements, and function calls—will be the most prepared to benefit from the content in this book.

This book was written with the following groups in mind:

Aspiring data scientists

These days, it seems like everyone wants to be a data scientist, and every company wants to hire data scientists. This book will help a beginner who is just entering the job market get the skills they need to work in the data science field. It can also help people who already have other careers and want to jump laterally to become data scientists or start doing more data science in their current roles.

Students

This book is suitable for an introductory class on data science at the undergraduate level or for interested students to read independently.

Professionals

Several types of professionals, including project managers, executive-level leaders, developers, and businesspeople in general, can benefit from understanding what their data scientist colleagues do all day. Gaining the skills in this book can help them work with data scientists more fruitfully.

Interested amateurs

You don't have to read this book just for career advancement purposes. Data science is a new, exciting field, and any interested amateur will find this book fascinating and edifying.

About This Book

This book provides an introduction to all of the most common techniques used by data scientists at the world's top businesses. You will also learn about ways that data science can be applied creatively to problems in various industries. Here is a summary of the how the chapters are organized.

Chapter 1: Exploratory Data Analysis   Explains the first step of every data science problem: exploring data, including reading data in Python, calculating summary statistics, visualizing data, and uncovering common-sense insights

Chapter 2: Forecasting   Covers linear regression, a popular technique from statistics that can be used to determine relationships between quantitative variables and even to predict the future

Chapter 3: Group Comparisons   Explores hypothesis testing, the standard statistical method for comparing measurements of groups

Chapter 4: A/B Testing   Discusses how to use experiments to determine which business practices work best

Chapter 5: Binary Classification   Covers logistic regression, a simple machine learning technique for classification into two categories

Chapter 6: Supervised Learning   Dives into several machine learning methods for prediction, including decision trees, random forests, and neural networks

Chapter 7: Unsupervised Learning   Presents two methods for clustering, another type of machine learning that can be used to find natural groups in unlabeled data

Chapter 8: Web Scraping   Explains methods for automatically downloading data from public-facing websites

Chapter 9: Recommendation Systems   Discusses how to build a system that can automatically recommend products to customers

Chapter 10: Natural Language Processing   Explores an advanced method that converts text to quantitative vectors that can be used for a variety of data science analyses

Chapter 11: Data Science in Other Languages   Covers both R and SQL, two other languages that are often used for data science applications

Setting Up the Environment

We'll implement the algorithms described in this book by using the Python language. Python is free and open source, and it runs on every major platform. You can use the following steps to install Python on Windows, macOS, and Linux.

Windows

To install Python on Windows, do the following:

1. Open the page dedicated to the latest version of Python for Windows: *https://www.python.org/downloads/windows/* (make sure you include the final slash).
2. Click the link for the Python release you want to download. To download the most recent release, click the link **Latest Python 3 Release - 3.X.Y**, where *3.X.Y* is the latest version number, like 3.10.4. The code in this book was tested on Python 3.8 and should work with later versions. If you're interested in downloading an older version, scroll down on this page to the Stable Releases section to find a release you prefer.
3. The link you clicked in step 2 takes you to a page dedicated to your chosen Python release. In the Files section, click the **Windows installer (64-bit)** link.
4. The link in step 3 downloads an *.exe* file to your computer. This is an installer file; double-click it to open it. It will execute the installation process automatically. Check the **Add Python 3.X to PATH** box, where *X* is the release number of the installer you downloaded, like 10. After that, click **Install Now** and choose the default options.
5. When you see the Setup was successful message, click **Close** to complete the installation process.

A new application is now on your computer. Its name is Python 3.*X*, where *X* is the version of Python 3 that you installed. In the Windows search bar, type **Python**, and click the application that appears. This will open a Python console. You can enter Python commands in this console, and they'll run there.

macOS

To install Python on macOS, do the following:

1. Open the page dedicated to the latest version of Python for macOS: *https://www.python.org/downloads/mac-osx/* (make sure you include the final slash).
2. Click the link for the Python release you want to download. To download the most recent release, click the link **Latest Python 3 Release - 3.X.Y**,

where 3.*X.Y* is the latest version number, like 3.10.4. The code in this book was tested on Python 3.8 and should work with later versions. If you're interested in downloading an older version, scroll down on this page to the Stable Releases section to find a release you prefer.

3. The link you clicked in step 2 takes you to a page dedicated to the latest Python release. In the Files section, click the **macOS 64-bit installer** link.

4. The link in step 3 downloads a *.pkg* file to your computer. This is an installer file; double-click it to open it. It will execute the installation process automatically. Choose the default options.

5. The installer will create a folder on your computer called **Python 3.*X***, where *X* is the number of the Python release you installed. In this folder, double-click the **IDLE icon**. This will open the **Python 3.*X.Y* Shell**, where 3.*X.Y* is your version number. This is a Python console where you can run any Python commands.

Linux

To install Python on Linux, do the following:

1. Determine which package manager your version of Linux uses. Two common examples of package managers are Yum and APT.

2. Open the Linux console (also called the *terminal*) and execute the following two commands:

```
> sudo apt-get update
> sudo apt-get install python3.11
```

If you are using Yum or another package manager, replace both instances of apt-get in these two lines with yum or the name of your package manager. Likewise, if you want to install a different version of Python, replace 3.11 (the latest version number at the time of this writing) with any other release number, like 3.8, one of the versions used to test the code in this book. To see the latest version of Python, go to *https://www.python.org/downloads/source/*. There, you will see a **Latest Python 3 Release - Python 3.*X.Y*** link, where 3.*X.Y* is a release number; use the first two numbers (for example, 3 and 11) in the previous installation command.

3. Run Python by executing the following command in the Linux console:

```
> python3
```

The Python console opens in the Linux console window. You can enter Python commands here.

Installing Packages with Python

When you install Python using the steps in the previous section, you're installing the *Python standard library*, or in more colloquial terms, *base Python*. Base Python enables you to run simple Python code and contains standard capabilities that are built into the Python language. Base Python is powerful, and you can do many remarkable things with it. But it can't do everything, and this is why kind, talented people in the Python community create Python packages.

Python *packages* (also called Python *libraries*) are add-ons to base Python that provide extra capabilities not present in base Python. For example, you may find that you have some data stored in Microsoft Excel format, and you may want to write Python code that will read this Excel data. There's no straightforward way to do this in base Python, but a package called *pandas* enables you to read Excel files in Python quite easily.

To use the pandas package, or any other Python package, you'll need to install it. A few packages are installed by default when you install base Python, but most packages need to be installed manually. To install any Python package manually, you'll need Python's standard package installation tool, pip.

If you have base Python installed, installing pip is straightforward. First, you will need to download a Python script from *https://bootstrap.pypa.io/get-pip.py*. As the name of this script suggests, it's a script that will help you get pip. Now, you will need to run this script. The way you run this script will depend on the operating system you're using:

- If you're using Windows, you need to open the command prompt. You can do this by clicking the Start button and entering **cmd** in the search bar. The command prompt program will appear as a suggestion in the Start menu, and you can click this to open the command prompt.

- If you're using macOS, you need to open the terminal. To open the terminal, you can open the Finder, open the */Applications/Utilities* folder, and then double-click **Terminal**.

- If you're using Linux, you need to open the terminal. Most Linux distributions have a shortcut to open the terminal available on the desktop by default.

After opening the command prompt (in Windows) or the terminal (in macOS or Linux), you need to run the following command:

```
> python3 get-pip.py
```

This will install pip on your computer. If you get an error when you run this command, it's possible that your *get-pip.py* file is stored in a location that Python is having trouble finding. Being more specific about the location of your files often helps, so you can try a command like the following instead:

```
> python3 C:/Users/AtticusFinch/Documents/get-pip.py
```

Here, we've specified a filepath (*C:/Users/AtticusFinch/Documents/get-pip.py*) that tells Python where to look for the *get-pip.py* file. You should alter this filepath so it matches the location of the *get-pip.py* file on your own computer; for example, you probably need to change AtticusFinch to your own name.

After you've installed pip, you'll be able to use it to install any other Python packages. For example, if you want to install the pandas package, you can install it with the following command:

```
> pip install pandas
```

You can replace pandas with the name of any other Python package you want to install. After installing pandas or any other Python package, you'll be able to use it in your Python scripts. We'll go over more details about how to use packages in Python in Chapter 1.

Other Tools

The previous sections contain details on how to install Python and how to manually install Python packages. If you can do those two things, you will be able to run all the code in this book.

Some Python users prefer to use other tools to run Python code. For example, a popular tool called Anaconda is also free to use and allows you to run Python code for data science. Anaconda includes base Python, plus many popular packages and other capabilities. If you'd like to download and use Anaconda for free, you can visit its web page at *https://www.anaconda.com/ products/distribution*. You may find that you like it, and you'll be able to use it to run any code in this book, but it's not required.

Project Jupyter provides another popular set of tools for running Python code. You can visit its website at *https://jupyter.org/* to learn about its most popular tools: JupyterLab and Jupyter Notebook. These tools allow users to run Python code in environments that are highly readable, interactive, shareable, and user-friendly. All of the Python code in this book was tested with Jupyter, but neither Jupyter nor Anaconda is required to run the code in this book: only base Python and pip (as described in the previous sections) are needed.

Summary

Data science can give you abilities that feel like magic: the ability to predict the future, the ability to multiply profits, the ability to automatically collect huge datasets, the ability to turn a word into a number, and more. Learning to do all these things well is not easy, and it takes serious study to make it to the most advanced level. But the difficulty of learning data science can lead to great rewards, and if you master the skills in this book, you can succeed in a data science career and also have a lot of fun. This book is an introduction to the main ideas of data science and how they're applied in business—it will get you started on the journey to becoming an expert data scientist in any field you choose.

1

EXPLORATORY DATA ANALYSIS

This is a data science book, so let's start by diving into some data. This is something you should get used to: the first step of every data science problem is exploring your data. Looking closely at its minutest details will help you understand it better and give you clearer ideas for next steps and more sophisticated analyses. It will also help you catch any errors or problems with your data as early as possible. These first steps in the data science process are referred to as *exploratory data analysis*.

We'll start this first chapter by introducing a business scenario and describing how data might be used to better run a business. We'll talk about reading data in Python and checking basic summary statistics. We'll then introduce some Python tools to create plots of data. We'll go over simple exploratory analyses we can perform and talk about the questions they can answer for us. Finally, we'll close with a discussion of how the analyses can help us improve business practices. The simple analyses that we'll do in this chapter are the same types of analyses that you can do as a first step of working on any data science problem you ever encounter. Let's begin!

Your First Day as CEO

Imagine you receive a job offer to be the CEO of a company in Washington, DC, that provides bicycles that people can rent for short periods to ride around the city. Even though you don't have any experience running bike-sharing companies, you accept the offer.

You show up to work on your first day and think about your business goals as a CEO. Some of the goals you might think about could be related to issues like customer satisfaction, employee morale, brand recognition, market share maximization, cost reduction, or revenue growth. How can you decide which of these goals you should pursue first, and how should you pursue it? For example, think about increasing customer satisfaction. Before focusing on that goal, you'd need to find out whether your customers are satisfied and, if not, discover what's making satisfaction suffer and how it can be improved. Or suppose you're more interested in working to increase revenue. You would need to know what your revenue is right now before figuring out how it could be increased. In other words, you won't be able to choose your initial focus until you better understand your company.

If you want to understand your company, you need data. You might try to look at charts and reports that summarize your company's data, but no prepared report can tell you as much as you'll learn by diving into the data yourself.

Finding Patterns in Datasets

Let's look at some data from a real bike-sharing service and imagine that this is data from your company. You can download this data from *https://bradfordtuckfield.com/hour.csv*. (This file is in a special format called *.csv*, which we'll talk more about soon.) You can open this file in a spreadsheet editor like Microsoft Excel or LibreOffice Calc; you should see something that looks like Figure 1-1.

NOTE *The original source of the bike-sharing data is Capital Bikeshare (*https://ride.capitalbikeshare.com/system-data*). The data was compiled and augmented by Hadi Fanaee-T and Joao Gama and posted online by Mark Kaghazgarian.*

instant	dteday	season	yr	mnth	hr	holiday	weekday	workingday	weathersit	temp	atemp	hum	windspeed	casual	registered	count
1	2011-01-01	1	0	1	0	0	6	0	1	0.24	0.2879	0.81	0	3	13	16
2	2011-01-01	1	0	1	1	0	6	0	1	0.22	0.2727	0.8	0	8	32	40
3	2011-01-01	1	0	1	2	0	6	0	1	0.22	0.2727	0.8	0	5	27	32
4	2011-01-01	1	0	1	3	0	6	0	1	0.24	0.2879	0.75	0	3	10	13
5	2011-01-01	1	0	1	4	0	6	0	1	0.24	0.2879	0.75	0	0	1	1
6	2011-01-01	1	0	1	5	0	6	0	2	0.24	0.2576	0.75	0.0896	0	1	1
7	2011-01-01	1	0	1	6	0	6	0	1	0.22	0.2727	0.8	0	2	0	2
8	2011-01-01	1	0	1	7	0	6	0	1	0.2	0.2576	0.86	0	1	2	3
9	2011-01-01	1	0	1	8	0	6	0	1	0.24	0.2879	0.75	0	1	7	8
10	2011-01-01	1	0	1	9	0	6	0	1	0.32	0.3485	0.76	0	8	6	14
11	2011-01-01	1	0	1	10	0	6	0	1	0.38	0.3939	0.76	0.2537	12	24	36
12	2011-01-01	1	0	1	11	0	6	0	1	0.36	0.3333	0.81	0.2836	26	30	56
13	2011-01-01	1	0	1	12	0	6	0	1	0.42	0.4242	0.77	0.2836	29	55	84
14	2011-01-01	1	0	1	13	0	6	0	2	0.46	0.4545	0.72	0.2985	47	47	94
15	2011-01-01	1	0	1	14	0	6	0	2	0.46	0.4545	0.72	0.2836	35	71	106
16	2011-01-01	1	0	1	15	0	6	0	2	0.44	0.4394	0.77	0.2985	40	70	110
17	2011-01-01	1	0	1	16	0	6	0	2	0.42	0.4242	0.82	0.2985	41	52	93
18	2011-01-01	1	0	1	17	0	6	0	2	0.44	0.4394	0.82	0.2836	15	52	67
19	2011-01-01	1	0	1	18	0	6	0	3	0.42	0.4242	0.88	0.2537	9	26	35
20	2011-01-01	1	0	1	19	0	6	0	3	0.42	0.4242	0.88	0.2537	6	31	37
21	2011-01-01	1	0	1	20	0	6	0	2	0.4	0.4091	0.87	0.2537	11	25	36
22	2011-01-01	1	0	1	21	0	6	0	2	0.4	0.4091	0.87	0.194	3	31	34
23	2011-01-01	1	0	1	22	0	6	0	2	0.4	0.4091	0.94	0.2239	11	17	28

Figure 1-1: Bike-sharing data, viewed in a spreadsheet

This dataset is no different from many other datasets that you've probably seen before: a rectangular array of rows and columns. In this dataset, each row represents information about a particular hour between midnight on January 1, 2011, and 11:59 PM on December 31, 2012—more than 17,000 hours total. The rows are arranged in order, so the first few rows give us information about the first few hours of 2011, and the last few rows relate to the last few hours of 2012.

Each column contains a particular metric that has been measured for each of these hours. For example, the windspeed column gives us hourly measurements of wind speed at a particular weather-recording station in Washington, DC. Notice that this measurement isn't in familiar units like miles per hour. Instead, the measurements have been transformed so that they're always between 0 and 1; all we need to know is that 1 represents a fast wind speed and 0 represents no wind.

If you look at the first few rows, you'll see that the windspeed value is 0 for each of these rows, meaning there was no measured wind for the first few hours of the bike-sharing service's existence. On the seventh row (counting the heading as the first row), you can see that there was finally some wind, and its measured speed was 0.0896. If you look at the hr column, you can see that this wind was recorded when hr = 5, or at 5 AM. We know that this row gives us information about January 1 because the dteday column on the seventh row has the value 2011-01-01.

Just by looking at a few values in the data, we can already start to tell a story, albeit an unexciting one: a still New Year's night that turned into a slightly less still New Year's morning. If we want to know some stories about the bike-sharing company and its performance instead of just the weather, we'll have to look at other, more relevant columns.

The columns with the most important information are the last three: casual, registered, and count. These columns indicate the number of people who used your company's bikes each hour. People who register with your service to get discounts and benefits are registered users, and their bike use is recorded in the registered column. But people can also use your bikes without registering, and their bike use is recorded in the casual column. The sum of the casual and registered columns is the total count of users during each hour, and it's recorded in the count column.

Now that you're familiar with some of the more relevant columns in this dataset, you can learn a great deal just by glancing at their numbers. Looking at the first 20 or so hours shown in Figure 1-1, for example, you can see that in most hours, you have more registered users than casual users (higher values in the registered column than the casual column). This is just a simple numeric fact, but as the CEO, you should think through its implications for your business. Having more registered than casual users might mean that you're doing well at convincing people to register, but it also might mean that using your service casually without registering isn't as easy as it should be. You'll have to think about which segment of customers is more important for you to target: the regular, registered users, like daily commuters, or the casual, infrequent users, like sightseeing tourists.

We can look more closely at the daily patterns of casual and registered users to see if we can learn more about them. Let's look at the hours shown in Figure 1-1 again. We see that casual users are sparse until the afternoon of the first day and peak around 1 PM. Registered users are relatively numerous even at 1 AM of the first day and peak at 2 PM. The differences between the behavior of registered and casual users are small but could be meaningful. For example, they could indicate demographic differences between these groups. This, in turn, could require using different marketing strategies targeted to each group.

Consider what we've done already: just by looking at a few columns of the first 24 rows of our data, we've already learned several important things about the company and started to get some business ideas. Data science has a reputation for requiring arcane knowledge about sophisticated math and computer science, but simply glancing at a dataset, thinking a little, and applying common sense can go a long way toward improving any business scenario.

Using .csv Files to Review and Store Data

Let's look even more closely at our data. If you open the data file (*hour.csv*) in a spreadsheet editor, it will look like Figure 1-1. However, you can also open this file in a text editor like Notepad (if you're using Windows) or TextEdit (if you're using macOS) or GNU Emacs or gedit (if you're using Linux). When you open this file in a text editor, it will look like Figure 1-2.

```
  1 instant,dteday,season,yr,mnth,hr,holiday,weekday,workingday,weathersit,temp,atemp,hum,windspeed,casual,registered,count
  2 1,2011-01-01,1,0,1,0,0,6,0,1,0.24,0.2879,0.81,0,3,13,16
  3 2,2011-01-01,1,0,1,1,0,6,0,1,0.22,0.2727,0.8,0,8,32,40
  4 3,2011-01-01,1,0,1,2,0,6,0,1,0.22,0.2727,0.8,0,5,27,32
  5 4,2011-01-01,1,0,1,3,0,6,0,1,0.24,0.2879,0.75,0,3,10,13
  6 5,2011-01-01,1,0,1,4,0,6,0,1,0.24,0.2879,0.75,0,0,1,1
  7 6,2011-01-01,1,0,1,5,0,6,0,2,0.24,0.2576,0.75,0.0896,0,1,1
  8 7,2011-01-01,1,0,1,6,0,6,0,1,0.22,0.2727,0.8,0,2,0,2
  9 8,2011-01-01,1,0,1,7,0,6,0,1,0.2,0.2576,0.86,0,1,2,3
 10 9,2011-01-01,1,0,1,8,0,6,0,1,0.24,0.2879,0.75,0,1,7,8
 11 10,2011-01-01,1,0,1,9,0,6,0,1,0.32,0.3485,0.76,0,8,6,14
 12 11,2011-01-01,1,0,1,10,0,6,0,1,0.38,0.3939,0.76,0.2537,12,24,36
 13 12,2011-01-01,1,0,1,11,0,6,0,1,0.36,0.3333,0.81,0.2836,26,30,56
 14 13,2011-01-01,1,0,1,12,0,6,0,1,0.42,0.4242,0.77,0.2836,29,55,84
 15 14,2011-01-01,1,0,1,13,0,6,0,2,0.46,0.4545,0.72,0.2985,47,47,94
 16 15,2011-01-01,1,0,1,14,0,6,0,2,0.46,0.4545,0.72,0.2836,35,71,106
 17 16,2011-01-01,1,0,1,15,0,6,0,2,0.44,0.4394,0.77,0.2985,40,70,110
 18 17,2011-01-01,1,0,1,16,0,6,0,2,0.42,0.4242,0.82,0.2985,41,52,93
 19 18,2011-01-01,1,0,1,17,0,6,0,2,0.44,0.4394,0.82,0.2836,15,52,67
 20 19,2011-01-01,1,0,1,18,0,6,0,3,0.42,0.4242,0.88,0.2537,9,26,35
 21 20,2011-01-01,1,0,1,19,0,6,0,3,0.42,0.4242,0.88,0.2537,6,31,37
 22 21,2011-01-01,1,0,1,20,0,6,0,2,0.4,0.4091,0.87,0.2537,11,25,36
 23 22,2011-01-01,1,0,1,21,0,6,0,2,0.4,0.4091,0.87,0.194,3,31,34
 24 23,2011-01-01,1,0,1,22,0,6,0,2,0.4,0.4091,0.94,0.2239,11,17,28
 25 24,2011-01-01,1,0,1,23,0,6,0,2,0.46,0.4545,0.88,0.2985,15,24,39
 26 25,2011-01-02,1,0,1,0,0,0,0,2,0.46,0.4545,0.88,0.2985,4,13,17
 27 26,2011-01-02,1,0,1,1,0,0,0,2,0.44,0.4394,0.94,0.2537,1,16,17
 28 27,2011-01-02,1,0,1,2,0,0,0,2,0.42,0.4242,1,0.2836,1,8,9
 29 28,2011-01-02,1,0,1,3,0,0,0,2,0.46,0.4545,0.94,0.194,2,4,6
 30 29,2011-01-02,1,0,1,4,0,0,0,2,0.46,0.4545,0.94,0.194,2,1,3
 31 30,2011-01-02,1,0,1,6,0,0,0,3,0.42,0.4242,0.77,0.2985,0,2,2
 32 31,2011-01-02,1,0,1,7,0,0,0,2,0.4,0.4091,0.76,0.194,0,1,1
 33 32,2011-01-02,1,0,1,8,0,0,0,3,0.4,0.4091,0.71,0.2239,0,8,8
```

Figure 1-2: Bike-sharing data viewed as raw text

This raw data (that is, every single text character) constitutes our *hour.csv* file, without the alignment of straight columns you'd see in a spreadsheet. Notice the many commas. This file's extension, *.csv*, is short for *comma-separated values* because the numeric values in each row are separated from each other by commas.

When you use a spreadsheet editor to open a *.csv* file, the editor will attempt to interpret every comma as a boundary between spreadsheet cells so that it can display the data in straight, aligned rows and columns. But the data itself is not stored that way: it's just raw text with rows of values, with each value separated from other values by commas.

The simplicity of *.csv* files means that they can be easily created, easily opened by many types of programs, and easily changed. That's why data scientists commonly store their data in *.csv* format.

Displaying Data with Python

Using Python will allow us to do more sophisticated analyses than are possible in text editors and spreadsheet programs. It will also allow us to automate our processes and run analyses more quickly. We can easily open *.csv* files in Python. The following three lines of Python code will read the *hour.csv* file into your Python session and display its first five rows:

```
import pandas as pd
hour=pd.read_csv('hour.csv')
print(hour.head())
```

We'll look more closely at the output of this snippet later. For now, let's look at the code itself. Its purpose is to read and display our data. The second line reads the data by using the read_csv() method. A *method* is a unit of code that performs a single, well-defined function. As its name suggests, read_csv() is specifically designed to read data that's stored in *.csv* files. After you run this line, the hour variable will contain all the data in the *hour.csv* file; then you can access this data in Python.

On the third line, we use the print() function to display (print) our data onscreen. We could change the third line to print(hour) to see the entire dataset printed out. But datasets can be very large and hard to read all at once. Therefore, we add the head() method because it returns only the dataset's first five rows.

Both read_csv() and head() can be very useful to us. But they're not part of the *Python standard library*—the standard Python capabilities installed by default. They are instead part of a package, a third-party body of code that's optional to install and use in Python scripts.

These two methods are part of a popular package called *pandas*, which contains code for working with data. That's why the first line of the previous snippet is import pandas as pd: this *imports*, or brings in, the pandas package so we can access it in our Python session. When we write as pd, this gives the package an *alias*, so every time we want to access a pandas capability, we can write pd instead of the full name pandas. So when we write pd.read_csv(), we're accessing the read_csv() method that's part of the pandas package.

If you get an error when you run import pandas as pd, it's possible that pandas is not installed on your computer. (Packages need to be installed before you can import them.) To install pandas, or any other Python package, you should use the standard Python package installer, called pip. You can find instructions for how to install pip and use it to install Python packages like pandas in this book's introduction. Throughout this book, every time you import a package, you should make sure that you've first installed it on your computer by using pip.

You might get another error when you run this snippet. One of the most common errors will occur when Python isn't able to find the *hour.csv* file. If that happens, Python will print out an error report. The last line of the error report might say this:

```
FileNotFoundError: [Errno 2] No such file or directory: 'hour.csv'
```

Even if you're not a Python expert, you can surmise what this means: Python tried to read the *hour.csv* file but wasn't able to find it. This can be a frustrating error, but one that's possible to resolve. First, make sure that you've downloaded the *hour.csv* file and that it has the name *hour.csv* on your computer. The filename on your computer needs to exactly match the filename in your Python code.

If the name *hour.csv* is spelled correctly in your Python code (entirely with lowercase letters), the problem is probably with the file's location. Remember that every file on your computer has a unique filepath that specifies exactly where you need to navigate to get to it. A filepath might look like this:

```
C:\Users\DonQuixote\Documents\hour.csv
```

This filepath is in the format used in the Windows operating system. If you're using Windows, try to make sure that your directories and filenames don't use any special characters (like characters from non-English alphabets) because filepaths with special characters can lead to errors. The following is another example of a filepath, one that's in the format used by Unix-style operating systems (including macOS and Linux):

```
/home/DonQuixote/Documents/hour.csv
```

You'll notice that Windows filepaths look different from macOS and Linux filepaths. In macOS and Linux, we use forward slashes exclusively, and we start with a slash (/) instead of a drive name like C:\. When you read a file into Python, the most straightforward way to avoid an error is to specify the full filepath, as follows:

```
import pandas as pd
hour=pd.read_csv('/home/DonQuixote/Documents/hour.csv')
print(hour.head())
```

When you run this snippet, you can replace the filepath in the read_csv() method with the filepath on your own computer. When you run the previous snippet, with the filepath correctly specified to match the location of *hour.csv* on your computer, you should get the following output:

```
   instant    dteday  season  yr  ...  windspeed  casual  registered  count
0        1  2011-01-01      1   0  ...        0.0       3          13     16
1        2  2011-01-01      1   0  ...        0.0       8          32     40
2        3  2011-01-01      1   0  ...        0.0       5          27     32
3        4  2011-01-01      1   0  ...        0.0       3          10     13
4        5  2011-01-01      1   0  ...        0.0       0           1      1

[5 rows x 17 columns]
```

This output shows the first five rows of our data. You can see that the data is arranged by column, in a way that looks similar to our spreadsheet output. Just as in Figure 1-1, each row contains numeric values related to a particular hour of the bike-sharing company's history.

Here, we see ellipses in place of some columns so that it's easier to read onscreen and not too hard to read or copy and paste into text documents. (You might see all the columns instead of ellipses—your display will depend on the details of how Python and pandas are configured on your computer.) Just as we did when we opened the file in a spreadsheet editor, we can start looking at some of these numbers to discover stories about the company's history and get ideas for running the business.

Calculating Summary Statistics

Besides just looking at our data, quantifying its important attributes will be helpful. We can start by calculating the mean of one of the columns, as follows:

```
print(hour['count'].mean())
```

Here, we access the count column of our hour dataset by using square brackets ([]) and the column name (count). If you run print(hour['count']) alone, you'll see the entire column printed to your screen. But we want just the *mean* of the column, not the column itself, so we add the mean() method—yet another capability provided by pandas. We see that the mean is about 189.46. This is interesting to know from a business perspective; it's a rough measurement of the size of the business over the two years covered by the data.

In addition to calculating the mean, we could calculate other important metrics as follows:

```
print(hour['count'].median())
print(hour['count'].std())
print(hour['registered'].min())
print(hour['registered'].max())
```

Here, we calculate the median of the count column by using the median() method. We also use the std() method to calculate a standard deviation of our count variable. (You may already know that a *standard deviation* is a measurement of how far spread out a set of numbers is. It's useful to help us understand the amount of variation that exists in ridership counts between hours in our data.) We also calculate the minimum and maximum of the registered variable, using the min() and max() methods, respectively. The number of registered users ranges from 0 to 886, and this tells us the hourly record you've set, and the record you'll need to break if you want your business to do better than it ever has before.

These simple calculations are called *summary statistics*, and they're useful to check for every dataset you ever work with. Checking the summary statistics of a dataset can help you better understand your data and, in this case, help you better understand your business.

As simple as these summary statistics might seem, many CEOs, if put on the spot, couldn't even tell you their company's exact number of customers. Knowing simple things like the mean number of customers on any hour of any day can help you understand how big your company is and how much room you have to grow.

These summary statistics can also be combined with other information to tell us even more. For example, if you look up how much your company charges for one hour of bike usage, you can multiply that by the mean of the count column to get your total revenue over the two years covered by the data.

You can check summary statistics manually by using pandas methods like mean() and median() as we did previously. But another method makes summary statistics easy to check:

```
print(hour.describe())
```

Here, we use the describe() method to check the summary statistics of all variables in the dataset. The output looks like this:

	instant	season	...	registered	count
count	17379.0000	17379.000000	...	17379.000000	17379.000000
mean	8690.0000	2.501640	...	153.786869	189.463088
std	5017.0295	1.106918	...	151.357286	181.387599
min	1.0000	1.000000	...	0.000000	1.000000
25%	4345.5000	2.000000	...	34.000000	40.000000
50%	8690.0000	3.000000	...	115.000000	142.000000
75%	13034.5000	3.000000	...	220.000000	281.000000
max	17379.0000	4.000000	...	886.000000	977.000000

```
[8 rows x 16 columns]
```

You can see that describe() provides an entire table to us, and this table contains several useful metrics, including the mean, minimum, and maximum of each of our variables. The output of describe() also contains percentiles. The 25% row, for example, contains the 25th percentile of each variable in the hour data. We can see that the 25th percentile of the count variable is 40, meaning that 25 percent of the hours in our dataset had 40 users or fewer, while 75 percent had more than 40 users.

The table that we get from the describe() method is also useful to help us check for problems with the data. It's common for datasets to contain major errors that can be spotted in the output of describe(). For example, if you run the describe() method on a dataset of people and see that their average age is 200, your data has errors. This may sound obvious, but that exact error (average ages greater than 200) was recently found in a well-known research paper published in a top academic journal—if only those researchers had used describe()! You should look at the output of describe() for every dataset you work with to make sure that all the values are at least plausible. If you find average ages over 200, or other data that doesn't look credible, you'll have to locate the problems in the data and fix them.

At this stage, we can already start to use what we've learned from the data to get ideas for improving the business. For example, we've seen that in the first 24 hours of our data, rider numbers at night are much lower than rider numbers during the day. We've also seen a wide variation in the hourly count of users: 25 percent of hours have fewer than 40 riders, but one hour had 886 riders. As the CEO, you may want more hours that have closer to 886 riders and fewer hours that have fewer than 40 riders.

You could pursue this goal in many ways. For example, you might lower prices during the night to get more customers at that time and therefore have fewer hours with low ridership. Just through simple exploration, you can continue to learn from the data and get ideas for improving the business.

Analyzing Subsets of Data

We've checked summary statistics related to the full dataset, and then considered offering lower prices at night to increase nighttime ridership. If we really want to pursue this idea, we should check summary statistics related to just the nighttime.

Nighttime Data

We can start by using the loc() method:

```
print(hour.loc[3,'count'])
```

This loc() method allows us to specify a subset of our full data. When we use loc(), we specify the subset we want to select by using square brackets with this pattern: [<row>,<column>]. Here, we specify [3,'count'], indicating that we want to select row 3 of our data and the count column. The output we get from this is 13, and if you look at the data in Figure 1-1 or Figure 1-2, you can see that this is correct.

One important thing to point out here is that the standard practice in Python, as well as in pandas, is to use *zero-based indexing*. We count from zero, so if our dataset has four rows, we label them row 0, row 1, row 2, and row 3. The fourth row of your data is called row 3, or we say its index is 3. Similarly, the third row of your data has index 2, the second row has index 1, and the first row has index 0. That's why when we run print(hour .loc[3,'count']), we get 13, which is the fourth value stored in the data (the value from the row with index 3), instead of 32, which is the third value stored in the data (the value from the row with index 2). Zero-based indexing doesn't feel natural to many people, but with experience, you can get used to it and feel comfortable with it.

In the previous snippet, we looked at a subset that consists of a single number (the count from a single row and a single column). But you may want to know about a subset that consists of multiple rows or multiple columns. By using a colon (:), we can specify a range of rows we want to look at:

```
print(hour.loc[2:4,'registered'])
```

In this snippet, we specify that we want values of the registered variable. By specifying 2:4 in the square brackets, we indicate that we want all the rows between row 2 and row 4, so we get three numbers as output: 27, 10, and 1. If you look at these rows, you can see that these observations are related to the hours 2 AM, 3 AM, and 4 AM. Instead of printing out all the data, we're printing out just three rows. Since we are printing out only a subset, we can call this process *subsetting*—selecting subsets of data. This can be useful when exploring and analyzing data.

Instead of looking at a few adjacent rows at a time, let's look at all the nighttime observations in our data. We can use logical conditions with the loc() method:

```
print(hour.loc[hour['hr']<5,'registered'].mean())
```

This snippet uses loc() to access a subset of the data, just as we've done before. However, instead of specifying particular row numbers, it specifies a logical condition: hour['hr']<5, meaning that it will select every row in our data for which the value of the hr variable is less than 5. This will give us a subset of the data corresponding to the earliest hours of the morning (midnight to 4 AM). We can specify multiple conditions for more complex logic. For example, we can check specifically for ridership counts on colder early mornings or warmer early mornings:

```
print(hour.loc[(hour['hr']<5) & (hour['temp']<.50),'count'].mean())
print(hour.loc[(hour['hr']<5) & (hour['temp']>.50),'count'].mean())
```

Here, we specify multiple logical conditions, separated by an & character to mean *and*, which indicates that two things must be true simultaneously. The first line selects rows that have an hr value less than 5 *and* a temp value less than 0.50. In this dataset, the temp variable records temperatures, but not on a Fahrenheit or Celsius scale that we're familiar with. Instead, it uses a special scale that puts all temperatures between 0 and 1, where 0 represents a very cold temperature, and 1 represents a very warm temperature. Whenever you're working with data, it's important to make sure you know exactly which units are used for each variable. We specify hour['temp']<.50 to select hours with colder temperatures and hour['temp']>.50 to select hours with warmer temperatures. Together, these lines allow us to compare average ridership on cold early mornings with average ridership on warm early mornings.

We can also use the | symbol to signify *or*. This could be useful in an example like this:

```
print(hour.loc[(hour['temp']>0.5) | (hour['hum']>0.5),'count'].mean())
```

This line selects the mean readership count for rows with either high temperatures *or* high humidity—both aren't required. Being able to select these complex conditions could help you choose ways to improve ridership during hours with uncomfortable weather.

Seasonal Data

A nighttime discount is not the only possible strategy for improving ridership and revenue. You could also consider specials during certain seasons or at certain times of the year. In our data, the season variable records 1 for winter, 2 for spring, 3 for summer, and 4 for fall. We can use the groupby() method to find the mean number of users during each of these seasons:

```
print(hour.groupby(['season'])['count'].mean())
```

Much of this snippet should look familiar. We're using print() to look at metrics related to the hour data. We use the mean() method, indicating that we're looking at averages. And we use ['count'] to access the count column of the data. So it's already clear that we're going to be looking at average ridership counts in our hour data.

The only new part is groupby(['season']). This is a method that splits the data into groups—in this case, one group for each unique value that appears in the season column. The output shows us the mean ridership counts for each individual season:

```
season
1    111.114569
2    208.344069
3    236.016237
4    198.868856
Name: count, dtype: float64
```

Interpreting this output is straightforward: in the first season (winter), average ridership per hour is about 111.115; in the second season (spring), average ridership per hour is about 208.344; and so on. A definite seasonal pattern exists: higher ridership in the spring and summer seasons, and lower ridership in the fall and winter. The groupby() method can also group on multiple columns, as follows:

```
print(hour.groupby(['season','holiday'])['count'].mean())
```

The result is the following:

```
season  holiday
1       0          112.685875
        1           72.042683
2       0          208.428472
        1          204.552083
3       0          235.976818
        1          237.822917
4       0          199.965998
        1          167.722222
Name: count, dtype: float64
```

Here, we specify two columns to group on: season and holiday. This splits our hourly data into the four individual seasons, and then splits each season into holidays (denoted by 1s) and non-holidays (denoted by 0s). It shows us average ridership counts on holidays and non-holidays separately for each season. The result is that we can see the differences between holidays and non-holidays seasonally. It seems like holidays in the colder seasons have ridership that's lower than that on non-holidays, and holidays in the warmer seasons have ridership that's roughly equal to that on non-holidays. Understanding these differences can help you make decisions about how to run the business and might give you ideas about strategies you can pursue during different seasons or different holidays.

This dataset is big, and there's no end to the different ways it can be examined. We've begun to look at a few subsets and started to get a few ideas. You should do much more: examine subsets related to all the columns and explore many perspectives on the data. Even without doing advanced statistics and machine learning, you can learn a great deal and get many useful ideas.

Visualizing Data with Matplotlib

Summary statistics are valuable and useful for exploration. However, there's an extremely important part of exploratory data analysis that we haven't done yet: *plotting*, or visualizing the data in organized charts.

Drawing and Displaying a Simple Plot

You should plot your data early and often every time you're doing data analysis. We'll use a popular plotting package called *Matplotlib*. We can draw a simple plot of our data as follows:

```
import matplotlib.pyplot as plt
fig, ax = plt.subplots(figsize=(10, 6))
ax.scatter(x = hour['instant'], y = hour['count'])
plt.show()
```

Here, we import the Matplotlib package, giving it the alias plt. Next, we create a figure, called fig, and an axis, called ax. The figure, fig, will contain all the information about whatever plot or group of plots we draw. The axis, ax, will give us access to useful methods for actually drawing plots. The subplots() method creates both of these for us, and inside that method, we can specify a figure size (figsize). In this case, we specify a figure size of (10,6), meaning that our figure will have a width of 10 inches and a height of 6 inches.

Next, we draw our plot by using the scatter() method. In scatter(), we specify x=hour['instant'] so the x-axis will show the instant variable in our hour data. We specify y=hour['count'] so the y-axis will show the count variable. Finally, we use plt.show() to display this plot onscreen. This snippet creates a plot that should look like Figure 1-3.

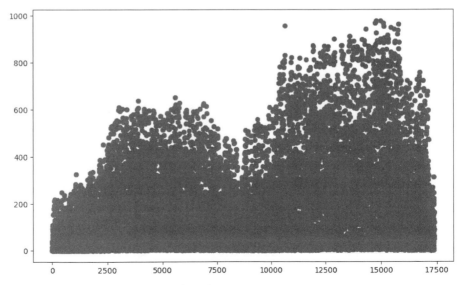

Figure 1-3: Ridership counts every hour for two years

In this plot, you can see that every single point is an hour whose information is recorded in the dataset. The first hour (the beginning of 2011) is the one that appears at the farthest left of the plot. The last hour (the end of 2012) is the one that appears at the farthest right, and all other hours proceed in order in between.

This plot, known as a *scatterplot*, is a good first plot to draw because it shows every observation in the data; it also makes relationships easy to visually identify. In this case, we can see a full representation of the seasonal variation that our groupby() statement previously gave us a hint about. We can also see the general growth of ridership over time.

Clarifying Plots with Titles and Labels

The plot in Figure 1-3 shows the data, but it's not as clearly presented as it should be. We can add titles and labels to our plot as follows:

```
fig, ax = plt.subplots(figsize=(10, 6))
ax.scatter(x = hour['instant'], y = hour['count'])
plt.xlabel("Hour")
plt.ylabel("Count")
plt.title("Ridership Count by Hour")
plt.show()
```

This snippet uses xlabel() to add a label to our x-axis, ylabel() to add a label to our y-axis, and title() to add a title to the plot. You can specify any text in these methods to get any labels you like. The output should look like Figure 1-4.

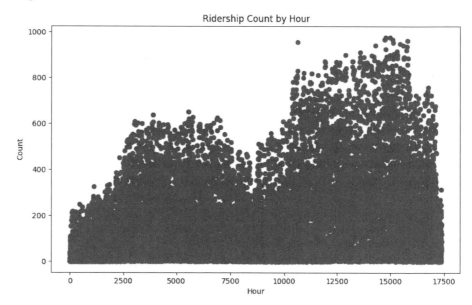

Figure 1-4: Ridership counts by hour, with axis labels and a title

Our dataset is very large, and looking at all the data at once is hard. Let's look at how to plot smaller subsets of our data.

Plotting Subsets of Data

We can use the subsetting we did previously to plot only a subset of the data:

```
hour_first48=hour.loc[0:48,:]
fig, ax = plt.subplots(figsize=(10, 6))
ax.scatter(x = hour_first48['instant'], y = hour_first48['count'])
plt.xlabel("Hour")
plt.ylabel("Count")
plt.title("Count by Hour - First Two Days")
plt.show()
```

Here, we define a new variable called hour_first48. This variable contains data related to row 0 through row 48 of the original data, corresponding roughly to the first two full days in the data.

Notice that we select this subset by writing hour.loc[0:48,:]. This is the same loc() method that we've used before. We use 0:48 to specify that we want the rows with indexes up to 48, but we don't specify any columns—we just write a colon (:) where we would normally specify column names to select. This is a useful shortcut: a colon alone placed there tells pandas that we want to select every column of the dataset, so we don't need to write out each column name individually. The plot of this subset looks like Figure 1-5.

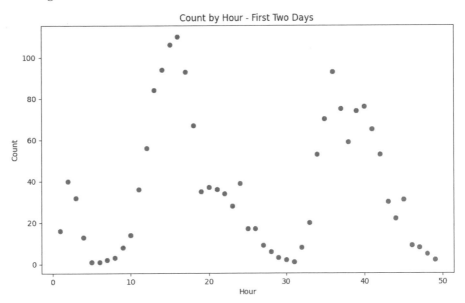

Figure 1-5: Ridership counts by hour for the first two days

By plotting only two days instead of two years of data, we avoid the problem of points overlapping and hiding one another. We can see every observation much more clearly. When you have a big dataset, it's a good idea to do both: plot the entire dataset at once (to understand the general, overall patterns) as well as plot smaller subsets of the data (to understand individual observations and smaller-scale patterns). In this case, we can see patterns within each day of the data in addition to the longer-term seasonal patterns within its years.

Testing Different Plot Types

We have many ways to change the appearance of a plot. Our scatter() function contains parameters that we can adjust to get different looks:

```
fig, ax = plt.subplots(figsize=(10, 6))
ax.scatter(x = hour_first48['instant'], y = hour_first48['count'],c='red',marker='+')
plt.xlabel("Hour")
plt.ylabel("Count")
plt.title("Count by Hour - First Two Days")
plt.show()
```

Here, we use the c argument to specify a color for our plot points (red). We also specify a marker argument to change the *marker style*, or the shape of the points that are drawn. By specifying + for our marker argument, we get plot points that look like little pluses instead of little dots. Figure 1-6 shows the output.

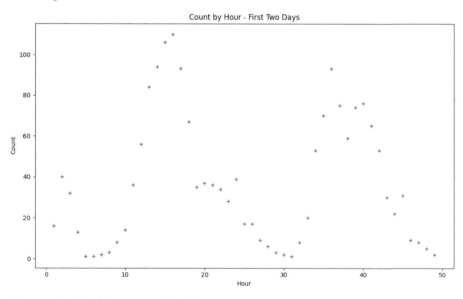

Figure 1-6: Ridership counts, with different style choices

This book isn't printed in color, so you will not see the specified red color displayed on this page. But you should see red points if you run this code at home.

Scatterplots are not the only type of plot we can draw. Let's try a line plot:

```
fig, ax = plt.subplots(figsize=(10, 6))
ax.plot(hour_first48['instant'], hour_first48['casual'],c='red',label='casual',linestyle='-')
ax.plot(hour_first48['instant'],\
hour_first48['registered'],c='blue',label='registered',linestyle='--')
ax.legend()
plt.show()
```

In this case, we use `ax.plot()` instead of `ax.scatter()` to draw the plot. The `ax.plot()` method allows us to draw a line plot. Here, we call `ax.plot()` twice to draw two lines on a single plot. This enables us to compare casual and registered users (Figure 1-7).

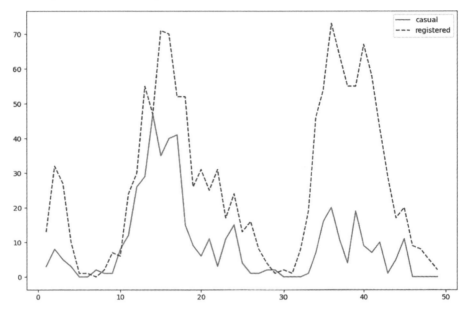

Figure 1-7: A line plot showing casual and registered riders over the first two days

This plot shows that the number of casual riders is almost always lower than the number of registered riders. The plot's legend indicates different colors for casual and registered users as well as the different line styles (solid for casual riders, dashed for registered riders). Run this code at home to see the colors and their contrast more clearly.

We can also try a different kind of plot:

```
import seaborn as sns
fig, ax = plt.subplots(figsize=(10, 6))
sns.boxplot(x='hr', y='registered', data=hour)
plt.xlabel("Hour")
plt.ylabel("Count")
plt.title("Counts by Hour")
plt.show()
```

This time, we import a package called *seaborn*. This package is based on Matplotlib, so it includes all the capabilities of Matplotlib, plus more features that help create beautiful, informative plots quickly. We use seaborn's boxplot() method to create a new kind of plot: a *box plot*. Figure 1-8 shows the box plots that this snippet creates.

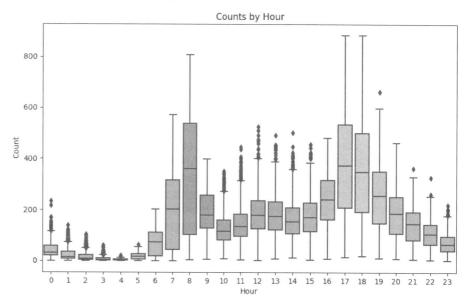

Figure 1-8: Box plots showing ridership counts grouped by the hour of the day

You can see 24 vertical box plots, drawn parallel to one another—each one representing information about a particular hour of the day. A box plot is a simple kind of plot, but one that gives a great deal of information. In a box plot, the upper and lower horizontal boundaries of each rectangle represent the 75th and 25th percentiles of the plotted data, respectively. The horizontal line inside the rectangle represents the median (or 50th percentile). The vertical lines extending from the top and bottom of each rectangle represent the full range of all observations that are not considered outliers. The individually drawn points beyond the ranges of the vertical lines are regarded as outliers.

Seeing the box plots together in Figure 1-8 enables you to compare ridership at different times of day. For example, the median ridership during hour 5 (around 5 AM) is quite low, but the median ridership at hour 6 (around 6 AM) is much higher. At hour 7 (around 7 AM), the median ridership is higher still. High ridership occurs again around 5 PM and 6 PM; maybe these peaks indicate that many of your customers use your bikes to commute to and from work.

As you might expect, we can draw many more types of plots. Another useful one is a *histogram*, which you can create as follows:

```
fig, ax = plt.subplots(figsize=(10, 6))
ax.hist(hour['count'],bins=80)
plt.xlabel("Ridership")
```

```
plt.ylabel("Frequency")
plt.title("Ridership Histogram")
plt.show()
```

This snippet uses the hist() command to draw a histogram. Figure 1-9 shows the output.

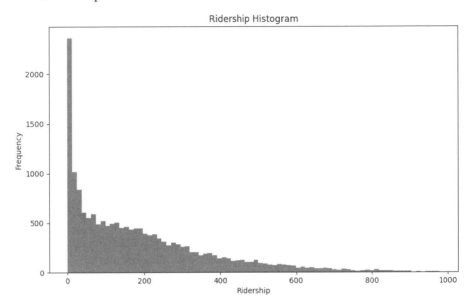

Figure 1-9: A histogram showing the frequency of each ridership count

In a histogram, the height of every bar represents frequency. In this case, our histogram shows the frequencies of every ridership count. For example, if you look at the x-axis around 800, you'll see bars that have a height close to 0. This means that very few hours in our dataset had around 800 riders. By contrast, at about 200 on the x-axis, you see higher bars, with height closer to 500. This indicates that for close to 500 individual hours in our data, ridership was close to 200. The pattern we see in this histogram is a common one for businesses: many hours have few customers, and few hours have many customers.

You could use this kind of histogram to think about the capacity of your company. For example, maybe your company has 1,000 bicycles available to rent today. You think that it might be good to save money by selling 200 of your bicycles—that way, you'll earn some extra cash and won't have to worry about maintenance and storage of superfluous bikes. This would leave you with 800 bicycles available to rent. By looking at the histogram, you can see exactly how much you would expect that change to impact your company: since only a small fraction of hours have demand higher than 800, this should have a relatively small impact on your capacity. You could look at the histogram to decide exactly how many of your bicycles you feel comfortable selling.

Another type of plot, a *pair plot*, draws every possible scatterplot for every possible pair of variables in your data:

```
thevariables=['hr','temp','windspeed']
hour_first100=hour.loc[0:100,thevariables]
sns.pairplot(hour_first100, corner=True)
plt.show()
```

Here, we create a thevariables variable, which is a list of three variables we'll plot. (We're plotting only three instead of all variables because of the limited space in the book.) We also create hour_first100, which is a subset of our full data containing only the rows with index 100 or less in the hour dataset. Again, the seaborn package helps us by providing the pairplot() method that we can call to create our plot. The result, Figure 1-10, is a collection of plots, including both scatterplots and histograms.

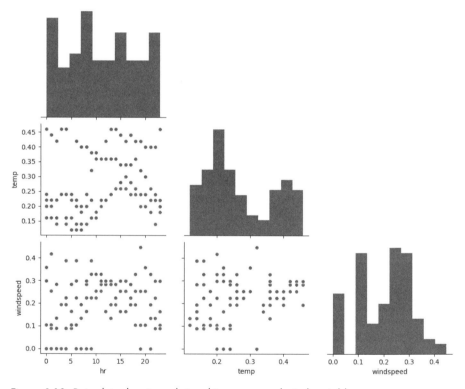

Figure 1-10: Pair plots showing relationships among selected variables

The pair plot shows scatterplots for every possible combination of variables in the subset of the data we selected, as well as histograms for the individual variables we selected. A lot of data is plotted here, but the scatterplots don't show much apparent relationship among the variables; these relationships appear to be essentially random.

Sometimes when we draw pair plots, we see more than just randomness. Instead, we can see clear relationships among variables. For example, if we had a measurement of snowfall in our data, we would see that as temperature goes up, snowfall levels go down, and vice versa. This type of clear relationship between variables is called *correlation*, and we'll explore it in the next section.

Exploring Correlations

Two variables are *correlated* if a change in one variable tends to occur together with a change in the other variable. We say that two variables are positively correlated if they change *together*: one variable tends to go up when the other goes up, and one variable tends to go down when the other goes down. We can find innumerable examples of positive correlations in the world. The number of domestic house cats in a city is positively correlated with the amount of cat food purchased in that city. If one of these variables is high, the other one also tends to be high, and if one of these variables is low, the other one also tends to be low.

We can also talk about negative correlations: two variables are negatively correlated if one tends to go up when the other goes down, or if one tends to go down when the other goes up. Negative correlations are also common in the world. For example, the average temperature of a city is negatively correlated with the average amount of money a typical resident spends on thick winter coats every year. In cities where one of these numbers is high, the other tends to be low, and in cities where one of these numbers is low, the other tends to be high.

In the world of data science, it's extremely important to find and understand correlations, both positive and negative ones. Your performance as CEO will improve if you can find and understand these correlations. For example, you might find that the count of riders is positively correlated with the temperature. If so, this means that ridership tends to be low when temperatures are low. You could even consider selling some of your bikes during seasons with low ridership to generate cash flow instead of letting many of your bikes sit idle. Exactly what you choose to do will depend on many other details of your situation, but understanding the data on a deep level will help you make the best possible business decisions.

Calculating Correlations

We can calculate correlations in Python:

```
print(hour['casual'].corr(hour['registered']))
print(hour['temp'].corr(hour['hum']))
```

Here, we use the corr() method, yet another capability provided by pandas. The corr() method calculates a number called the *correlation coefficient*. We can calculate many types of correlation coefficients, but by default, corr() calculates the Pearson correlation coefficient. This is the most commonly used correlation coefficient, so whenever we refer to a correlation coefficient in this book, we'll be referring to the Pearson correlation coefficient.

The Pearson correlation coefficient is a number that's always between –1 and 1, and it's often named with the variable *r*. It's meant to describe the relationship between two variables; its sign describes the type of correlation, and its size describes the strength of the correlation. If the correlation coefficient *r* is a positive number, our two variables are positively correlated, and if *r* is a negative number, they're negatively correlated. If the correlation coefficient is 0, or very close to 0, we say that the variables are *uncorrelated*.

In this case, the first line of this snippet calculates the correlation coefficient describing the relationship between the casual and registered variables in our data. For these variables, *r* is about 0.51, a positive number that indicates a positive correlation.

Understanding Strong vs. Weak Correlations

In addition to noticing whether correlation coefficients are positive, negative, or 0, we pay attention to their exact *magnitude*, or size. If a correlation coefficient is large (far from 0 and close to either 1 or –1), we often say that the correlation is *strong*. Take a look at Figure 1-11 to see examples of correlations.

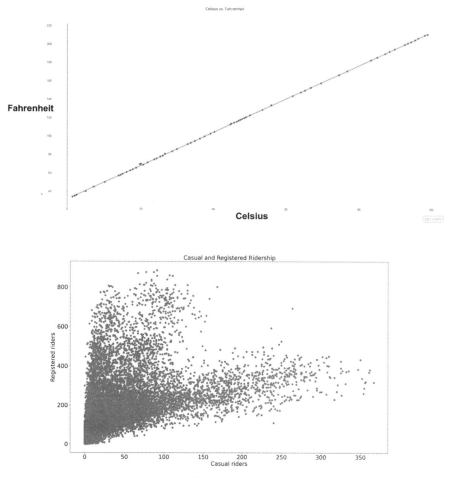

Figure 1-11: Positively correlated variables

Here, you can see two plots. The first plot shows the relationship between Fahrenheit and Celsius temperatures. You can see that Fahrenheit and Celsius are positively correlated: when one goes up, the other goes up, and vice versa. The second plot shows the relationship between casual and registered ridership in your company. Again, we see a positive correlation: when casual ridership goes up, registered ridership tends to go up as well, and vice versa.

The two correlations in Figure 1-11 are both positive, but we can see a qualitative difference between them. The relationship between Fahrenheit and Celsius is deterministic: knowing the Fahrenheit temperature allows us to know the Celsius temperature exactly, with no uncertainty or guesswork. This kind of deterministic positive correlation that appears as a straight line on a plot is also called a *perfect* correlation, and when we measure a correlation coefficient for a perfect positive correlation, we'll find that $r = 1$.

By contrast, the relationship between casual and registered ridership is *not* deterministic. Often a higher number of casual riders corresponds to a higher number of registered riders. But sometimes it doesn't; we can't perfectly predict one variable by using the other one. When two variables are correlated but don't have a deterministic relationship, we say that the relationship between the two variables has "noise," or randomness.

Randomness is hard to define precisely, but you can think of it as unpredictability. When you know a Fahrenheit temperature, you can predict the Celsius temperature with perfect accuracy. By contrast, when you know the casual ridership, you can predict the registered ridership, but your prediction may not be perfectly accurate. When unpredictability like this exists, the two variables will have a correlation coefficient that's less than 1. In this case, we can calculate the correlation of casual and registered ridership and find that $r = 0.51$.

You can think of the size of the correlation coefficient as a measure of the amount of randomness in the relationship between two variables. A larger correlation coefficient corresponds to less randomness (closer to a deterministic relationship, like the relationship between Fahrenheit and Celsius). A smaller correlation coefficient corresponds to more randomness and less predictability. You can think of a 0 correlation coefficient, indicating no relationship at all between variables, as an indication of pure randomness, or pure noise.

You can look at Figure 1-12 to see examples of negative correlations of different magnitudes.

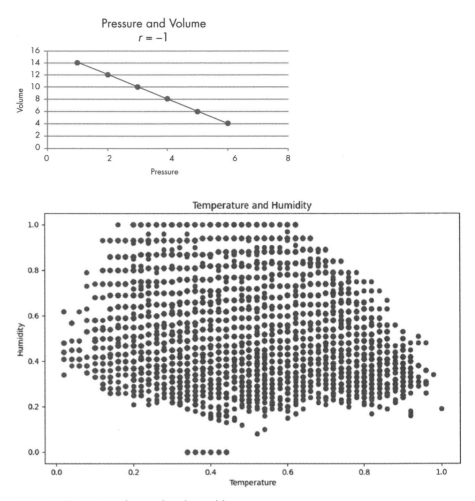

Figure 1-12: Negatively correlated variables

Here, we see the same ideas as in Figure 1-11. The first plot shows a *perfect* negative correlation: this time, the deterministic relationship between pressure and volume. The correlation here is exactly $r = -1$, indicating that no randomness occurs in the relationship between the variables; each variable is perfectly predictable by using the other one.

The second plot shows the relationship between temperature and humidity in our data. These two variables also have a negative correlation, but with a much smaller coefficient: r is about -0.07. Just as we did with the positive correlations in Figure 1-11, we can interpret these correlation coefficients as measurements of randomness: a correlation coefficient with a larger magnitude (meaning that it's closer to 1 or -1) is a correlation that's highly predictable and not very random, while a coefficient with a smaller magnitude (closer to 0) is a correlation that has more randomness. When we see $r = -0.07$ here, we interpret that to mean that temperature and humidity are negatively correlated, but their correlation is very weak—it's not far from pure randomness.

One important thing to remember when you look at correlations is a famous saying: "Correlation does not imply causation." When we observe strong correlations, all we can be certain of is that two variables tend to change together; we can't be certain that one causes the other.

For example, suppose we study Silicon Valley startups and find that their monthly revenues are correlated with the number of Ping-Pong tables they purchase. We may hastily conclude from this correlation that Ping-Pong tables are causing revenue to increase; maybe the relaxation and camaraderie that they facilitate leads to higher productivity, or maybe the fun atmosphere they create leads to better retention and hiring success.

On the other hand, these ideas may be completely mistaken, and maybe the causation flows in the opposite direction; companies that have success (totally independent of their Ping-Pong tables) have higher revenues, and since their budget has suddenly increased, they use some of their new extra money for a fun purchase like a Ping-Pong table. In that case, revenue would be causing Ping-Pong table purchases, not the other way around.

Finally, the correlation could be mere coincidence. Maybe Ping-Pong tables don't lead to higher revenues, and revenues don't lead to more Ping-Pong tables, but instead we've observed a *spurious correlation:* a correlation that occurs only by coincidence and does not indicate any causation or special relationship. A correlation could also be due to an *omitted variable*, something we haven't observed but is independently causing revenue increases and Ping-Pong table purchases simultaneously.

In any case, the important thing is to always be cautious when you find and interpret correlations. Correlations mean that two variables tend to change together, and they can help us make predictions, but they don't necessarily imply that one variable causes the other, or even that they have any real relationship.

Discovering and understanding correlation coefficients can help you in your CEO duties, especially when you find surprising correlations. For example, you may find a strong, positive correlation between the size of groups that rent bicycles together and their level of customer satisfaction after the rental. Maybe this can give you some ideas about encouraging people to rent bikes with their friends as a chance to get more satisfied customers. Finding correlations, and understanding the magnitude of correlations and what that tells you about predictability, can be valuable in business.

Finding Correlations Between Variables

We can do more than calculate individual correlations between pairs of variables. We can go further by creating a *correlation matrix*, which is a matrix (or rectangular array) of numbers, each of whose elements is the correlation coefficient measuring the relationship between two particular variables. A correlation matrix will show the relationships among all of our variables:

```
thenames=['hr','temp','windspeed']
cor_matrix = hour[thenames].corr()
print(cor_matrix)
```

Here, we use the same corr() method that we've used before. When we use corr() without any arguments inside the parentheses, it creates a correlation matrix for all the variables in a dataset. In this case, we create a smaller correlation matrix that shows correlations among just three selected variables. The correlation matrix that we calculate here looks like this:

```
            hr       temp  windspeed
hr         1.000000  0.137603   0.137252
temp       0.137603  1.000000  -0.023125
windspeed  0.137252 -0.023125   1.000000
```

Here, we have a 3×3 matrix. Every entry in this matrix is a correlation coefficient. For example, in the second row, third column, you can see that the correlation between windspeed and temp is about $r = -0.023$. Technically, this is a negative correlation, though it's so close to 0 that we would typically describe the two variables as uncorrelated.

You also can see that three correlations in the matrix are equal to 1.0. That's expected: these perfect correlations are measuring the correlation of each variable with itself (the correlation of hr with hr, temp with temp, and windspeed with windspeed). Every variable will always have a perfect correlation with itself. Creating a correlation matrix can be a quick, simple way to find correlations among all the variables in your data and find any surprising positive or negative correlations.

Creating Heat Maps

After creating a correlation matrix, we can create a plot of all these correlations to make the matrix more easily readable:

```
plt.figure(figsize=(14,10))
corr = hour[thenames].corr()
sns.heatmap(corr, annot=True,cmap='binary',
        fmt=".3f",
        xticklabels=thenames,
        yticklabels=thenames)
plt.show()
```

Here, we create a heat map. In this type of plot, the color or darkness of a cell indicates the value of the number in that cell. The heat map in Figure 1-13 shows measurements of correlations between variables.

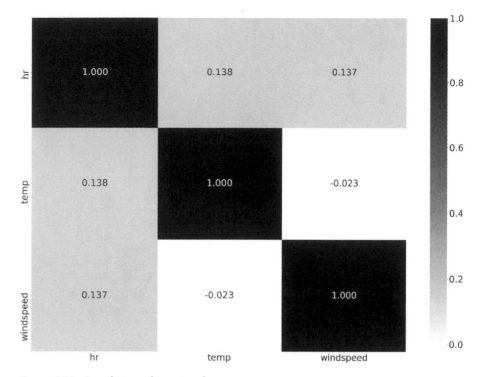

Figure 1-13: Correlations shown in a heat map

This heat map shows a collection of nine rectangles. As the legend on the right indicates, a darker fill in a rectangle indicates that a particular correlation is higher, and a lighter fill indicates that a particular correlation is lower. A heat map of a correlation matrix can provide an even quicker way to check for patterns and relationships among variables, since strong relationships will quickly catch the eye.

If you prefer a color plot instead of a grayscale one, you can change the `cmap='binary'` parameter in the `sns.heatmap()` method. This `cmap` parameter refers to the *color map* of the heat map, and by choosing a different `cmap` value, you can get different color schemes. For example, if you use `cmap='coolwarm'`, you'll see a heat map in which higher values are represented by reddish colors and lower values are represented by bluish colors.

Heat maps can be drawn for variables other than correlation matrices. For example, we can draw a heat map showing the number of riders at each hour throughout a week:

```
# Create a pivot table
df_hm =hour.pivot_table(index = 'hr',columns ='weekday',values ='count')
# Draw a heatmap
plt.figure(figsize = (20,10)) # To resize the plot
sns.heatmap(df_hm,  fmt="d", cmap='binary',linewidths=.5, vmin = 0)
plt.show()
```

To create this plot, we have to create a pivot table, a table of grouped values. If you've spent a lot of time working with Excel or other spreadsheet programs, you've likely encountered pivot tables before. Here, our pivot table has grouped values from our full dataset based on their day of the week and hour of the day. We have the average ridership for each hour (0 through 23) of each day (Sunday through Saturday). After creating a pivot table with data grouped in this way, we can use the same heatmap() method to create the heat map shown in Figure 1-14.

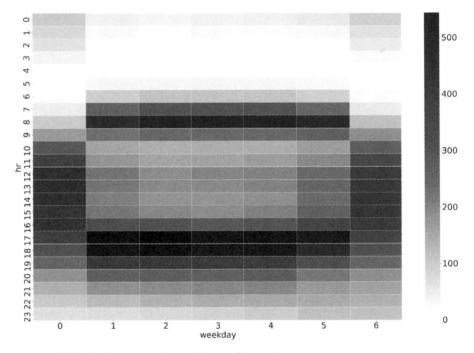

Figure 1-14: Ridership counts for each hour of every day

This heat map contains darker rectangles for hours that had more riders and lighter rectangles for hours that had fewer riders. We can see commuters who spike in activity around 8 AM and 5 PM. We can also see weekend outings on Saturday and Sunday afternoons.

From a business perspective, this heat map could give us any number of business ideas. For instance, seeing the spike in ridership around 8 AM on weekdays could give you an idea for increasing your revenue. Just as we imagined providing discounts during times of low activity, we might also consider the mirror image strategy: surge pricing (temporarily higher prices) during especially active times. Other transportation companies like Uber, Lyft, and Grab use this surge pricing strategy, not only to increase revenue but also to ensure high availability of their products.

Exploring Further

So far, we've looked at only one dataset, and we've done only a few of the infinite explorations that are possible with it. As you continue from your first morning as CEO to your first afternoon, then your second day, and further on, you will need to make many decisions about your business and the way it operates. The exploration that we've done in this chapter can be applied to any other business question you ever encounter. For example, you might consider bundling bike rentals with refreshing drinks and earning extra revenue that way (not to mention keeping your riders healthier and safer). Analyzing data related to your customers, their riding patterns, and how thirsty they get during bike rides could help you figure out whether this strategy is a good idea.

Other analyses could be related to the repairs your bikes need. How often are your bikes being repaired, and how much do repairs cost? You could check for the times of repairs and make sure they're not being done during peak hours. You could check the costs of repairs of various types of bikes. You could check a histogram of the prices of repairs and check whether any outliers are increasing your costs too much. These explorations would help you better understand your business and help you get ideas for running it better.

So far, our analyses have not been extremely sophisticated; mostly we've calculated only summary statistics and drawn plots. But these simple calculations and plots, when combined with common sense, can be valuable as a first step in making business decisions. Some CEOs don't look at data enough, and others want to look at data but depend on staff to provide reports to them, and those reports may be slow or imperfect. A CEO who can confidently check data related to their company is a CEO who can be effective. CEOs can become good at data, and this can combine with their business knowledge to make them even better at their jobs. Similarly, data scientists can become good at business, and when their data skills are combined with business acumen, they can really become a force to be reckoned with.

Summary

In this chapter, we started with a simple business scenario: becoming a CEO and making decisions related to running a business better. We went over some ideas for what a CEO needs to do and how exploratory data analysis can be helpful. We covered how to read data into Python, calculate summary statistics, draw plots, and interpret results in a business context. In the next chapter, we'll go over linear regression, a more sophisticated method that can be used not only for exploration but also for forecasting. Let's continue!

2

FORECASTING

Let's look at some data science tools that can help you predict the future. In this chapter, we'll introduce a simple business scenario in which a company needs to forecast customer demand. We'll then talk about how tools from data science can be applied to make an accurate forecast and how that forecast can lead to better business decision-making.

We'll use linear regression for our forecasting, and we'll discuss both univariate and multivariate linear regression. Finally, we'll look at extrapolation of regression lines and how to evaluate various regression models to choose the best one.

Predicting Customer Demand

Imagine that you're running a car dealership in Quebec, Canada. You are using a standard business model for retail: you buy cars from a manufacturer at a low price and then sell those cars to individual customers at higher prices. Every month, you need to decide how many cars you'll order from the manufacturer. If you order too many cars, you'll be unable to sell them all quickly, resulting in high storage costs or cash flow problems. If you order too few cars, you won't be able to meet your customers' demands.

Ordering the right number of cars is important. But what is the right number? The answer depends on certain business considerations, such as the cash in your bank account and how much you want to grow—but in a typical month, the right number of cars to order is exactly the number of cars that customers will want to buy during the coming month. Since we can't see into the future, we need to forecast the demand and place an order based on our forecast.

We can choose from several proven quantitative methods to obtain a forecast of next month's demand. One of the best methods is *linear regression*. In the remainder of this chapter, we'll explain how to use linear regression for forecasting. We'll use past data to predict future data, to learn the number of cars we need to order. We'll start simply, just by reading in and looking at some data, and then proceed to the other steps of the forecasting process.

Cleaning Erroneous Data

The data we'll analyze to forecast the future is a record of the number of cars sold by dealerships in Quebec, Canada, for each of 108 consecutive months. This data was originally made available online by Rob Hyndman, a statistics professor and forecasting guru. You can download the data from *https://bradfordtuckfield.com/carsales.csv*.

This data is old; the most recent month recorded is December 1968. Therefore, for this scenario, we'll be imagining that we live in December 1968, and we'll make forecasts for January 1969. The forecasting principles we'll discuss will be evergreen, so if you can use data from 1968 to forecast results in 1969, you'll be able to use data from year n to forecast results from year $n + 1$, for $n = 2,023$ or 3,023 or any other number.

Save this file into the same directory where you're running Python. Then we'll read our data by using Python's pandas package:

```
import pandas as pd
carsales=pd.read_csv('carsales.csv')
```

Here, we import pandas and give it the alias pd. We then use its read_csv() method to read our data into Python and store it in the variable carsales. The pandas package we import and use here is a powerful module that makes working with data in Python easier. The carsales object we create is a pandas dataframe, which is the standard pandas format for storing data in a Python session. Because the object is stored as a pandas dataframe, we'll be able to use many helpful pandas methods to work with it, just as we did in Chapter 1. Let's start by using the head() method that enables us to inspect pandas dataframes:

```
>>> print(carsales.head())
      Month  Monthly car sales in Quebec 1960-1968
0  1960-01                                 6550.0
1  1960-02                                 8728.0
2  1960-03                                12026.0
3  1960-04                                14395.0
4  1960-05                                14587.0
```

By looking at these rows, we can notice a few important points. First, we can see the column names. The column names in this dataset are Month and Monthly car sales in Quebec 1960-1968. The second column name will be easier to work with if we shorten it. We can do this easily in Python:

```
carsales.columns= ['month','sales']
```

In this snippet, we access the columns of our dataframe and redefine them to have shorter names (month and sales, respectively).

Just as the head() method prints the top five rows of a dataset, the tail() method prints the bottom five rows. If you run print(carsales.tail()), you'll see the following output:

```
>>> print(carsales.tail())
                                     month    sales
104                                1968-09  14385.0
105                                1968-10  21342.0
106                                1968-11  17180.0
107                                1968-12  14577.0
108  Monthly car sales in Quebec 1960-1968      NaN
```

We can see that the column names are shorter now and easier to read. But we also see that the very last row doesn't contain car sales data. Instead, its first entry is a *tag*, or label, that tells us about the whole dataset. Its second entry is NaN, which stands for *not a number*, meaning that the entry contains no data or undefined data. We don't need the label entry or the empty (NaN) entry, so let's remove the entire last row (row 108):

```
carsales=carsales.loc[0:107,:].copy()
```

Here, we use the pandas loc() method to specify a selection of rows that we want to keep: in this case, all the rows between row 0 and row 107, inclusive. We use the colon (:) after the comma to indicate that we want to keep both of the dataset's columns. We store the result in our carsales variable, thereby removing the superfluous row 108. If you run **print(carsales.tail())** again, you'll see that that row has been removed.

Another thing we can see by looking at the head and tail of our data is the format of the month data. The first entry is 1960-01 (January of 1960), the second entry is 1960-02 (February of 1960), and so on.

As data scientists, we're interested in doing numeric analyses using math, statistics, and other quantitative methods. Dates can present several tedious challenges that make it hard to do math and statistics the way we want to. The first challenge is that dates are sometimes not stored in a numeric data type. Here, the dates are stored as *strings*, or collections of characters.

To see why this is an issue, try `print(1960+1)` in the Python console; you'll notice that the result is 1961. Python has seen that we're working with two numbers, and it's added them in the way we expect. Then, try `print('1960'+'1')` in the Python console; now you get 19601 as the result. Instead of adding two numbers, Python has seen that we've input strings and assumes that the + sign means that we want to do *concatenation*, simply fusing the strings together in a way that doesn't follow the rules of math.

Another challenge with dates is that even when they're in numeric form, they follow logic that is different from the logic of natural numbers. For example, if we add 1 to month 11, we get month 12, which follows the arithmetic rule that 11 + 1 = 12. But if we add 1 to month 12, we get month 1 again (since every December is followed by January of the next year), which is not consistent with the simple arithmetic of 12 + 1 = 13.

In this case, the simplest way to address the issues with the data type of our date data is to define a new variable called `period`. We can define it as follows:

```
carsales['period']=list(range(108))
```

Our new `period` variable is just a list of all the numbers from 0 to 107. We'll refer to January 1960 as period 0, February 1960 as period 1, and so on until December 1968, the last month in our data, which we'll call period 107. This new variable is numeric, so we can add to it, subtract from it, or do any other mathematical operation with it. Also, it will follow the rules of standard arithmetic, with period 13 coming after period 12, as we expect in numeric variables. This simple solution is possible because in this particular dataset, the rows are organized in chronological order, so we can be sure that each period number is being assigned to the correct month.

These simple tasks, like adding a numeric column for months, removing an extra row, and changing column names, are part of *data cleaning*. This is not a glamorous or particularly exciting process, but doing it right is extremely important because it lays a foundation for the more thrilling steps of the data science process.

Plotting Data to Find Trends

After these basic data-cleaning tasks, we should definitely plot the data. Plotting should be done early and often in every data science project. Let's use the Matplotlib module to create a simple plot of our data:

```
from matplotlib import pyplot as plt
plt.scatter(carsales['period'],carsales['sales'])
```

```
plt.title('Car Sales by Month')
plt.xlabel('Month')
plt.ylabel('Sales')
plt.show()
```

In this snippet, we import the Matplotlib `pyplot` module and give it the alias `plt`. Then, we use the `scatter()` method to create a scatterplot of all the sales numbers in our data, organized by period (month). We also use a few lines to add axis labels and a plot title and then show the plot. Figure 2-1 shows the result.

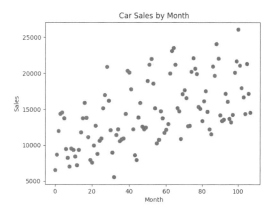

Figure 2-1: Car sales by month over nine years

This simple plot shows our `period` variable on the x-axis and `sales` on the y-axis. Each point represents one row of data or, in other words, the number of car sales for one particular month.

See what interesting information pops out at you in this plot. Probably the most obvious thing is the gradual upward trend from left to right: sales appear to be increasing gradually over time. Other than this trend, the data seems noisy and scattered, with huge variations between one month and another. The variations within a year or season look random, noisy, and unpredictable. The linear regression method that we'll implement next will attempt to capture the order and patterns in our data, and help us be less distracted by the randomness and noise.

So far, all we've done is read in the data and draw a simple plot. But already we're starting to see patterns that will be useful for making accurate forecasts. Let's go on to some more serious forecasting steps.

Performing Linear Regression

Now that we've cleaned the data, plotted it, and noticed some basic patterns, we're ready to do forecasting in earnest. We'll use linear regression for our forecasts. *Linear regression* is an essential part of every data scientist's toolkit: it finds a line that captures a noisy relationship between variables, and we can use that line to make predictions about things we've never seen.

Linear regression was invented more than a century before the term *machine learning* was coined, and it has historically been thought of as part of pure statistics. However, since it bears such a strong resemblance to many common machine learning methods, and since it shares some common theoretical foundations with machine learning, linear regression is sometimes considered part of the machine learning field. Like all the best scientific tools, it allows us to pull order from chaos.

In this case, we have the chaos of car sales in Quebec, where seasonal variations, time trends, and plain randomness mingle together in a noisy dataset. When we apply simple linear regression to this data, our output will be a straight line that captures an underlying structure that will help us make sound forecasts for the future. Figure 2-2 shows an example of a typical output of linear regression.

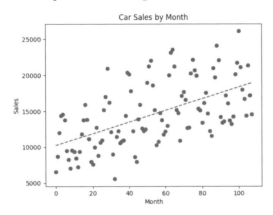

Figure 2-2: A dashed line showing a typical output of linear regression

In this plot, you can see the points representing the data, just as in Figure 2-1. Again, we see the chaos of our dataset: great variations occur between months across the whole dataset.

The dashed line that progresses slightly upward from left to right represents the output of a linear regression. It's called a *regression line*, and we often say that this regression line *fits* the data. In other words, it goes through what looks like roughly the center of the cloud constituted by all the points together. It gets close to many of the points of our data, and no data point is particularly far away from it. It's as if the line expresses or reveals the fundamental relationship between time and sales (a relationship of gradual growth). The notion of a line fitting a set of points is fundamental to linear regression. In fact, for reasons we'll discuss later, a regression line is sometimes called the *line of best fit* to a dataset.

Since our regression line is a straight line, it doesn't have the random variation of the real data. The line proceeds in a predictable way. By removing that randomness, the regression line shows us a clear representation of the underlying pattern of the data. In this case, the regression line shows us that the data has a general trend upward over time, and if we measure the regression line carefully, we can find exactly the slope and height of that trend.

We can interpret the value of the regression line for any particular month as the number of car sales expected in that month. Later we'll extrapolate our simple line forward into the future (by continuing to draw it with the same slope until it extends past the right edge of the plot) to generate forecasts for sales in future months.

Let's run the code that performs linear regression and outputs a regression line. We'll use methods for linear regression that are very particular about the *shape* of the data we use, meaning whether sales numbers are stored as 108 rows × 1 column or 108 columns × 1 row. In this case, our linear regression code will run more smoothly if our data is stored as 108 rows of 1 list each, where each list contains one number. To get our data in this shape, we'll use the pandas reshape() method as follows:

```
x = carsales['period'].values.reshape(-1,1)
y = carsales['sales'].values.reshape(-1,1)
```

If you run print(x) and print(y), you can see the new shape of the data: 108 rows of one-element lists. Actually performing the linear regression takes little code. We can do the whole thing, including importing the relevant module, with three lines:

```
from sklearn.linear_model import LinearRegression
regressor = LinearRegression()
regressor.fit(x, y)
```

Here, we import the linear regression capability from the scikit-learn package, which can be referred to by its standard abbreviation, sklearn. This package, which is extremely popular in the machine learning world, provides many useful machine learning capabilities, including linear regression. After importing sklearn, we define the variable regressor. A *regressor*, as its name tautologically suggests, is a Python object that we'll use to perform regression. After creating the regressor, we tell it to fit our x and y variables. We are telling it to calculate the line shown in Figure 2-2 that fits the data by matching its location and general trend.

A more quantitative way to describe what *fitting our regression* means is that it's determining precise, optimized values for two numbers: a coefficient and an intercept. After running the preceding snippet, we can look at both of these numbers as follows:

```
print(regressor.coef_)
print(regressor.intercept_)
```

This code prints out two numbers that are output by the regressor's fit() method: an intercept, which you should see is about 10,250.8; and a variable called coef_, which is short for *coefficients*, and should be equal to about 81.2. Together, these two numbers specify the exact position and trend of the dashed regression line you see in Figure 2-2. You'll see how they do this in the next section.

Applying Algebra to the Regression Line

To see how these two numbers specify the regression line, think back to your high school math classes. You may remember learning that every straight line can be expressed in a form like this:

$$y = m \cdot x + b$$

Here, m is a slope, or coefficient, and b is the intercept (technically a *y-intercept*—the exact place where the line crosses the plot's y-axis). In this case, the value of the coef_ variable we found, about 81.2, is the value of m, and the value of the intercept variable we found, about 10,250.8, is the value of b. So, what we have learned from our regression process is that the relationship between time period and car sales can be expressed, at least approximately, as follows:

$$car\ sales = 81.2 \cdot period + 10250.8$$

The chaos of the car sales dataset's apparently random variation (shown in Figure 2-1) is now reduced to the order of this simple equation. The line that this equation describes is the dashed line in Figure 2-2. We can think of every point on that line as a prediction of how many car sales are expected at each time period, ignoring the distracting randomness and noise.

The m and b values in our equation have useful interpretations. The interpretation of the line's slope, 81.2, is the monthly growth trend of car sales. Based on the data we've observed in the past, we conclude that car sales in Quebec grow by about 81.2 cars per month. Randomness and other variation remain, but a growth of 81.2 is what we approximately expect. The interpretation of the intercept variable, 10,250.8, is the *baseline* value of car sales: the expected car sales in month 0 after "removing" or ignoring the chaos of seasonal variation, the passage of time, and other influences.

The equation that linear regression finds can also be called a *model*, a quantitative description of how two or more variables relate to each other. So when we perform the preceding steps, we can say that we *fit a regression*, or equivalently we can say that we *trained a model*. Our regression, or equivalently our model, tells us that we expect to sell about 10,250.8 cars at the beginning of the time frame in our data, and we expect to sell about 81.2 more cars every month than we sold in the previous month.

It's natural to wonder how our regressor determined that 81.2 and 10,250.8 (the coef_ and intercept outputs of our regressor) are the best values for m and b in our regression line. The line they specify looks good enough in Figure 2-2, but it's not the only line we could draw through our cloud of points. A literally infinite number of conceivable lines also go through our cloud and could be said to fit our data. For example, we might hypothesize that the following line is a better approximation of the relationship between time period and sales:

$$car\ sales = 125 \cdot period + 8000$$

Let's call this new line our *hypothesized line*. If we use it as a model of our data, we have a new *m* and *b*, and so we have a new interpretation. In particular, the slope of this line is 125, which we would interpret as an expectation that monthly car sales will increase by about 125 every month—significantly higher than 81.2, the estimate from our regression line. Let's plot our regression line and this new hypothesized line together with the data as follows:

```
plt.scatter(carsales['period'],carsales['sales'])
plt.plot(carsales['period'],[81.2 * i + 10250.8 for i in \
carsales['period']],'r-',label='Regression Line')
plt.plot(carsales['period'],[125 * i + 8000 for i in
carsales['period']],'r--',label='Hypothesized Line')
plt.legend(loc="upper left")
plt.title('Car Sales by Month')
plt.xlabel('Month')
plt.ylabel('Sales')
plt.show()
```

You can see the output of this snippet in Figure 2-3, where we've drawn the data, our regression line (the shallow solid line), and our new hypothesized line (the steeper dashed line).

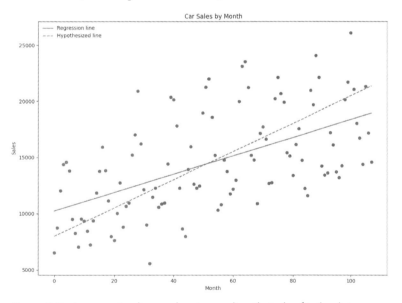

Figure 2-3: A regression line and a steeper line that also fits the data

Both lines go through our cloud of points. Both show an upward trend over time. Both are reasonable candidates to be approximations of the relationship between time and sales, and both could be said to fit the data. Why has our regressor output one line instead of the other? We said that the regression line output by the linear regression process is the *line of best fit*. What is it that enables us to say that it fits better than any other line?

Calculating Error Measurements

We can find the answer by looking at measurements related to *regression errors*. Remember that we interpret each point of a regression line as our prediction of what value we expect in the data. Figure 2-4 shows a regression line and the data used to create it.

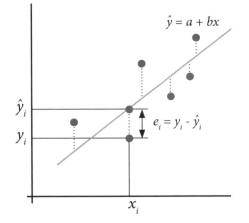

Figure 2-4: Regression errors: vertical distances between points and a regression line

You can see that this regression line is a good fit to the data, meaning it gets close to most of the illustrated points. However, it's not a perfect fit. For every data point, we can calculate the vertical distance between the data point and the regression line. The regression line predicts a certain value, and the point in the data has a particular distance from that prediction. This distance between a predicted and an actual value of a data point is called the regression's *error* relative to that point. In Figure 2-4, the variable e_i is an error measurement for one of the points in the data. You can see that e_i is the vertical distance between a particular point and the regression line. We can calculate this distance for every point in our data.

Calculating the error relative to each data point will give us a way to quantify how well any line fits our data. Lines with low errors fit the data well, and lines with high errors fit the data poorly. That's why we say that measuring regression errors is one way to measure a regression line's *goodness of fit*, the degree to which a line fits the data well.

Let's calculate those error measurements for our car sales regression. We'll calculate each point of the lines we're interested in and compare those points to each point of our dataset:

```
saleslist=carsales['sales'].tolist()
regressionline=[81.2 * i + 10250.8 for i in carsales['period']]
hypothesizedline=[125 * i + 8000 for i in carsales['period']]
error1=[(x-y) for x, y in zip(regressionline,saleslist)]
error2=[(x-y) for x, y in zip(hypothesizedline,saleslist)]
```

In this snippet, we create `saleslist`, a variable that includes the raw car sales numbers for every month. Then we create two variables, `regressionline` and `hypothesizedline`. These variables record every point on the regression and hypothesized lines, respectively. We want to measure how far each true sales number is from both of these lines, so we create two more variables: `error1` to record the distance between true sales numbers and the regression line, and `error2` to record the distance between true sales numbers and the hypothesized line.

We can print out these variables to look at what errors we find for both of our lines:

```
print(error1)
print(error2)
```

When you look at these lists of errors, you can see 108 separate measurements of how far these lines are from the raw data. These 108 measurements are an expression of how well these lines fit the raw data. However, looking at all 216 of these measurements at once is difficult. It would be easier if we could boil down all this information indicating how well a line fits to just one number. The following snippet shows one way to do this:

```
import numpy as np

error1abs=[abs(value) for value in error1]
error2abs=[abs(value) for value in error2]

print(np.mean(error1abs))
print(np.mean(error2abs))
```

In this snippet, we import Python's NumPy package. NumPy is used often in data science, especially for calculations with arrays and matrices. Here, we import it because it gives us the ability to find the mean of a list. Then we define two new variables: `error1abs` and `error2abs`, each containing a list of the absolute values of our error measurements for our two respective lines. Finally, we take the means of these lists.

The means that we find are called the *mean absolute error (MAE)* measurements of each line. Hopefully, the MAE feels like an intuitive measurement of error to you: it's just the average vertical distance between a line and the points in a dataset. A line that gets very close to the points in a dataset will have a low MAE, and a line that is very far from most points will have a higher MAE.

The MAE is a reasonable way to express the degree of goodness of fit of a regression line or any other line. The lower the MAE, the better. In this case, we can see that the MAE for our regression line is 3,154.4, while the MAE for our hypothesized line is 3,239.8. At least according to this measurement, the regression line fits the data better than our hypothesized line.

The MAE has an easy interpretation: it's the average error we expect to have if we use a particular line for prediction. When we say that the MAE for our regression line is 3,154.4, we mean that if we use this regression line to make predictions, we expect our predictions to be wrong by about 3,154.4 on average (either 3,154.4 too low or too high).

For example, suppose we predict that three months from now, we will sell exactly 20,000 cars. We wait three months, count our monthly sales, and find that we actually sold 23,154 cars instead of 20,000. Our prediction was wrong; we underestimated car sales by 3,154. So, we're not perfect at prediction, and the size of our prediction error tells us exactly how imperfect we are. Is the size of our error a surprise? The MAE we just measured (3,154.4) tells us that having an error this high isn't surprising—in fact, underestimating by 3,154 is (after rounding) exactly the size of error we expect to encounter in any month when we're using this regression. Sometimes we'll overestimate instead of underestimating, and sometimes we'll have lower or higher errors than 3,154. Regardless, the MAE is telling us that having an error of about 3,154 is what we expect when using this regression for this prediction scenario.

MAE is not the only measurement that indicates how well a line fits a dataset. Let's look at another possible measurement:

```
error1squared=[(value)**2 for value in error1]
error2squared=[(value)**2 for value in error2]

print(np.sqrt(np.mean(error1squared)))
print(np.sqrt(np.mean(error2squared)))
```

Here, we create lists of the squared values of each error. Then we take the square root of the sum of these errors. This measurement is called the *root mean squared error (RMSE)*. Lower RMSE values indicate a line that is a better fit—one that's expected to make better predictions.

We can create simple Python functions that perform calculations of MAE and RMSE:

```
def get_mae(line,actual):
    error=[(x-y) for x,y in zip(line,actual)]
    errorabs=[abs(value) for value in error]
    mae=np.mean(errorabs)
    return(mae)

def get_rmse(line,actual):
    error=[(x-y) for x,y in zip(line,actual)]
    errorsquared=[(value)**2 for value in error]
    rmse=np.sqrt(np.mean(errorsquared))
    return(rmse)
```

These functions just calculate MAE and RMSE, respectively, exactly as we did previously. If you run print(get_rmse(regressionline,saleslist)), you can see that the RMSE of our regression line is about 3,725, and if you run print(get_rmse(hypothesizedline,saleslist)), you can see that the RMSE of our hypothesized line is about 3,969.

You'll notice that the RMSE of our regression line is smaller than the RMSE of our hypothesized line. This enables us to say that the regression line is a better fit to the data than the hypothesized line, according to the RMSE metric.

It's not a coincidence that our regression line has a lower RMSE than our hypothesized line. When we ran the command regressor.fit(x,y) in Python earlier, the regressor.fit() method performed linear algebraic calculations that were invented by the great mathematician Adrien-Marie Legendre and first published in 1805. Legendre's calculations take a collection of points as an input, and their output is the intercept and coefficients that minimize the value of the RMSE. In other words, the line whose coefficients are determined by Legendre's method is mathematically guaranteed to have a lower RMSE than any of the other infinite possible lines that we could draw to try to fit our data. When we call the regression line the line of best fit, we mean that it is mathematically guaranteed to have the lowest possible RMSE of all possible lines that use the variables we specified. This guarantee is a reason for the enduring popularity of linear regression, and why it's still a standard way to find a line that fits a dataset after all these years.

The line that the regressor outputs is the best-fit line, not just in the loose sense that it looks like it fits the cloud very well, but in the strict quantitative sense that out of all the infinite lines that go through the cloud of points, it is guaranteed to have the lowest RMSE. You can feel free to try other straight lines and check their RMSE values—you won't find one that performs better than our regression line.

Using Regression to Forecast Future Trends

So far, we've used linear regression to find the line that is the best fit of our historical data. But our historical data is all from the past, so we haven't done any real forecasting yet. Going from a linear regression to a forecast is simple: we just need to extrapolate.

The dashed regression line we drew in Figure 2-2 stops at the edges of our plot, at month 0 on the left and month 107 on the right, but there's no reason it needs to stop there. If we continue to draw our regression line farther to the right, we can see the values we expect for any month, however far in the future. Of course, we'll keep the same slope and intercept as we extend the line in this way. Let's write code that will do this:

```
x_extended = np.append(carsales['period'], np.arange(108, 116))
```

Here, we create the variable x_extended. This variable is a combination of two sets of numbers. First, it includes the values of our dataset's period column that records the periods from 0 to 107 in order. Second, it includes all the numbers 108 through 115 in order—these are meant to represent future months after the end of our data (month 108, month 109, . . . all the way to month 115). We combine these two things by using the np.append() method, and the end result is an extended version of our original x variable.

Next, we can use our regressor's predict method to calculate the values that will be on our regression line for each of the month numbers in x_extended:

```
x_extended=x_extended.reshape(-1,1)
extended_prediction=regressor.predict(x_extended)
```

Now we have the forecast values stored in the variable extended_prediction. If you look at extended_prediction, you can see what these predictions are. These predictions follow a simple pattern: each is about 81.2 higher than the previous one. This is because 81.2 is the slope of our regression line. Remember, 81.2 is not just the slope of the line but also the size of the increase we expect in car sales every month, ignoring randomness and seasonal variation.

The prediction method we used here is helpful, but we don't really need it. We can get any values we want on our regression line just by plugging in numbers to our regression equation:

$$car\ sales = 81.2 \cdot period + 10250.8$$

However we get the next predicted values, we can plot them and see what they look like on a graph (Figure 2-5):

```
plt.scatter(carsales['period'],carsales['sales'])
plt.plot(x_extended,extended_prediction,'r--')
plt.title('Car Sales by Month')
plt.xlabel('Month')
plt.ylabel('Sales')
plt.show()
```

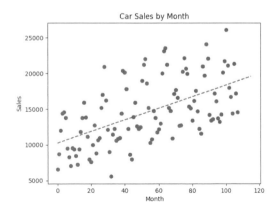

Figure 2-5: A regression line extrapolated several periods forward, for forecasting

This plot will probably not surprise you. It looks almost identical to Figure 2-2, and it's supposed to. The only difference is that we've extended our regression line out a few more periods to the right, to see what car sales we expect—that is, how many we forecast—in the near future. This extrapolation of a regression line is a simple but effective way to forecast.

We've accomplished forecasting with linear regression, but there's more we can do to improve our forecasts. In the next sections, we'll talk about ways to evaluate and improve the performance of our forecasts.

Trying More Regression Models

The linear regression we did in the previous sections is a simple kind called *univariate linear regression*. This type of regression uses only one variable to predict one other variable. In our case, we used the period variable alone to predict sales. Using only one variable has a couple of advantages: first, it is easy; and second, it creates a simple, straight line that expresses some order in the data without also including its random noise. But we have other options.

Multivariate Linear Regression to Predict Sales

If we use other variables to predict sales as well as just the period, we can perform a more complex kind of regression called *multivariate linear regression*. The details of multivariate linear regression are essentially the same as univariate linear regression; the only real difference is the number of variables we use for prediction. We can use any variables we like for multivariate regression: gross domestic product (GDP) growth rates, population estimates, car prices, inflation rates, or anything else we want.

For now, we're limited because our dataset doesn't contain any of those variables. It contains only the period and the sales. However, we can still perform multivariate regression, by using variables that we derive from the period variable. For example, we could use $period^2$ as a new variable in a multivariate regression, or log(*period*), or any other mathematical transformation of the period variable.

Remember that when we performed regression before, we found the m and the b (slope and intercept) variables in the following equation:

$$y = m \cdot x + b$$

When we use multiple variables to predict car sales, we're also finding slope and intercept variables. The only difference is that we're also finding more variables. If we're using three variables to do prediction (which we can call x_1, x_2, and x_3), then we're finding the m_1, m_2, m_3, and b variables in the following equation:

$$y = m_1 \cdot x_1 + m_2 \cdot x_2 + m_3 \cdot x_3 + b$$

The idea is the same as in univariate regression, but we end up with more slopes for more predictor variables. If we want to use *period*, $period^2$, and $period^3$ to predict car sales in our regression, we'll need to estimate the m_1, m_2, m_3, and b variables in Equation 2-1:

$$car\ sales = m_1 \cdot period + m_2 \cdot period^2 + m_3 \cdot period^3 + b$$

Equation 2-1: An equation for multivariate regression using our car sales data

Let's look at the code that will create these transformations of our period variable and do linear regression with three variables:

```python
carsales['quadratic']=carsales['period'].apply(lambda x: x**2)
carsales['cubic']=carsales['period'].apply(lambda x: x**3)

x3 = carsales.loc[:,['period','quadratic','cubic']].values.reshape(-1,3)
y = carsales['sales'].values.reshape(-1,1)

regressor_cubic = LinearRegression()
regressor_cubic.fit(x3, y)
plt.scatter(carsales['period'],carsales['sales'])
plt.plot(x,regressor.predict(x),'r-')
plt.plot(x,regressor_cubic.predict(x3),'r--')
plt.title('Car Sales by Month')
plt.xlabel('Month')
plt.ylabel('Sales')
plt.show()
```

In this snippet, we define two new variables: quadratic, whose value is equal to $period^2$, and cubic, whose value is equal to $period^3$. Then, we define a new x3 dataframe that includes all three of these new variables, and we reshape it so that they will be the right shape for our regressor. The right shape for this three-variable multivariate regression is an array of 108 rows, in which each row is a list of the values of our three variables for a particular month. As long as the data is in the right shape, we can use the fit() method for any univariate or multivariate linear regression with any number of variables. After calling fit(), we calculate the values predicted by this regression for our data and plot them. This snippet creates the plot in Figure 2-6.

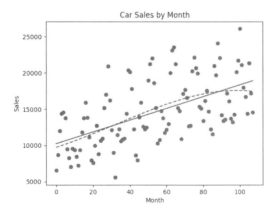

Figure 2-6: A curve that also fits the data

Here, you can see two regression lines. One is the (solid) straight line that is the result of our previous (univariate) regression. The other, newer regression line is not a straight line, but rather a (dashed) curve—a *cubic curve*, to be precise. Linear regression was originally designed to work with straight lines (hence the name *linear*), but we can also use it to find best-fit curves and nonlinear functions like the cubic polynomial in Figure 2-6.

Whether we find a best-fit straight line or a best-fit curve, the linear regression methods that we're using are exactly the same. Similarly, using multiple variables for prediction is not really different from univariate regression with one variable: the output still fits our data, and in fact, our new curve goes very close to the straight line. Every time we select different variables for our regression, the output will look a little different: it may have a different shape or a different curve. But it will always fit the data. In this case, if you want to know the unknown variables in Equation 2-1, we can print them out as follows:

```
print(regressor_cubic.coef_)
print(regressor_cubic.intercept_)
```

The outputs from these `print()` statements are the following:

```
[[ 8.13410634e+01  7.90279561e-01 -8.19451188e-03]]
[9746.41276055]
```

These outputs enable us to fill in all the variables in Equation 2-1 to get an equation for estimating car sales using a cubic polynomial of the period:

$$car\ sales = 81.34 \cdot period + 0.79 \cdot period^2 - 0.008 \cdot period^3 + 9746.41$$

One important thing to notice about Figure 2-6 is the different behavior of our regression lines during the last few periods, on the right side of the plot. The straight line from our univariate regression increases by about 81.2 every period, and when we extrapolate it farther to the right, it will continue to predict increases of about 81.2 every period. By contrast, the curved line from our multivariate regression begins to curve downward on the right side of the plot. If we extrapolated it farther to the right, it would predict a decrease in car sales every month forever.

These two lines, though they behave similarly and are both the result of linear regression, make opposite predictions about the future: one predicts growth, and the other predicts contraction. Later in the chapter, we'll talk more about how to choose which regression line to use for forecasting.

Trigonometry to Capture Variations

There's no limit to the number of variables we can add to a multivariate regression. Each selection of variables will lead to a curve with a slightly different shape. One of the difficult choices we have to make in every regression problem is which variables to add to the regression.

In this case, the univariate regression line (the straight line in Figure 2-2) and the cubic regression line (the curved line in Figure 2-6) are both acceptable and can be used to forecast the future. However, though they both pass through what looks like the middle of our cloud of points, there is so much variation that they don't capture—sales for many individual months are much higher or much lower than these lines. Ideally, we could find a collection of variables that, when fit using a linear regression, lead to a curve that better fits some of this variation. In this case, making one small change to the way we plot our data can make what we should do next clearer.

Let's change Figure 2-1 from a scatterplot to a line plot, by making just one small change in our code (shown in bold):

```
from matplotlib import pyplot as plt
plt.plot(carsales['period'],carsales['sales'])
plt.title('Car Sales by Month')
plt.xlabel('Month')
plt.ylabel('Sales')
plt.show()
```

Figure 2-7 shows the new plot.

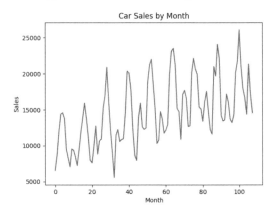

Figure 2-7: A line plot makes the patterns within years (high summers and low winters) more apparent.

This new plot shows the same data, but plotted as a line rather than a collection of points. With a line plot, another pattern becomes much clearer. We can see that the noisy ups and downs of monthly sales within individual years are more ordered than they looked in the scatterplot.

In particular, our data includes nine years of sales figures, and exactly nine major peaks are apparent in the contour of the line plot. What looked like totally random noise actually has some structure: a predictable peak in sales occurs every summer, with a corresponding trough every winter. If you think about it a little more, you might realize why variation could exist within a year: it's because this data comes from Quebec, where very cold winters are associated with lower activity levels, and beautiful warm summers are associated with going outside and shopping and taking long road trips that require cars.

Now that you can see the way the number of car sales goes up and down during a year, maybe it reminds you of a mathematical function. In fact, the pattern of periodic increases and decreases looks like a trigonometric curve, like a sine or cosine curve. Figure 2-8 shows an example of sine and cosine curves.

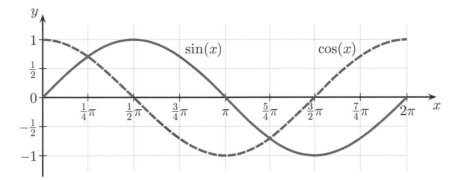

Figure 2-8: A plot of a sine curve and a cosine curve

Let's try a regression that uses the sine and cosine of the period in a multivariate regression:

```python
import math
carsales['sin_period']=carsales['period'].apply(lambda x: math.sin(x*2*math.pi/12))
carsales['cos_period']=carsales['period'].apply(lambda x: math.cos(x*2*math.pi/12))

x_trig = carsales.loc[:,['period','sin_period','cos_period']].values.reshape(-1,3)
y = carsales['sales'].values.reshape(-1,1)

regressor_trig = LinearRegression()
regressor_trig.fit(x_trig, y)

plt.plot(carsales['period'],carsales['sales'])
plt.plot(x,regressor_trig.predict(x_trig),'r--')
plt.title('Car Sales by Month')
plt.xlabel('Month')
plt.ylabel('Sales')
plt.show()
```

In this snippet, we define sine and cosine transformations of the period variable, and then we fit a regression that uses these new variables as predictors. Finally, we plot the result, which is shown in Figure 2-9.

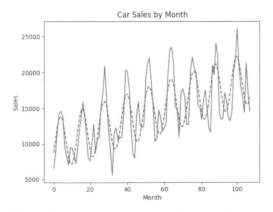

Figure 2-9: A trigonometric curve fit to our data

In Figure 2-9, you can see the raw sales data plotted as a solid line, and the trigonometric regression curve plotted as a dashed line. You can see that we're really getting somewhere now. The regression that relies on trigonometric functions seems to fit the data especially well. In particular, it seems to go up during the yearly peaks and down during the yearly troughs, thereby getting much closer to the true sales numbers. We can verify that this trigonometric curve has a lower RMSE than the straight line as follows:

```
trig_line=regressor_trig.predict(x_trig)[:, 0]
print(get_rmse(trig_line,saleslist))
```

The RMSE we get as output is the lowest one we've seen yet: about 2,681. It is not entirely a coincidence that trigonometric functions enable us to fit the data well. In fact, the increases and decreases in temperature during seasons on our planet are due to a change in the angle of the Earth during its revolution around the sun. The change in the angle of the Earth with respect to the sun follows a curve that's like a sine curve, and therefore temperature changes throughout each year also follow sine-like curves. If car sales are reacting to winter and summer weather changes due to temperature, it makes sense that they would also follow sine-like curves. Regardless of whether we found the trigonometric model by blind chance, by looking at our scatterplot in Figure 2-1, or because we know about the astronomy of the Earth's rotation around the sun, it seems like we've found a good regression curve that fits the data well.

Choosing the Best Regression to Use for Forecasting

We've observed that the regression line that includes terms for the sine and cosine of the period seem to fit the data well. When we say that this line fits the data well, we mean that, qualitatively, the dashed line in Figure 2-9 gets quite close to the solid line. More precisely, we mean that quantitatively, the RMSE for the trigonometric line is lower than the RMSE for the other lines we've looked at. Whenever we find a model with a lower RMSE, we are getting a model that fits our data better.

The natural temptation is to keep looking for new regression specifications that have lower and lower RMSEs. For example, let's try a new regression specification that includes seven prediction terms to forecast sales, and find the RMSE for that model:

```
carsales['squareroot']=carsales['period'].apply(lambda x: x**0.5)
carsales['exponent15']=carsales['period'].apply(lambda x: x**1.5)
carsales['log']=carsales['period'].apply(lambda x: math.log(x+1))

x_complex = carsales.loc[:,['period','log','sin_period','cos_period', \
'squareroot','exponent15','log','quadratic', 'cubic']].values.reshape(-1,9)
y = carsales['sales'].values.reshape(-1,1)

regressor_complex = LinearRegression()
regressor_complex.fit(x_complex,y)
```

```
complex_line=[prediction for sublist in regressor_complex.predict(x_complex) \
for prediction in sublist]
print(get_rmse(complex_line,saleslist))
```

In this snippet, we repeated steps that we've done before: define some variables, use the variables in a linear regression, and check the RMSE of the regression. Notice the backslash (\) at the end of a few of the lines. These are *line continuation characters*: they're telling Python that the line they're on and the next line should be treated as one single line of code. We are using them here because the full line doesn't fit on the book's page. At home, you can use line continuation characters, or you can ignore them if you're able to type the full lines without breaks.

At the end of the preceding snippet, we check the RMSE for this new regression model, and we find that it's about 2,610: even lower than the RMSE for the trigonometric model shown in Figure 2-9. If RMSE is our metric for judging how well a model fits, and we have gotten the lowest RMSE yet, it probably seems natural to conclude that this is our best model yet, and we should use this model for forecasting.

But be careful; this apparently reasonable conclusion is not correct. The approach we've been taking to model selection has a problem: it doesn't fully resemble the reality of forecasting as we encounter it in real life. Think about what we've done. We've used past data to fit a regression line and then judged how good that regression line is, based on how close it gets to past data points (its RMSE). We're using the *past* both for fitting our regression line and for judging its performance. In a real-world forecasting scenario, we'll use the past to fit our regression line, but we should use the *future* for judging its performance. A forecasting method is worthwhile only if it can predict the unknown future.

When we're choosing the best regression line to use for forecasting, we want to find a way to evaluate various regression lines based on their performance on future data. This is not possible because the future hasn't happened yet, so we can't ever have future data. But we can make a small change in the way we perform and evaluate regressions so that our measurements of performance on past data give a good estimate of how they'll perform when predicting the future.

What we need to do is split our full dataset into two separate, mutually exclusive subsets: a *training set*, consisting of the majority of our data, and a *test set*, consisting of the rest. We'll use only the training set to fit our regressions, or in other words, to *train* them. After fitting/training our regressions, we'll use the test set to evaluate how good the regressions are, using metrics like RMSE or MAE.

This simple change makes an important difference. Instead of evaluating performance based on the same data used to fit our regressions, we are evaluating based on separate data that was not used during the fitting process. Our test set is from the past, but it's *as if* it's from the future, since it's not used to determine the coefficients and intercept in our regression, and it's used only to test how good the regression's predictions are. Since the test set hasn't been used to fit our regressions, we sometimes say that the regressions haven't *learned from* the test data, or that it's *as if* the test data is from the future. By having some data that's as if it's from the future, our regression evaluation more closely resembles a true forecasting process, where prediction of the future is the most important goal.

Let's look at the code to accomplish this training/test split, and then we'll see what makes it work so well:

```
x_complex_train = carsales.loc[0:80,['period','log','sin_period','cos_period','squareroot', \
'exponent15','log','quadratic','cubic']].values.reshape(-1,9)
y_train = carsales.loc[0:80,'sales'].values.reshape(-1,1)

x_complex_test = carsales.loc[81:107,['period','log','sin_period','cos_period','squareroot', \
'exponent15','log','quadratic','cubic']].values.reshape(-1,9)
y_test = carsales.loc[81:107,'sales'].values.reshape(-1,1)

regressor_complex.fit(x_complex_train, y_train)
```

Here, we split the data into two sets: a training set and a test set. We use the training set to train the data (to fit a regression line). We can then use the test set to test how well our regression performs. If you think about this approach, it resembles an actual forecasting situation: we train a model knowing only the past, but the model has to do well on data that wasn't used to train it (the future, or data that's as if it's from the future). Creating a test set like this is essentially creating a simulated future.

In the preceding snippet, we use the first 81 time periods as our training data and the rest (27 time periods) as our test data. In percentage terms, we use 75 percent of our data for training and reserve about 25 percent for testing. Splitting training and test data in proportions close to this is common: 70 percent training data and 30 percent testing data is also common, as are 80/20 and 90/10 splits. We usually keep the large majority of our data in the training set since finding the right regression line is crucial, and using more data for training can help us find the best regression line (the one with the most predictive accuracy). At the same time, we need more than a negligible amount of data in the test set, since we also need to get an accurate estimate of how our regression is expected to perform with new data.

After we've created training and test sets, we can test our different regression models on the test set and check the RMSE or the MAE for each model. The model that has the lowest RMSE or MAE on the test set is a reasonable choice for the model we can use for forecasts of the actual future. Let's check the RMSE for several of the regressions we've run so far:

```
x_train = carsales.loc[0:80,['period']].values.reshape(-1,1)
x_test = carsales.loc[81:107,['period']].values.reshape(-1,1)
x_trig_train = carsales.loc[0:80,['period','sin_period','cos_period']].values.reshape(-1,3)
x_trig_test = carsales.loc[81:107,['period','sin_period','cos_period']].values.reshape(-1,3)

regressor.fit(x_train, y_train)
regressor_trig.fit(x_trig_train, y_train)
```

```
complex_test_predictions=[prediction for sublist in \
    regressor_complex.predict(x_complex_test) for prediction in sublist]
test_predictions=[prediction for sublist in regressor.predict(x_test) for \
    prediction in sublist]
trig_test_predictions=[prediction for sublist in \
    regressor_trig.predict(x_trig_test) for prediction in sublist]

print(get_rmse(test_predictions,saleslist[81:107]))
print(get_rmse(trig_test_predictions,saleslist[81:107]))
print(get_rmse(complex_test_predictions,saleslist[81:107]))
```

After you run the preceding snippet, you can see that our univariate regression has an RMSE of about 4,116 on the test set. The trigonometric multivariate regression has an RMSE of about 3,461—much better than the univariate regression. By contrast, the complex regression model that includes nine prediction terms has an RMSE of about 6,006 on the test set—an awful performance. Though it had excellent performance on the training set, we find that it has awful performance on the test set.

This complex model shows a particularly bad example of *overfitting*. In this common machine learning problem, a model is too complex and fits the data's noise and coincidences instead of the data's true patterns. Overfitting often happens when our attempts to get low errors on a training set lead to us getting much higher errors on a test set.

For example, suppose that by some coincidence, car sales in Quebec spiked every time the star Betelgeuse had a V-band magnitude greater than 0.6 between 1960 and 1968. If we included Betelguese's V-band magnitude as a parameter in our regressions, we would find that our RMSE was quite low when predicting 1960 to 1968 because of this coincidence. Finding a low RMSE might make us quite confident that we had a great model that would perform well. We might extrapolate this pattern into the future and forecast future sales spikes at future high points of Betelgeuse's brightness cycle. However, since the past relationship between Betelgeuse and car sales was only coincidental, extrapolating this pattern into the future would give us huge errors; it would cause RMSE on future predictions to be quite high. The Betelgeuse/car sales relationship was only noise, and our regressions are supposed to capture only true signals, not noise. Including Betelguese's brightness measurements in our regression would be an example of overfitting, since our zeal to decrease RMSE for the past would lead us to increase RMSE in the future.

This example should make it clear that using error measurements on a training set to choose the best model could lead us to choose a model that has high error measurements on the test set. For that reason, error measurement on the test set is the right metric to use to compare models in all forecasting tasks. As a general rule, you can expect overfitting to happen when you've included too many irrelevant variables in your regression. So, you can avoid overfitting by removing the irrelevant variables (like the brightness of Betelgeuse) from your regressions.

The problem is that we're not always entirely sure which variables are irrelevant and which ones are actually useful. That's why we have to try several models and check performance. Find the model that has the lowest RMSE on the test set, and that will be the one that has the right mix of variables and doesn't lead you to get distracted by coincidences and overfit.

Now that we've compared models based on their RMSE on the test set, we can choose the trigonometric model as our best model so far. We can extrapolate one period forward in this model and determine a forecast for consumer demand next month, just as we extrapolated for our univariate model before. We can report this number back to the business as an estimate based on rigorous linear regression analysis. Not only that, we can explain why we made this prediction and why we used our model, including the idea of the best-fit line, the trigonometric modeling of the seasons, and the favorable (low) errors on the test set. If no objections or countervailing business considerations arise, we can order this number of cars next month, and we can expect that customers will want to purchase close to this number of cars.

Exploring Further

Linear regression and forecasting are both topics that can fill many textbooks. If you continue in your data science education, you'll have a chance to learn many of the subtleties and nuances related to these subjects.

One thing you should consider studying if you want to get to an advanced level in data science is the linear algebra behind linear regression. You can think of each observation in your data as a row of a matrix, and then you can use matrix multiplication and matrix inversion to calculate the line of best fit, instead of relying on a Python library to do the calculations for you. If you deeply explore these linear algebra concepts, you'll learn about the mathematical assumptions underlying linear regression. Understanding these mathematical assumptions will enable you to more accurately judge whether linear regression is the best method to use with your data, or whether you should use some of the methods described later in the book instead (especially the supervised learning topics discussed in Chapter 6).

Another issue you should become familiar with is the limitation of linear regression as a forecasting method. As the name indicates, linear regression is a linear method, and it's meant to be used with variables that have linear relationships. For example, if customers order about 10 more units of your product each week than they did the previous week, a linear relationship exists between time and customer demand, and linear regression would be a perfect method to measure that increase and forecast future customer demand. On the other hand, if your sales double every week for a year and then suddenly crash and then slowly rise again for a while, the relationship between time and sales would be highly nonlinear, and linear regression may not yield accurate predictions.

Similarly, remember that when we use linear regression for forecasting, we are extrapolating past growth to predict future growth. If certain circumstances aren't present or accounted for in your historical data, your linear regression won't be able to accurately predict their occurrence in the future. For example, if you use data from steady, prosperous years as your training data, you'll probably predict steady, prosperous growth in the future. Instead, you may find that a global financial crisis or pandemic changes everything, and since the regression's training data didn't include a pandemic, no prediction of any pandemic will be given for the future. Regression works only when the future resembles the past. Some events like wars and pandemics are so inherently unpredictable that regression can never give us completely accurate predictions about them. In those cases, preparation is more important than forecasting; make sure your business is ready for hard times and surprises instead of assuming that linear regression will always give you completely correct answers. Though forecasting is important and linear regression is powerful, it's important to remember that these limitations exist.

Summary

We began this chapter with a common business scenario: a company needs to decide how much new inventory it should order. We used linear regression as our main forecasting tool, and we looked a little at the programming side of it (how to write code for regression), the statistical side of it (which error metrics we can use to determine a model's goodness of fit), and the math side of it (why our particular line is the best-fit line). After we went through all these aspects of the problem, we arrived at a model that we thought was best, which we could use to obtain a forecast of next month's consumer demand.

This scenario—considering a business problem and using programming, mathematical theory, and common sense to find a data-driven solution—is typical of data science. In the remaining chapters, we'll examine other business scenarios and talk about how to use data science to find ideal solutions to them. In the next chapter, we'll go over data distributions and show how to test two groups to see whether they're significantly different from each other.

3

GROUP COMPARISONS

In this chapter, we'll discuss how to make intelligent comparisons between groups, using examples from business scenarios. We'll start small by looking at one group alone. We'll see which descriptive statistics most succinctly describe it, draw plots that capture its essence, and compare various samples from it. We'll then be ready to reason about samples from two groups. We'll conclude by looking at statistical significance tests: the t-test and the Mann-Whitney U test.

Reading Population Data

Let's start by reading in some data. This data records measurements of 1,034 professional baseball players, including their height, weight, and age at the time of measurement. You can download this data directly from *https://bradfordtuckfield.com/mlb.csv*. Its original source is the Statistics Online Computational Resource (SOCR) website (*https://web.archive .org/web/20220629205951/https://wiki.stat.ucla.edu/socr/index.php/SOCR _Data_MLB_HeightsWeights*).

```
import pandas as pd
mlb=pd.read_csv('mlb.csv')
print(mlb.head())
print(mlb.shape)
```

In this snippet, we import pandas and use its read_csv() method to read in our data. This is all simple data ingestion, just as we did in Chapters 1 and 2. After you run this snippet, you should see the following output:

```
             name team       position  height  weight    age
0    Adam_Donachie  BAL        Catcher      74   180.0  22.99
1        Paul_Bako  BAL        Catcher      74   215.0  34.69
2  Ramon_Hernandez  BAL        Catcher      72   210.0  30.78
3     Kevin_Millar  BAL  First_Baseman      72   210.0  35.43
4      Chris_Gomez  BAL  First_Baseman      73   188.0  35.71
(1034, 6)
```

The last line of the output shows the *shape* of the data, the number of rows and columns in the dataset. We can see that our data has 1,034 rows and 6 columns. We have one row for each person who was measured, and one column for each fact recorded about each person. These 1,034 people are collectively called our *population*, which, in the world of statistics, means any set of similar items that are being studied to answer a particular question.

Summary Statistics

Doing exploratory analysis every time we get a new dataset is useful. One thing we can do is run print(mlb.describe()) to see our summary statistics all at once:

	height	weight	age
count	1034.000000	1033.000000	1034.000000
mean	73.697292	201.689255	28.736712
std	2.305818	20.991491	4.320310
min	67.000000	150.000000	20.900000
25%	72.000000	187.000000	25.440000
50%	74.000000	200.000000	27.925000
75%	75.000000	215.000000	31.232500
max	83.000000	290.000000	48.520000

Plotting the data early and often is also a good idea in any data analysis effort. We'll create a box plot with the following code:

```
import matplotlib.pyplot as plt
fig1, ax1 = plt.subplots()
ax1.boxplot([mlb['height']])
ax1.set_ylabel('Height (Inches)')
plt.title('MLB Player Heights')
plt.xticks([1], ['Full Population'])
plt.show()
```

Here, we import Matplotlib to create plots. We use its `boxplot()` command to create a box plot of all the heights in our population. You can see the results in Figure 3-1.

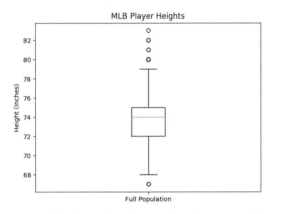

Figure 3-1: A box plot showing the distribution of heights of our Major League Baseball (MLB) population

This box plot is similar to the box plots we looked at in Chapter 1. Remember that box plots show the range and distribution of data. Here, we can see that the minimum value of height in the data is around 67, and the maximum is around 83. The median (the horizontal line in the middle of the box) is around 74 inches. We can see that Matplotlib regards several of the points as outliers, and that's why they're drawn as circles beyond the range of the vertical lines extending from the top and bottom of the box. Box plots provide a simple way to explore our population and understand it better.

Random Samples

In many common scenarios, we're interested in studying a population, but we don't have access to the full population, so we study a small part, or *sample*, instead. For example, medical researchers may want to create a drug that can cure a disease for all women over 50 years old. The researchers don't have a way to contact all women in the world who are over 50, so instead they recruit a sample of that full population, maybe a few hundred people. They study the effect of their drug on this sample. They hope that their sample resembles the full population, so that if the drug works on the sample, it will also work on the full population.

Recruiting a sample is something you should do carefully, to make sure the sample resembles the full population as much as possible. For example, if you recruit participants at an Olympic training facility, your sample will contain people who are healthier than average, so you may create a drug that works for extremely healthy people but not for the general population. If you recruit participants at a Polish community festival, you might create a drug that works for Eastern Europeans but not for others. The best way to collect a sample that resembles the full population is to take a random sample. By selecting randomly from a full population, you expect to have equal likelihood of selecting each different type of person.

Let's look at samples of our baseball player population, which we can create in Python as follows:

```
sample1=mlb.sample(n=30,random_state=8675309)
sample2=mlb.sample(n=30,random_state=1729)
```

Here, we use the convenient pandas `sample()` method. This method randomly selects 30 baseball players for both of our samples, `sample1` and `sample2`. Setting the `random_state` parameter is not necessary. But we set it here because it ensures that you'll get the same results as we do when you run the same code.

You may wonder why we select 30 samples and not 20 or 40 or some other number. In fact, we could easily select any other number of samples by changing n=30 to n=20 or n=40 or anything else we prefer. When we choose a large n for our random sample, we expect the sample to closely resemble the full population. But sometimes recruiting participants can be challenging, so we want to choose a small n to avoid the difficulty of recruiting. In the world of statistics, choosing $n = 30$ is a common convention; when we choose samples that have at least size 30, we feel reasonably confident that our samples are big enough to make our statistical calculations give us good results.

Let's also create a third sample, which we'll define manually as follows:

```
sample3=[71, 72, 73, 74, 74, 76, 75, 75, 75, 76, 75, 77, 76, 75, 77, 76, 75,\
76, 76, 75, 75, 81,77, 75, 77, 75, 77, 77, 75, 75]
```

We know that `sample1` and `sample2` are random samples from our baseball player population, since we created them using `sample()`. But it's not yet clear where the measurements in `sample3` came from. Later, you'll learn how to use statistical tests to reason about whether `sample3` is likely to be a random sample from our population of baseball players, or whether it is more likely to be associated with a different population, like basketball players or another group. Keep thinking about `sample3`, because reasoning about where `sample3` came from (and in general, whether two given samples come from the same population) will be the central goal of this chapter.

Let's look at a plot of these samples to see whether they resemble each other and the full population:

```
import numpy as np
fig1, ax1 = plt.subplots()
ax1.boxplot([mlb['height'],sample1['height'],sample2['height'],np.array(sample3)])
ax1.set_ylabel('Height (Inches)')
plt.title('MLB Player Heights')
plt.xticks([1,2,3,4], ['Full Population','Sample 1','Sample 2','Sample 3'])
plt.show()
```

Here, we use the same box plot code we used before, but instead of plotting only one dataset, we plot four datasets: the distribution of heights of the full population and the distribution of heights of all three samples separately. We can see the results in Figure 3-2.

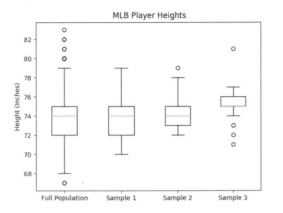

Figure 3-2: Box plots of our full MLB population (far left), two samples from the population (middle), and a mystery sample that may or may not be from our population (right)

We can see that none of these box plots are quite identical, but they definitely bear some resemblance to one another. We see some similar median values and 75th percentile values, as well as some similar maxima. The similarity in the first three box plots should match your intuition: when we take large enough random samples from a population, the samples should resemble the population and should resemble one another. We can also check simple summary statistics related to each sample, like the mean:

```
print(np.mean(sample1['height']))
print(np.mean(sample2['height']))
print(np.mean(sample3))
```

Here, we check the mean height in all our samples. The mean height for `sample1` is 73.8, while the mean height for `sample2` is 74.4, and the mean height for sample3 is 75.4. These means are relatively close to the mean height of the full population, 73.7. In this context, the mean height of the full population has a special name; it's called the population's *expected value*. If we take a random sample from our population, we expect that the mean height of our sample will be about the same as the population's expected value for height, 73.7. At least two of our samples are random samples from the population, and we see that their means are indeed close to our expected value.

When we look at the box plot of sample3, we can see that it doesn't seem to resemble the other three box plots as much as they resemble each other. We may interpret this as evidence that it isn't a random sample from our population of baseball players. On the other hand, it doesn't look different enough from the population or other samples that we can be immediately certain that it isn't a random sample from our population. We need to learn more before we can feel certain about whether sample3 is a random draw from our population or whether it comes from some other population.

So far, we've used vague and impressionistic language to talk about our samples: they *resemble* each other, and they have means that are *relatively close* or *about the same* as our expectations. If we want to make concrete, evidence-based decisions, we need to be more precise. In the next section, we'll explore quantitative methods that statisticians have developed for reasoning about the differences between groups, including some easy-to-use tests that help us decide whether two groups come from the same population.

Differences Between Sample Data

We saw a difference of about 0.6 inches between sample1 and sample2 and a difference of more than 1.6 inches between sample1 and sample3. Here's the important question we would like to answer: Do we believe that sample3 is a random sample from the same population as sample1 and sample2? We need a method more reliable than intuition to say, for example, that a difference of 0.6 inches between sample means is plausible or probable, while a difference of 1.6 inches between sample means makes it implausible that the samples come from the same population. How big of a difference between sample means would make it implausible that two samples come from the same population?

To answer this question, we need to understand the size differences we should expect between random samples from our population. So far, we've looked at only two random samples from our population. Instead of trying to generalize based on only two samples, let's look at a large collection of samples and see how much they tend to differ from one another. This will help us understand which variations are plausible and which variations are implausible.

Here's some code to get a collection of 2,000 sample means and their differences:

```
alldifferences=[]
for i in range(1000):
    newsample1=mlb.sample(n=30,random_state=i*2)
    newsample2=mlb.sample(n=30,random_state=i*2+1)
    alldifferences.append(newsample1['height'].mean()-newsample2['height'].mean())

print(alldifferences[0:10])
```

In this snippet, we create the `alldifferences` variable as an empty list. Then we create a loop that goes through 1,000 iterations. In each iteration, we create two new samples and append the difference between their sample means to our `alldifferences` list. The final result is a completely filled-in `alldifferences`, a list of 1,000 differences between randomly selected samples. After running this snippet, you should see the following output:

```
[0.8333333333333286, -0.30000000000001137, -0.10000000000000853,\
-0.1666666666666572, 0.06666666666667709, -0.9666666666666686,\
0.7999999999999972, 0.9333333333333371, -0.5333333333333314,\
-0.20000000000000284]
```

You can see that the first two samples we checked have means that are about 0.83 inches apart. The second pair of samples has means that are about 0.3 inches apart. The sixth pair of samples has means that are almost a full inch apart from each other (about −0.97 inches), while the fifth pair of samples has means that are nearly identical, only about 0.07 inches apart. Looking at these 10 numbers, we can see that 0.6 is not an implausible difference between two samples from our population, since several of our first 10 differences are greater in magnitude than 0.6. However, none of the differences we've seen so far are greater than 1 inch in magnitude, so 1.6 inches is starting to seem more implausible.

We can see a fuller representation of our 1,000 differences by drawing a plot of the `alldifferences` list:

```
import seaborn as sns
sns.set()
ax=sns.distplot(alldifferences).set_title("Differences Between Sample Means")
plt.xlabel('Difference Between Means (Inches)')
plt.ylabel('Relative Frequency')
plt.show()
```

Here, we import the seaborn package because it can make beautiful plots. We use its `distplot()` method to plot the differences we find. You can see the results in Figure 3-3.

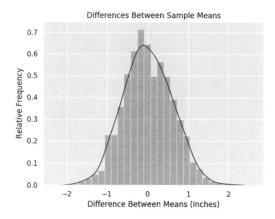

Figure 3-3: A histogram showing the distribution of differences between mean heights of random samples, creating an approximate bell curve pattern

In this histogram, each bar represents a relative frequency; it represents how likely each observation is compared to other observations. There's a high bar at the point marked 0 on the x-axis. This indicates a relatively high number of differences in our `alldifferences` list that are very close to 0. A much lower bar appears at $x = 1$. This indicates relatively few cases in which the difference between the sample means is about 1. The full shape of the plot should make solid intuitive sense: it's rare for our random samples to be very different from each other, because they're samples from the same population and we expect their means to be roughly the same.

The shape that the bars make in Figure 3-3 resembles a bell. You can see that we've drawn a line over the bars that shows this general bell shape. The curve that this plot approximates is called a *bell curve*. Approximate bell curves are found in many situations. One powerful theoretical result in statistics is called the *central limit theorem,* and it states that under a certain set of common conditions, differences between means of samples will be distributed in a shape that's approximately a bell curve. The technical conditions that make this theorem true are that the random samples are independent and *identically distributed* (that is, random draws from the same population) and that the population has a finite expected value and a finite variance. The fact that we see approximate bell curves in so many domains provides evidence that these technical conditions are often met.

Once we know the shape and size of the bell curve in Figure 3-3, we can reason more accurately about difficult statistical questions. Let's return to the question of `sample3`. Given what we know so far, do we believe that `sample3` is a random sample from our population of baseball players? We saw that the difference between the mean of `sample3` and the mean of `sample1` is about 1.6 inches. When we look at Figure 3-3, we can see that the bell curve is extremely low there, close to 0. This means that random samples from our population only rarely differ by as much as 1.6 inches. This makes it seem relatively implausible that `sample3` is a random sample from our baseball player population. We can find out how implausible it is by checking exactly how many of our differences have magnitude greater than or equal to 1.6 inches:

```
largedifferences=[diff for diff in alldifferences if abs(diff)>=1.6]
print(len(largedifferences))
```

In this snippet, we create `largedifferences`, a list that contains all elements of `alldifferences` with magnitude greater than or equal to 1.6. We then check the length of the `largedifferences` list. We find that the list has only eight elements, meaning random samples from our `mlb` population have means that differ by 1.6 or more only about 8 in 1,000 times, or 0.8 percent of the time. This value, 0.8 percent or 0.008, is a calculated likelihood. We can think of it as our best estimate of the probability that the mean heights of two random samples from the `mlb` population differ by 1.6 inches or more. This probability is often called a *p-value*, where *p* is short for *probability*.

If we assume that `sample3` is a random sample from our `mlb` population, we have to believe that this rare difference, something whose extremity occurs less than 1 percent of the time, has happened naturally. The low likelihood of this event may convince us to reject the idea that `sample3` comes from the same population as `sample1`. In other words, the low *p*-value causes us to reject the notion that these two groups come from the same population. The lower the *p*-value, the more confident we feel about rejecting the notion that the groups come from the same population, because low *p*-values require us to believe in more and more unlikely coincidences. By contrast, consider how common it is that differences between sample means from our population are 0.6 inches or more:

```
smalldifferences=[diff for diff in alldifferences if abs(diff)>=0.6]
print(len(smalldifferences))
```

Here, we create `smalldifferences`, a list containing every element of `alldifferences` that has magnitude greater than or equal to 0.6 inches. We can see that differences of this magnitude occur about 31.4 percent of the time. In this case, we would say that our *p*-value is 0.314. If `sample1` and `sample2` come from the same population, we would have to believe that this size of difference, which occurs about 31 percent of the time, occurred in our case. It's not hard to believe that something with 31 percent probability occurred, so we conclude that the difference between `sample1` and `sample2` is plausible; we're willing to accept that, though not identical, they're random samples from the same population.

The *p*-values we've calculated here have led us to accept the notion that `sample1` and `sample2` come from the same population, and to reject the notion that `sample1` and `sample3` come from the same population. You can see how important the size of a *p*-value is in our efforts to compare groups.

Performing Hypothesis Testing

We've outlined all the ingredients needed for a method of statistical reasoning called *hypothesis testing*. We can formalize this method of reasoning in more scientific terms. We're trying to determine whether sample3 is a random sample from the same population as sample1. In scientific terms, we can say that we're considering two separate hypotheses:

Hypothesis 0 sample1 and sample3 are random samples from the same population.

Hypothesis 1 sample1 and sample3 are not random samples from the same population.

In the common statistical parlance, we call Hypothesis 0 the *null hypothesis*, and we call Hypothesis 1 the *alternative hypothesis*. The null hypothesis asserts that both samples are randomly drawn from one population (our baseball player dataset), with just one mean and one standard deviation. The alternative hypothesis asserts that the samples are randomly drawn from two totally different populations, each with its own mean, its own standard deviation, and all of its own unique characteristics. The way we choose between these two hypotheses is by following the same reasoning we followed previously:

1. Assume that Hypothesis 0, the null hypothesis, is true.
2. Find how likely we are to observe sample means that differ by as much as our observed sample means, assuming that Hypothesis 0 is true. The likelihood of this occurring is called the *p*-value.
3. If the *p*-value is small enough, we reject Hypothesis 0, and we're therefore willing to accept Hypothesis 1.

Notice that step 3 is stated vaguely: it doesn't specify how small the *p*-value should be to justify rejecting the null hypothesis. The reason for this vagueness is that there's no mathematically dictated choice for how small the *p*-value needs to be. We can choose whatever level of smallness we think is appropriate to justify rejecting Hypothesis 0, based on our own judgment and intuitions. The *p*-value size that we believe justifies rejecting Hypothesis 0 is called the *significance level*.

The most common significance level used in empirical research is 5 percent, meaning that we consider the rejection of the null hypothesis justified if $p < 0.05$. In the case of sample1 and sample3, we can justify rejecting Hypothesis 0 at a significance level as low as 1 percent, because we found $p < 0.01$. When we find a *p*-value that's less than our chosen significance level, we say that the difference between our groups is *statistically significant*. The recommended practice is to choose the significance level that we want to use before we do any calculations; that way, we avoid the temptation to choose a significance level that confirms whichever hypothesis we want to be confirmed.

The t-Test

We don't have to go through the whole process of calculating means, creating a histogram, and manually calculating *p*-values every time we want to do hypothesis testing. Statisticians have discovered succinct equations that define how likely two groups are to come from the same population. They've created a relatively simple test called a *t-test* that does the process of hypothesis testing quickly and painlessly, without requiring a for loop or a histogram. We can do a t-test to test our Hypothesis 0 and Hypothesis 1. We'll check whether sample1 and sample2 come from the same population as follows:

```
import scipy.stats
scipy.stats.ttest_ind(sample1['height'],sample2['height'])
```

Here, we import the scipy.stats module. The SciPy package that this module is a part of is a popular Python library that includes, among other things, many statistical tests that could be useful as you get more advanced in statistics and data science. After importing this module, we use its ttest_ind command to check for differences between our samples. Its output is the following:

```
Ttest_indResult(statistic=-1.0839563860213952, pvalue=0.2828695892305152)
```

Here, the *p*-value is relatively high (about 0.283), certainly higher than a 0.05 significance threshold. (It differs a little from the 0.314 *p*-value we calculated earlier because that *p*-value calculation method was an approximate method, and this one is more mathematically exact.) This high *p*-value indicates that it is plausible that these are samples from the same population. This is not surprising because we know that they are from the same population (we created them ourselves). In this case, we decide not to reject our null hypothesis, and we accept (until any other evidence convinces us otherwise) that sample1 and sample2 come from the same population. You can also run scipy .stats.ttest_ind(sample1['height'],sample3) to compare sample1 and sample3, and if you do, you'll find a low *p*-value (less than 0.05), which justifies rejecting the null hypothesis that sample1 and sample3 come from the same population.

Several types of t-tests exist, as well as other hypothesis tests besides the t-test. The ttest_ind command we've used so far has an _ind suffix to indicate that it's meant to be used for independent samples. Here, *independent* means just what we would expect: no meaningful, consistent relationship exists between the individuals in one sample and the individuals in the other—the samples consist of different people who were randomly selected.

If we have *related* rather than independent samples, we can use another command, scipy.stats.ttest_rel, which performs another type of t-test that is mathematically a little different from ttest_ind. The ttest_rel command would be appropriate when observations in different samples have a meaningful relationship to each other—for example, if they're two different exam scores for the same student, or two different medical test results for the same patient.

Another type of t-test, the *Welch's t-test*, is designed for comparing samples when we don't want to assume that the samples have equal variance. You can implement Welch's t-test in Python by adding `equal_var=False` to the t-test command.

The t-test is a *parametric test*, meaning that it relies on assumptions about the distribution of the data in our population. The t-test relies on several technical assumptions: first, that the groups being compared should have sample means that follow a bell curve; second, that the variances of the groups being compared should be identical (unless using Welch's t-test); and third, that the two groups are independent of each other. If these assumptions are not met, the t-test is not completely accurate, though it's rarely too far from the truth even if the assumptions are not met.

In some cases, we'd prefer to perform hypothesis testing with a test that didn't make these strong assumptions that may not be true. If so, we can rely on a body of knowledge called *nonparametric statistics*, which provides tools for hypothesis testing and other statistical reasoning that make fewer assumptions about the distribution of our data (for example, we don't need to work with populations whose sample means follow bell curves). One hypothesis test from nonparametric statistics is called the *Mann-Whitney U test* (or the *Wilcoxon rank-sum test*), and we can implement it easily in Python as follows:

```
scipy.stats.mannwhitneyu(sample1['height'],sample2['height'])
```

This test requires only one line, since the SciPy package includes an implementation of the Mann-Whitney U test. Just like the t-test, all we need to input is the data we're comparing, and the code will output a *p*-value. If you want to have a deep understanding of the various kinds of hypothesis tests and exactly when to use them, you should read some advanced theoretical statistics textbooks. For now, the simple independent sample t-test we've used is quite robust and should work in most practical scenarios.

Nuances of Hypothesis Testing

Hypothesis testing using a null hypothesis and a t-test is common enough to be called *popular*, but it's not as beloved as most popular things are. Students tend to dislike it because it's not intuitive to most people, and it requires some tortured reasoning to understand. Teachers sometimes dislike it because their students dislike it and struggle to learn it. Many methodological researchers find it irritating because it's so common at all levels for people to misunderstand and misinterpret t-tests, *p*-values, and hypothesis tests in general. The antipathy toward hypothesis testing has even led some respected scientific journals to ban it from their publications, although this has been rare.

Most of the negative feelings toward hypothesis testing are the result of misunderstanding. Researchers misunderstand some nuances of hypothesis testing and misuse it, and then mistakes in research result, which methodological sticklers resent. Since these misunderstandings are common even among professionals, it's worthwhile to mention some of them here and try to explain nuances that will help you avoid some of these same mistakes.

One important point to remember is what a *p*-value tells you: it tells you the likelihood of observing data, after assuming a null hypothesis to be true. People often think or wish it told them the converse: the likelihood of a hypothesis's truth, given some observed data. Always remember that a *p*-value should not be interpreted directly as a probability of a hypothesis being true. So, when we see that the *p*-value for comparing the heights of `sample1` and `sample3` is $p = 0.008$, we can't say, "These samples have only a 0.8 percent probability of coming from the same population," nor can we say, "The null hypothesis has a 0.8 percent probability of being true." We can say only, "If the null hypothesis is true, something with 0.8 percent probability occurred." This enables us to decide whether to reject the null hypothesis, but it doesn't enable us to say exactly how likely either hypothesis is to be true.

Another important nuance is the difference between accepting a hypothesis and failing to reject it. Hypothesis testing has only two possible outcomes: either we reject a null hypothesis, or we decide not to reject the null hypothesis. Failing to reject something is not quite the same as wholeheartedly accepting it, and just because a *p*-value is not below a significance threshold does not mean that two groups are certainly the same. Just because one t-test fails to lead to a rejection of the null hypothesis does not mean that the null hypothesis is certainly true.

Similarly, just because one *p*-value seems to justify a rejection of a null hypothesis does not mean that the null hypothesis is certainly false. This is especially true when we have limited data; difficult, noisy measurements; or a reason to doubt our measurements. Hypothesis testing does not let us take uncertain data and have perfect certainty about hypotheses. Rather, it provides one piece of evidence that we have to understand properly and then weigh together with a great deal of other evidence.

Another important concept to remember is the Anna Karenina principle. Leo Tolstoy wrote in *Anna Karenina* that "all happy families are alike; each unhappy family is unhappy in its own way." Statistics has an analogous principle: all acceptances of the null hypothesis are alike, but each rejection of the null hypothesis happens for a different reason. The null hypothesis states that two samples are random draws from the same population. If we reject the null hypothesis, any one or more of a number of things could be true: our two samples could be random draws from different populations, or both could be samples from the same population but not randomly selected, or a source of sampling bias could be present, or blind luck might be occurring. Just because we are confident about rejecting the null hypothesis doesn't mean we can be confident about which part of the null hypothesis is incorrect. As empirical researchers like to say, "Further research is needed."

A final nuance to remember is the difference between *statistical significance* and *practical significance*. It's possible for one sample of athletes to have mean height 73.11 and another sample of athletes to have mean height 73.12, and for these two means to have a statistically significant difference according to a t-test. We can justifiably conclude that these two groups are not random samples from the same population and treat them differently because of their different mean height. However, even if this difference of 0.01 inches is statistically significant, it's not clear that this difference has practical significance. Members of these two groups should be able to wear the same clothes, sit on the same seats on airplanes, and reach the same high cupboards (on average). We have no reason to suppose that one group would be better than the other group at baseball in any practically important sense. In this case, we might wish to ignore the results of a t-test, since even though a statistically detectable difference exists, it's not a difference that has any practical consequence. Practical significance is always an important thing to consider during the process of hypothesis testing.

Now that we've discussed hypothesis testing and its thorny theoretical nuances, let's turn to a practical business example.

Comparing Groups in a Practical Context

So far, this chapter has focused on statistical theory. But for data scientists, theoretical considerations always take place within a practical context. Let's switch from our baseball example to a marketing example. Suppose you're running a company that manufactures computers. To keep in touch with customers and increase sales, your company maintains email lists: interested customers can sign up for a topic they're interested in and receive periodic emails from your company related to that topic. For now, you have only two email lists: the desktop list and the laptop list, designed for customers who are interested in your desktop computers and your laptop computers, respectively.

Until now, desktops and laptops have been the only products your company makes. But soon you'll be releasing a new set of products that have been in development for several years: top-of-the-line web servers. It's a natural product line for your company, since you already manufacture computer hardware and already have many tech clients who need server infrastructure. But since this product line is new, almost no one knows about it. Your marketing team is planning to email the subscribers on your email lists to tell them about your great new products and hopefully get started on the right foot with high sales of the new servers.

The marketing team members want to make this email campaign as effective as possible. They have a discussion with you about the campaign strategy. They could design one email and send it to every person on both email lists, or they could design one email message for the desktop subscribers and a different email message for the laptop subscribers. The experts on your marketing team know a lot about targeting: for example, they know that the email messages that extroverts react to most positively are different from the email messages that introverts react to most positively. Other personal characteristics—including age, income, and culture—also have strong effects on responses to advertising.

We need to know whether the desktop subscribers have different characteristics than the laptop subscribers. If the two groups are essentially the same, we can save the marketing team members some time and have them send the same email to everyone. If the two groups are significantly different in ways we understand, we can craft better messages that appeal to each group and improve sales numbers.

We can start our investigation by reading in our data. We'll read in two fabricated datasets (not based on real people or products, just created to illustrate the points in the chapter). You can download these two datasets from *https://bradfordtuckfield.com/desktop.csv* and *https://bradfordtuckfield.com/laptop.csv*, and then read them into Python as follows:

```
desktop=pd.read_csv('desktop.csv')
laptop=pd.read_csv('laptop.csv')
```

You can run print(desktop.head()) and print(laptop.head()) to see the first five rows of each dataset. You'll notice that both datasets have four columns:

userid Contains a unique number identifying a particular user

spending Contains a record of how much that user has spent at your company's website

age Holds the user's age, which you may have recorded during a separate survey

visits Holds the number of times the user has visited pages on your website

Our goal is to determine whether the users described in the desktop dataframe and the users described in the laptop dataframe differ significantly from each other. Let's draw some plots and see whether any immediately apparent differences exist.

We can start with a plot of the amounts that subscribers to each list have spent on our company's products. We'll create a box plot with the following code:

```
import matplotlib.pyplot as plt
sns.reset_orig()
fig1, ax1 = plt.subplots()
ax1.set_title('Spending by Desktop and Laptop Subscribers')
ax1.boxplot([desktop['spending'].values,laptop['spending'].values])
ax1.set_ylabel('Spending ($)')
plt.xticks([1,2], ['Desktop Subscribers','Laptop Subscribers'])
plt.show()
```

Here, we import Matplotlib to create plots. We use its boxplot() command with data from desktop's spending column and laptop's spending column. You can see the results in Figure 3-4.

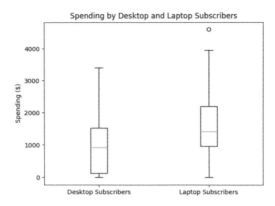

Figure 3-4: Box plots showing the spending levels of subscribers to the desktop email list (left) and subscribers of the laptop email list (right)

We can learn a few things by looking at these box plots. Both groups have minima at 0. Laptop subscribers have a higher 25th percentile, 50th percentile, and 75th percentile, as well as a high outlier that is higher than any observations in the desktop subscriber group. On the other hand, the distributions don't seem terribly different either; desktop subscribers don't seem totally different from laptop subscribers. We have groups that are different, but not too different. We should look more closely and see if some more precise quantitative metrics will help us judge how different they are.

Besides plotting, we can do simple calculations that get summary statistics for our data. In the following snippet, we'll get some of these descriptive statistics:

```
print(np.mean(desktop['age']))
print(np.mean(laptop['age']))
print(np.median(desktop['age']))
print(np.median(laptop['age']))
print(np.quantile(laptop['spending'],.25))
print(np.quantile(desktop['spending'],.75))
print(np.std(desktop['age']))
```

In this snippet, we check the mean age of desktop subscribers and laptop subscribers. The results reveal that the mean desktop subscriber is about 35.8 years old, and the mean laptop subscriber is about 38.7 years old. We can conclude that these groups are different, in the sense that they're not identical. But it's not clear whether the groups are different enough that we should tell our marketing group to create two separate emails instead of one. To make that judgment, we need to use our hypothesis-testing framework. We can specify our null hypothesis and alternative hypothesis as follows:

Hypothesis 0   The two email lists are random samples from the same population.

Hypothesis 1   The two email lists are not random samples from the same population.

Hypothesis 0, our null hypothesis, is describing a world in which there's a population of people who are interested in computers, both laptops and desktops. People from this population sign up for your company's email lists occasionally. But when they sign up for a list, they choose completely at random which of your two lists they sign up for. In this world, your lists have superficial differences, but they are truly two random samples from the same population and don't differ in any essential ways that would warrant different treatment by your company.

Hypothesis 1, the alternative hypothesis, describes a world in which the null hypothesis is not true. This would mean that your subscribers' membership on different email lists is the result at least partially of underlying differences in people who like desktops and people who like laptops. If Hypothesis 0 is true, it would be reasonable to send the same marketing email to both groups. If Hypothesis 1 is true, sending different marketing emails to each group makes more sense. A business decision now depends on the result of a statistical test.

Let's run our t-test and see whether our two subscriber groups actually differ from each other. First, we should specify a significance level. Let's use the 5 percent significance level that's common in research. We can run our t-test with only one line of code:

```
scipy.stats.ttest_ind(desktop['spending'],laptop['spending'])
```

When you look at the results from our t-test, you can see that our p-value is about 0.04. Since we use the common 5 percent significance level, this p-value is low enough for us to conclude that the desktop and laptop groups are not random draws from the same population, so we can reject the null hypothesis. It appears that desktop and laptop email subscribers are at least slightly different in a detectable way.

After finding these differences, we can talk to our company's marketing team and collectively make a decision about whether to design different email campaigns for the different groups. Suppose that the team decides to do so. We can feel proud of ourselves that our statistical analysis has led to a practical decision that we feel is justified. We didn't only analyze data; we used the data to make a decision. This is common in data science: we use our data analysis for data-driven decision-making to improve business outcomes.

But what next? We have come so far in this chapter only to make one decision: a yes/no decision to send different emails to both of our subscriber lists. The next set of questions we need to ask is about how our emails to each group should differ: What should their content be, how should we design them, and how will we know whether we're doing it right? In the next chapter, we'll talk about A/B testing, a powerful framework for answering these difficult questions.

Summary

In this chapter, we talked about populations and samples, as well as how samples that come from the same population should resemble each other. We introduced hypothesis testing, including the t-test, an easy, useful tool for detecting whether two groups are likely to be random draws from the same population. We discussed some business scenarios where the t-test would be useful, including a marketing scenario and a decision about whether to send different emails to different email lists.

The next chapter will build on the tools we introduced here. Instead of just comparing groups, we'll discuss how to run experiments and then use group comparison tools to check for the differences between our experimental treatments.

4

A/B TESTING

In the preceding chapter, we discussed the scientific practice of observing two groups and making quantitative judgments about how they relate to each other. But scientists (including data scientists) do more than just observe preexisting differences. A huge part of science consists of creating differences experimentally and then drawing conclusions. In this chapter, we'll discuss how to conduct those kinds of experiments in business.

We'll start by discussing the need for experimentation and our motivations for testing. We'll cover how to properly set up experiments, including the need for randomization. Next, we'll detail the steps of A/B testing and the champion/challenger framework. We'll conclude by describing nuances like the exploration/exploitation trade-off, as well as ethical concerns.

The Need for Experimentation

Let's return to the scenario we outlined in the second half of Chapter 3. Imagine that you're running a computer company and maintain email marketing lists that your customers can choose to subscribe to. One email list is designed for customers who are interested in your desktop computers, and the other email list is for customers interested in your laptops. You can download two fabricated datasets for this scenario from *https:// bradfordtuckfield.com/desktop.csv* and *https://bradfordtuckfield.com/laptop.csv*. If you save them to the same directory you're running Python from, you can read these hypothetical lists into Python as follows:

```
import pandas as pd
desktop=pd.read_csv('desktop.csv')
laptop=pd.read_csv('laptop.csv')
```

You can run `print(desktop.head())` and `print(laptop.head())` to see the first five rows of each dataset.

In Chapter 3, you learned how to use simple t-tests to detect differences between our datasets, as follows:

```
import scipy.stats
print(scipy.stats.ttest_ind(desktop['spending'],laptop['spending']))
print(scipy.stats.ttest_ind(desktop['age'],laptop['age']))
print(scipy.stats.ttest_ind(desktop['visits'],laptop['visits']))
```

Here, we import the SciPy package's stats module so we can use it for t-tests. Then we print the results of three separate t-tests: one comparing the spending of desktop and laptop subscribers, one comparing the ages of desktop and laptop subscribers, and one comparing the number of recorded website visits of desktop and laptop subscribers. We can see that the first p-value is less than 0.05, indicating that these groups are significantly different in their spending levels (at the 5 percent significance level), just as we concluded in Chapter 3.

After determining that desktop subscribers are different from laptop subscribers, we can conclude that we should send them different marketing emails. However, this fact alone is not enough to completely guide our marketing strategy. Just knowing that our desktop subscriber group spends a little less than the laptop subscriber group doesn't tell us whether crafting long messages or short ones would lead to better sales, or whether using red text or blue text would get us more clicks, or whether informal or formal language would improve customer loyalty most. In some cases, past research published in academic marketing journals can give us hints about what will work best. But even when relevant research exists, every company has its own unique set of customers that may not respond to marketing in exactly the same way that past research indicates.

We need a way to generate new data that's never been collected or published before, so we can use that data to answer new questions about the new situations that we regularly face. Only if we can generate this kind of new data can we reliably learn about what will work best in our efforts to grow our business with our particular set of unique customers. We'll spend the rest of this chapter discussing an approach that will accomplish this.

A/B testing, the focus of this chapter, uses experiments to help businesses determine which practices will give them the greatest chances of success. It consists of a few steps: experimental design, random assignment into treatment and control groups, careful measurement of outcomes, and finally, statistical comparison of outcomes between groups.

The way we'll do statistical comparisons will be familiar: we'll use the t-tests introduced in the previous chapter. While t-tests are a part of the A/B testing process, they are not the only part. A/B testing is a process for collecting new data, which can then be analyzed using tests like the t-test. Since we've already introduced t-tests, we won't focus on them in this chapter. Instead, we'll focus on all the other steps of A/B testing.

Running Experiments to Test New Hypotheses

Let's consider just one hypothesis about our customers that might interest us. Suppose we're interested in studying whether changing the color of text in our marketing emails from black to blue will increase the revenue we earn as a result of the emails. Let's express two hypotheses related to this:

Hypothesis 0 Changing the color of text in our emails from black to blue will have no effect on revenues.

Hypothesis 1 Changing the color of text in our emails from black to blue will lead to a change in revenues (either an increase or a decrease).

We can use the testing hypothesis framework covered in Chapter 3 to test our null hypothesis (Hypothesis 0) and decide whether we want to reject it in favor of its alternative hypothesis (Hypothesis 1). The only difference is that in Chapter 3, we tested hypotheses related to data we had already collected. Here, our datasets do not include information about blue-text and black-text emails. So, extra steps are required before we perform hypothesis testing: designing an experiment, running an experiment, and collecting data related to the experiment's results.

Running experiments may not sound so difficult, but some tricky parts are important to get exactly right. To do the hypothesis test we just outlined, we'll need data from two groups: a group that has received a blue-text email and a group that has received a black-text email. We'll need to know how much revenue we received from each member of the group that received the blue-text email and how much revenue we received from each member of the group that received the black-text email.

After we have that, we can do a simple t-test to determine whether the revenue collected from the blue-text group differed significantly from the revenue collected from the black-text group. In this chapter, we'll use a 5 percent significance level for all of our tests—that is, we'll reject the null hypothesis and accept our alternative hypothesis if our p-value is less than 0.05. When we do our t-test, if the revenues are significantly different, we can reject our null hypothesis (Hypothesis 0).

Otherwise, we won't reject our null hypothesis, and until something convinces us otherwise, we'll accept its assertion that blue and black text lead to equal revenues.

We need to split our population of interest into two subgroups and send a blue-text email to one subgroup and a black-text email to our other subgroup so we can compare revenues from each group. For now, let's focus on desktop subscribers only and split our desktop dataframe into two subgroups.

We can split a group into two subgroups in many ways. One possible choice is to split our dataset into a group of younger people and a group of older people. We might split our data this way because we believe that younger people and older people might be interested in different products, or we might do it this way just because age is one of the few variables that appears in our data. Later, we'll see that this way of splitting our group into subgroups will lead to problems in our analysis, and we'll discuss better ways to create subgroups. But since this method of splitting into subgroups is simple and easy, let's start by trying it to see what happens:

```
import numpy as np
medianage=np.median(desktop['age'])
groupa=desktop.loc[desktop['age']<=medianage,:]
groupb=desktop.loc[desktop['age']>medianage,:]
```

Here, we import the NumPy package, giving it the alias np, so we can use its median() method. Then we simply take the median age of our group of desktop subscribers and create groupa, a subset of our desktop subscribers whose age is below or equal to the median age, and groupb, a subset of our desktop subscribers whose age is above the median age.

After creating groupa and groupb, you can send these two dataframes to your marketing team members and instruct them to send different emails to each group. Suppose they send the black-text email to groupa and the blue-text email to groupb. In every email, they include links to new products they want to sell, and by tracking who clicks which links and their purchases, the team members can measure the total revenue earned from each individual email recipient.

Let's read in some fabricated data that shows hypothetical outcomes for members of our two groups. This data can be downloaded from *https://bradfordtuckfield.com/emailresults1.csv*; store it in the same directory where you run Python. Then you can read it into your Python session as follows:

```
emailresults1=pd.read_csv('emailresults1.csv')
```

If you run **print(emailresults1.head())** in Python, you can see the first rows of this new data. It's a simple dataset: each row corresponds to one individual desktop email subscriber, whose ID is identified in the userid column. The revenue column records the revenue your company earned from each user as a result of this email campaign.

It will be useful to have this new revenue information in the same dataframe as our other information about each user. Let's join the datasets:

```
groupa_withrevenue=groupa.merge(emailresults1,on='userid')
groupb_withrevenue=groupb.merge(emailresults1,on='userid')
```

In this snippet, we use the pandas `merge()` method to combine our dataframes. We specify `on='userid'`, meaning that we take the row of `emailresults1` that corresponds to a particular `userid` and merge it with the row of `groupa` that corresponds to that same `userid`. The end result of using `merge()` is a dataframe in which every row corresponds to a particular user identified by their unique `userid`. The columns tell us not only about their characteristics like age but also about the revenue we earned from them as a result of our recent email campaign.

After preparing our data, it's simple to perform a t-test to check whether our groups are different. We can do it in one line, as follows:

```
print(scipy.stats.ttest_ind(groupa_withrevenue['revenue'],groupb_withrevenue['revenue']))
```

When you run this code, you'll get the following result:

```
Ttest_indResult(statistic=-2.186454851070545, pvalue=0.03730073920038287)
```

The important part of this output is the `pvalue` variable, which tells us the p-value of our test. We can see that the result says that $p = 0.037$, approximately. Since $p < 0.05$, we can conclude that this is a statistically significant difference. We can check the size of the difference:

```
print(np.mean(groupb_withrevenue['revenue'])-np.mean(groupa_withrevenue['revenue']))
```

The output is 125.0. The average `groupb` customer has outspent the average `groupa` customer by $125. This difference is statistically significant, so we reject Hypothesis 0 in favor of Hypothesis 1, concluding (for now, at least) that the blue text in marketing emails leads to about $125 more in revenue per user than black text.

What we have just done was an *experiment*. We split a population into two groups, performed different actions on each group, and compared the results. In the context of business, such an experiment is often called an *A/B test*. The *A/B* part of the name refers to the two groups, Group A and Group B, whose different responses to emails we compared. Every A/B test follows the same pattern we went through here: a split into two groups, application of a different treatment (for example, sending different emails) to each group, and statistical analysis to compare the groups' outcomes and draw conclusions about which treatment is better.

Now that we've successfully conducted an A/B test, we may want to conclude that the effect of blue text is to increase spending by $125. However, something is wrong with the A/B test we ran: it's *confounded*. To see what we mean, consider Table 4-1.

Table 4-1: Differences Between Groups

	Group A	Group B
Personal characteristics	Younger (Same as B in other ways)	Older (Same as A in other ways)
Email text color	Black	Blue
Average revenue per user	$104	$229

We can see the important features of Group A and Group B. Our t-test comparing spending found that their spending levels were significantly different. We want an explanation for why they're different, and any explanation of different outcomes will have to rely on the differences listed in Table 4-1. We want to be able to conclude that the difference in spending can be explained by the difference in the text color. However, that difference coexists with another difference: age.

We can't be certain that the difference in spending levels is due to text color rather than age. For example, perhaps no one even noticed the text difference, but older people tend to be wealthier and more eager to buy your products than young people. If so, our A/B test didn't test for the effect of blue text, but rather for the effect of age or wealth. We intended to study only the effect of text color in this A/B test, and now we don't know whether we truly studied that or whether we studied age, wealth, or something else. It would be better if our A/B test had a simpler, non-confounded design like the one illustrated in Table 4-2.

Table 4-2: A Non-confounded A/B Test Design

	Group C	Group D
Personal characteristics	(Same as D in every way)	(Same as C in every way)
Email text color	Black	Blue
Average revenue per user	$104	$229

Table 4-2 imagines that we had split the users into hypothetical groups called C and D, which are identical in all personal characteristics, but differ only in the text of the emails they received. In this hypothetical scenario, the spending difference can be explained only by the different text colors sent to each group because that's the only difference between them. We should have split our groups in a way that ensured that the only differences between groups were in our experimental treatment, not in the group members' preexisting characteristics. If we had done so, we would have avoided having a confounded experiment.

Understanding the Math of A/B Testing

We can also express these notions mathematically. We can use the common statistical notation $E()$ to refer to the expected value. So $E(A's\ revenue$

with blk text) will mean *the expected value of revenue we would earn by sending a black-text email to Group A*. We can write two simple equations that describe the relationship between the revenue we expect to earn from black text, the effect of our experiment, and the revenue we expect to earn from blue text:

$$E(A\text{'s revenue with blk text}) + E(\text{effect of changing blk} \rightarrow \text{blue on } A) = E(A\text{'s revenue with blue text})$$
$$E(B\text{'s revenue with blk text}) + E(\text{effect of changing blk} \rightarrow \text{blue on } B) = E(B\text{'s revenue with blue text})$$

To decide whether to reject Hypothesis 0, we need to solve for the effect sizes: E(*effect of changing blk* → *blue on A*) and E(*effect of changing blk* → *blue on B*). If either of these effect sizes is different from 0, we should reject Hypothesis 0. By performing our experiment, we found E(*A's revenue with blk text*) = 104 and E(*B's revenue with blue text*) = 229. After knowing these values, we have the following equations:

$$104 + E(\text{effect of changing blk} \rightarrow \text{blue on } A) = E(A\text{'s revenue with blue text})$$
$$E(B\text{'s revenue with blk text}) + E(\text{effect of changing blk} \rightarrow \text{blue on } B) = 229$$

But this still leaves many variables we don't know, and we're not yet able to solve for E(*effect of changing blk* → *blue on A*) and E(*effect of changing blk* → *blue on B*). The only way we'll be able to solve for our effect sizes will be if we can simplify these two equations. For example, if we knew that E(*A's revenue with blk text*) = E(*B's revenue with blk text*), and E(*effect of changing blk* → *blue on A*) = E(*effect of changing blk* → *blue on B*), and E(*A's revenue with blue Text*) = E(*B's revenue with blue text*), then we could reduce these two equations to just one simple equation. If we knew that our groups were identical before our experiment, we would know that all of these expected values were equal, and we could simplify our two equations to the following easily solvable equation:

$$104 + E(\text{effect of changing blk} \rightarrow \text{blue on everyone}) = 229$$

With this, we can be sure that the effect of blue text is a $125 revenue increase. This is why we consider it so important to design non-confounded experiments in which the groups have equal expected values for personal characteristics. By doing so, we're able to solve the preceding equations and be confident that our measured effect size is actually the effect of what we're studying and not the result of different underlying characteristics.

Translating the Math into Practice

We know what to do mathematically, but we need to translate that into practical action. How should we ensure that E(*A's revenue with blk text*) = E(*B's revenue with blk text*), and how should we ensure that the other expected values are all the same? In other words, how can we ensure that our study design looks like Table 4-2 instead of Table 4-1? We need to find a way to select subgroups of our desktop subscriber list that are expected to be identical.

The simplest way to select subgroups that are expected to be identical is to select them randomly. We mentioned this briefly in Chapter 3: every random sample from a population has an expected value equal to the population mean. So, we expect that two random samples from the same population won't differ from each other significantly.

Let's perform an A/B test on our laptop subscriber list, but this time we'll use randomization to select our groups to avoid having a confounded experimental design. Suppose that in this new A/B test, we want to test whether adding a picture to a marketing email will improve revenue. We can proceed just as we did before: we split the laptop subscriber list into two subgroups, and we send different emails to each subgroup. The difference is that this time, instead of splitting based on age, we perform a random split:

```
np.random.seed(18811015)
laptop.loc[:,'groupassignment1']=1*(np.random.random(len(laptop.index))>0.5)
groupc=laptop.loc[laptop['groupassignment1']==0,:].copy()
groupd=laptop.loc[laptop['groupassignment1']==1,:].copy()
```

In this snippet, we use the NumPy random.random() method to generate a column that consists of randomly generated 0s and 1s. We can interpret a 0 to mean that a user belongs to Group C, and a 1 to mean that a user belongs to group D. When we generate 0s and 1s randomly like this, the groups could end up with different sizes. However, here we use a *random seed* (in the first line, np.random.seed(18811015)). Every time anyone uses this random seed, their "randomly" generated column of 0s and 1s will be identical. That means that if you use this random seed, your results at home should be the same as the results here in the book. Using a random seed is not necessary, but if you use the same random seed we used here, you should find that both Group C and Group D have 15 members.

After generating this random column of 0s and 1s that indicates the group assignment of each customer, we create two smaller dataframes, groupc and groupd, that contain user IDs and information about the users in each subgroup.

You can send the group membership information to your marketing team members and ask them to send the right emails to the right groups. One group, either C or D, should receive an email without a picture, and the other group, either D or C, should receive an email with a picture. Then, suppose that the marketing team sends you a file containing the results of this latest A/B test. You can download a fabricated dataset containing hypothetical results from *https://bradfordtuckfield.com/emailresults2.csv*. After you store it in the same place where you're running Python, let's read the results of this email campaign into Python as follows:

```
emailresults2=pd.read_csv('emailresults2.csv')
```

Again, let's join our email results to our group dataframes, just as we did before:

```
groupc_withrevenue=groupc.merge(emailresults2,on='userid')
groupd_withrevenue=groupd.merge(emailresults2,on='userid')
```

And again, we can use a t-test to check whether the revenue resulting from Group C is different from the revenue we get from Group D:

```
print(scipy.stats.ttest_ind(groupc_withrevenue['revenue'],groupd_withrevenue['revenue']))
```

We find that the *p*-value is less than 0.05, indicating that the difference between the groups is statistically significant. This time, our experiment isn't confounded, because we used random assignment to ensure that the differences between groups are the result of our different emails, not the result of different characteristics of each group. Since our experiment isn't confounded, and since we find a significant difference between the revenues earned from Group C and Group D, we conclude that including the picture in the email has a nonzero effect. If the marketing team tells us that it sent the picture only to Group D, we can find the estimated size of the effect easily:

```
print(np.mean(groupd_withrevenue['revenue'])-np.mean(groupc_withrevenue['revenue']))
```

We calculate the estimated effect here with subtraction: the mean revenue obtained from subjects in Group D minus the mean revenue obtained from subjects in Group C. The difference between mean revenue from Group C and mean revenue from Group D, about $260, is the size of the effect of our experiment.

The process we follow for A/B testing is really quite simple, but it's also powerful. We can use it for a wide variety of questions that we might want to answer. Anytime you're unsure about an approach to take in business, especially in user interactions and product design, considering an A/B test as an approach to learn the answer is worthwhile. Now that you know the process, let's move on and understand its nuances.

Optimizing with the Champion/Challenger Framework

When we've crafted a great email, we might call it our *champion* email design: the one that, according to what we know so far, we think will perform the best. After we have a champion email design, we may wish to stop doing A/B testing and simply rest on our laurels, collecting money indefinitely from our "perfect" email campaigns.

But this isn't a good idea, for a few reasons. The first is that times change. Fads in design and marketing change quickly, and a marketing effort that seems exciting and effective today may soon seem dated and outmoded. Like all champions, your champion email design will become weaker and less effective as it ages. Even if design and marketing fads *don't* change, your champion will eventually seem boring as the novelty wears off: new stimuli are more likely to get people's attention.

Another reason that you shouldn't stop A/B testing is that your customer base will change. You'll lose some old customers and gain new ones. You'll release new products and enter new markets. As your customer mix changes, the types of emails that they tend to respond to will change as well, and constant A/B testing will enable you to keep up with their changing characteristics and preferences.

A final reason to continue A/B testing is that although your champion likely is good, you might not have optimized it in every possible way. A dimension you haven't tested yet could enable you to have an even better champion that gets even better performance. If we can successfully run one A/B test and learn one thing, we'll naturally want to continue to use our A/B testing skills to learn more and more and to increase profits higher and higher.

Suppose you have a champion email and want to continue A/B testing to try to improve it. You do another random split of your users, into a new Group A and a new Group B. You send the champion email to Group A. You send another email to Group B that differs from the champion email in one way that you want to learn about; for example, maybe it uses formal rather than informal language. When we compare the revenues from Group A and Group B after the email campaign, we'll be able to see whether this new email performs better than the champion email.

Since the new email is in direct competition with the champion email, we call it the *challenger*. If the champion performs better than the challenger, the champion retains its champion status. If the challenger performs better than the champion, that challenger becomes the new champion.

This process can continue indefinitely: we have a champion that represents the state of the art of whatever we're doing (marketing emails, in this case). We constantly test the champion by putting it in direct competition with a succession of challengers in A/B tests. Each challenger that leads to significantly better outcomes than the champion becomes the new champion and is, in turn, put into competition against new challengers later.

This endless process is called the *champion/challenger framework* for A/B tests. It's meant to lead to continuous improvement, continuous refinement, and asymptotic optimization to get to the best-possible performance in all aspects of business. The biggest tech companies in the world run literally hundreds of A/B tests per day, with hundreds of challengers taking on hundreds of champions, sometimes defeating them and sometimes being defeated. The champion/challenger framework is a common approach for setting up and running A/B tests for the most important and most challenging parts of your business.

Preventing Mistakes with Twyman's Law and A/A Testing

A/B testing is a relatively simple process from beginning to end. Nevertheless, we are all human and make mistakes. In any data science effort, not just A/B testing, it's important to proceed carefully and constantly check whether we've done something wrong. One piece of evidence that often indicates that we've done something wrong is that things are going too well.

How could it be bad for things to go too well? Consider a simple example. You perform an A/B test: Group A gets one email, and Group B gets a different one. You measure revenue from each group afterward and find that the average revenue earned from members of Group A is about $25, while the average revenue earned from members of Group B is $99,999. You feel thrilled about the enormous revenue you earned from Group B. You call all your colleagues to an emergency meeting and tell them to stop everything they're doing and immediately work on implementing the email that Group B got and pivot the whole company strategy around this miracle email.

As your colleagues are working around the clock on sending the new email to everyone they know, you start to feel a nagging sense of doubt. You think about how unlikely it is that a single email campaign could plausibly earn almost $100,000 in revenue per recipient, especially when your other campaigns are earning only about $25 per user. You think about how $99,999, the amount of revenue you supposedly earned per user, is five identical digits repeated. Maybe you remember a conversation you had with a database administrator who told you that your company database automatically inserts 99999 every time a database error occurs or data is missing. Suddenly, you realize that your email campaign didn't really earn $99,999 per user, but rather a database error for Group B caused the appearance of the apparently miraculous result.

A/B testing is a simple process from a data science point of view, but it can be quite complex from a practical and social point of view. For example, in any company larger than a tiny startup, the creative people designing marketing emails will be different from the technology people who maintain the databases that record revenues per user. Other groups may be involved in little parts of A/B testing: maybe a group that maintains the software used to schedule and send out emails, maybe a group that creates art that the email marketing team asks for, and maybe others.

With all these groups and steps involved, many possible chances exist for miscommunication and small errors. Maybe two different emails are designed, but the person who's in charge of sending them out doesn't understand A/B testing and copies and pastes the same email to both groups. Maybe they accidentally paste in something that's not even supposed to be in the A/B test at all. In our example, maybe the database that records revenues encounters an error and puts 99999 in the results as an error code, which others mistakenly interpret as a high revenue. No matter how careful we try to be, mistakes and miscommunications will always find a way to happen.

The inevitability of mistakes should lead us to be naturally suspicious of anything that seems too good, bad, interesting, or strange to be true. This natural suspicion is advocated by *Twyman's law*, which states that "any figure that looks interesting or different is usually wrong." This law has been restated in several ways, including "any statistic that appears interesting is almost certainly a mistake" and "the more unusual or interesting the data, the more likely it is to have been the result of an error."

Besides extreme carefulness and natural suspicion of good news, we have another good way to prevent the kinds of interpretive mistakes that Twyman's law warns against: *A/A testing*. This type of testing is just what it sounds like; we go through the steps of randomization, treatment, and comparison of two groups just as in A/B testing, but instead of sending two different emails to our two randomized groups, we send the identical email to each group. In this case, we expect the null hypothesis to be true, and we won't be gullibly convinced by a group that appears to get $100,000 more revenue than the other group.

If we consistently find that A/A tests lead to statistically significant differences between groups, we can conclude that our process has a problem: a database gone haywire, a t-test being run incorrectly, an email being pasted wrong, randomization performed incorrectly, or something else. An A/A test would also help us realize that the first test described in this chapter (where Group A consists of younger people and Group B consists of older people) was confounded, since we would know that differences between the results of an A/A test must be due to the differences in age rather than differences between emails. A/A testing can be a useful sanity check that can prevent us from getting carried away by the kind of unusual, interesting, too-good-to-be-true results that Twyman's law warns us about.

Understanding Effect Sizes

In the first A/B test we ran, we observed a difference of $125 between the Group A users who received a black-text email and the Group B users who received a blue-text email. This $125 difference between groups is also called the A/B test's *effect size*. It's natural to try to form a judgment about whether we should consider this $125 effect size a small effect, a medium effect, or a large effect.

To judge whether an effect is small or large, we have to compare it to something else. Consider the following list of nominal GDP figures (in US dollars, as of 2019) for Malaysia, Myanmar, and the Marshall Islands, respectively:

```
gdps=[365303000000,65994000000,220000000]
```

When we look at these numbers, $125 starts to seem pretty small. For example, consider the standard deviation of our gdps list:

```
print(np.std(gdps))
```

The result is 158884197328.32672, or about $158,884,197,328 (almost $159 billion). The standard deviation is a common way to measure how dispersed a dataset is. If we observe a difference between two countries' GDPs that's about $80 billion, we don't think of that as outrageously big or outrageously small, because it means those countries are about half of a standard deviation apart, a common magnitude of difference. Instead of expressing the difference as an $80 billion difference, you might say that the two countries' GDPs differed by about half of a standard deviation, and expect to be understood by anyone with some statistical training.

By contrast, if someone tells you that two countries have GDPs that differ by 112 trillion kyat (the currency of Myanmar), you might be unsure whether that difference is large or small if you've never learned the value of 1 kyat (112 trillion kyat is equal to about $80 billion at the time of writing). Many currencies exist in the world, and their relative and absolute values change all the time. A standard deviation, on the other hand, isn't specific to any particular country and is not affected by inflation, making it a useful unit of measurement.

We can use standard deviations as measurements in other domains as well. Someone from Europe may be used to using meters to express heights. When you tell your European data scientist friend about a man who's 75 inches tall, they may feel puzzled about whether that's tall or short or average if they're not used to conversion from inches. But, if you tell them that he's about two standard deviations taller than the mean, they should immediately be able to understand that he's pretty tall but not a record-breaking height. Observing someone who's more than three standard deviations above the mean height will be much rarer, and we can know that whether we're measuring in meters or inches or any other units.

When we talk about the $125 effect size of our A/B test, let's try to think of it in terms of standard deviations as well. Compared to the standard deviation of the GDP measurements we've seen, $125 is small potatoes:

```
print(125/np.std(gdps))
```

The output is about $7.9 \cdot 10^{-10}$, which shows us that the $125 effect size is a little more than 1 one-billionth of the standard deviation of our GDP figures. Compared to the world of GDP measurements, a $125 difference in GDP is like being a micrometer taller than your friend—not even enough to notice without extremely precise measurement technology.

By contrast, suppose we conduct a survey of the prices of burgers at local restaurants. Maybe we find the following prices:

```
burgers=[9.0,12.99,10.50]
```

We can check this standard deviation as well:

```
print(np.std(burgers))
```

The standard deviation of our burger price data is about 1.65. So, two countries' GDPs differing by about $80 billion is roughly comparable to two burger prices differing by about 80 cents: both represent about half of a standard deviation in their respective domains. When we compare a $125 effect size to this, we see that it's huge:

```
print(125/np.std(burgers))
```

We see that \$125 is about 75.9 burger price standard deviations. Seeing a \$125 difference in burger prices in your town is therefore something like seeing a man who is over 20 feet tall—unheard of.

By measuring our effect size in terms of the standard deviation of different datasets, we can easily make comparisons, not just between different domains with the same units (GDP in dollars versus burger prices in dollars) but also between different domains that use totally different units (burger prices in dollars versus height in inches). The metric we've calculated several times here—an effect size divided by a relevant standard deviation—is called *Cohen's d*, a common metric for measuring effect sizes. Cohen's d is just the number of standard deviations that two populations' means are apart from each other. We can calculate Cohen's d for our first A/B test as follows:

```
print(125/np.std(emailresults1['revenue']))
```

We see that the result is about 0.76. A common convention when we're working with Cohen's d is to say that if Cohen's d is about 0.2 or lower, we have a small effect; if Cohen's d is about 0.5, we have a medium effect; and if Cohen's d is around 0.8 or even higher, we have a large effect. Since our result is about 0.76—quite close to 0.8—we can say that we're working with a large effect size.

Calculating the Significance of Data

We typically use statistical significance as the key piece of evidence that convinces us that an effect that we study in an A/B test is real. Mathematically, statistical significance depends on three things:

- The size of the effect being studied (like the increase in revenue that results from changing an email's text color). Bigger effects make statistical significance more likely.

- The size of the sample being studied (the number of people on a subscriber list who are receiving our marketing emails). Bigger samples make statistical significance more likely.

- The significance threshold we're using (typically 0.05). A higher threshold makes statistical significance more likely.

If we have a big sample size, and we're studying a big effect, our t-tests will likely reach statistical significance. On the other hand, if we study an effect that's very small, with a sample that's very small, we may have predestined our own failure: the probability that we detect a statistically significant result is essentially 0—even if the email truly does have an effect. Since running an A/B test costs time and money, we'd rather not waste resources running tests like this that are predestined to fail to reach statistical significance.

The probability that a correctly run A/B test will reject a false null hypothesis is called the A/B test's *statistical power*. If changing the color of text leads to a \$125 increase in revenue per user, we can say that \$125 is the effect size, and since the effect size is nonzero, we know the null hypothesis (that changing the text color has no effect on revenue) is false. But if we study this true effect by using a sample of only three or four email subscribers, it's very possible that, by chance, none of these subscribers purchase anything, so we fail to detect the true $125 effect. By contrast, if we study the effect of changing the text color by using an email list of a million subscribers, we're much more likely to detect the $125 effect and measure it as statistically significant. With the million-subscriber list, we have greater statistical power.

We can import a module into Python that makes calculating statistical power easy:

```
from statsmodels.stats.power import TTestIndPower
```

To calculate power with this module, we'll need to define parameters for the three things that determine statistical significance (see the preceding bulleted list). We'll define alpha, which is our chosen statistical significance threshold, as discussed in Chapter 3:

```
alpha=0.05
```

We choose the standard 0.05 threshold for alpha, as is standard in much empirical research. We also need to define our sample size. Suppose we're running an A/B test on a group of email subscribers that consists of 90 people total. That means we'll have 45 people in Group A and 45 people in Group B, so we define the number of observations in each of our groups as 45. We'll store this number in a variable called nobs, short for *number of observations*:

```
nobs=45
```

We also have to define an estimated effect size. In our previous A/B test, we observed an effect size of $125. However, for the statistical power calculations this module performs, we can't express the effect size in dollar units or units of any other currency. We'll use Cohen's *d* instead, and we'll specify a medium size:

```
effectsize=0.5
```

Finally, we can use a function that will take the three parameters we've defined and calculate the statistical power we should expect:

```
analysis = TTestIndPower()
power = analysis.solve_power(effect_size=effectsize, nobs1=nobs, alpha=alpha)
```

If you run print(power), you can see that the estimated statistical power for our hypothetical A/B test is about 0.65. This means that we expect about a 65 percent chance of detecting an effect from our A/B test and about a 35 percent chance that even though a true effect exists, our A/B test doesn't find it. These odds might seem unfavorable if a given

A/B test is expected to be expensive; you'll have to make your own decisions about the minimum level of power that is acceptable to you. Power calculations can help at the planning stage to understand what to expect and be prepared. One common convention is to authorize only A/B tests that are expected to have at least 80 percent power.

You can also use the same solve_power() method we used in the previous snippet to "reverse" the power calculation: you'd start by assuming a certain power level and then calculate the parameters required to achieve that level of statistical power. For example, in the following snippet, we define power, alpha, and our effect size, and run the solve_power() command not to calculate the power but to calculate observations, the number of observations we'll need in each group to achieve the power level we specified:

```
analysis = TTestIndPower()
alpha = 0.05
effect = 0.5
power = 0.8
observations = analysis.solve_power(effect_size=effect, power=power, alpha=alpha)
```

If you run print(observations), you'll see that the result is about 63.8. This means that if we want to have 80 percent statistical power for our planned A/B test, we'll need to recruit at least 64 participants for both groups. Being able to perform these kinds of calculations can be helpful in the planning stages of A/B tests.

Applications and Advanced Considerations

So far, we've considered only A/B tests related to marketing emails. But A/B tests are applicable to a wide variety of business challenges beyond optimal email design. One of the most common applications of A/B testing is user interface/experience design. A website might randomly assign visitors to two groups (called Group A and Group B, as usual) and show different versions of the site to each group. The site can then measure which version leads to more user satisfaction, higher revenue, more link clicks, more time spent on the site, or whatever else interests the company. The whole process can be completely automated, which is what enables the high-speed, high-volume A/B testing that today's top tech companies are doing.

E-commerce companies run tests, including A/B tests, on product pricing. By running an A/B test on pricing, you can measure what economists call the *price elasticity of demand*, meaning how much demand changes in response to price changes. If your A/B test finds only a very small change in demand when you increase the price, you should increase the price for everyone and take advantage of their greater willingness to pay. If your A/B test finds that demand drops off significantly when you increase the price slightly, you can conclude that customers are sensitive to price, and their purchase decisions depend heavily on price considerations. If customers are sensitive to price and constantly thinking about it, they'll likely respond positively to a price decrease. If so, you should decrease the price for everyone instead, and expect a large increase in demand. Some businesses have to set prices based on intuition or other painstaking calculations, but A/B testing makes determining the right price relatively simple.

Email design, user-interface design, and product pricing are all common concerns for *business-to-consumer (B2C)* business models, in which businesses sell directly to consumers. B2C scenarios are a natural fit for A/B testing because the number of customers, products, and transactions tends to be higher for B2C businesses than for other businesses, so we can get large sample sizes and higher statistical power.

This doesn't mean that business-to-business (B2B) companies can't do A/B testing. Indeed, A/B testing has been practiced for centuries around the world and in many domains, though it used to be called just *science*. For example, medical researchers do *randomized controlled trials* for new drugs, with an approach that's often essentially the same as A/B testing in a champion/challenger framework. Businesses of all kinds have always needed to learn about the market and their customers, and A/B testing is a natural, rigorous way to learn nearly anything.

As you apply A/B testing in your business, you should try to learn as much as you can about it, beyond the content in the limited space of this chapter. One huge field you might want to wade into is Bayesian statistics. Some data scientists prefer to use Bayesian methods instead of significance tests and *p*-values to test for the success of A/B tests.

Another interesting, useful topic to learn more about is the *exploration/exploitation trade-off* in A/B tests. In this trade-off, two goals are in constant tension: to explore (for example, to run A/B tests with possibly bad email designs to learn which is best) and to exploit (for example, to send out only the champion email because it seems to perform the best). Exploration can lead to missed opportunities if one of your challengers performs much worse than the champion; you would have been better off just sending out the champion to everyone. Exploitation can lead to missed opportunities if your champion is not as good as another challenger that you haven't tested yet because you're too busy exploiting your champion to do the requisite exploration.

In operations research, you'll find a huge body of research on the *multi-armed bandit problem*, which is a mathematical formalization of the exploration/exploitation dilemma. If you're really interested in doing A/B testing optimally, you can peer into some of the strategies that researchers have come up with to solve the multi-armed bandit problem and run A/B tests as efficiently as possible.

The Ethics of A/B Testing

A/B testing is fraught with difficult ethical issues. This may seem surprising, but remember, A/B testing is an experimental method in which we intentionally alter human subjects' experiences in order to study the results for our own gain. This means that A/B testing is human experimentation. Think about other examples of human experimentation to see why people have ethical concerns about it:

1. Jonas Salk developed an untested, unprecedented polio vaccine, tried it on himself and his family, and then tried it on millions of American children to ensure that it worked. (It worked and helped eliminate a terrible disease from much of the world.)

2. My grandmother made a pie for her grandchildren, observed how we reacted to it, and then the next day made a different pie and checked whether we reacted more or less positively. (Both were delicious.)

3. A professor posed as a student and emailed 6,300 professors to ask them to schedule time to talk to her, lying about herself and her intentions in an attempt to determine whether her false persona would be a target of discrimination so she could publish a paper about the replies. She didn't compensate any of the unwitting study participants for the deception or the schedule disruption, nor did she receive their consent beforehand to be an experimental subject. (Every detail of this study was approved by a university ethics board.)

4. A corporation intentionally manipulated the emotions of its users to better understand and sell products to them.

5. Josef Mengele performed painful and deadly sadistic experiments on unwilling human subjects in the Auschwitz concentration camp.

6. You perform an A/B test.

The first five entries on this list of human experiments actually happened, and all but the second inspired public discussions about ethics among social scientists. You'll have to decide whether the sixth will happen and what position you will take concerning the ethical issues involved. Because of the broad range of activities that could be called human experimentation, making a single ethical judgment about all of its forms isn't possible. We have to consider several important ethical concepts when we're deciding whether our A/B tests make us a hero like my grandmother or Salk, a villain like Mengele, or something in between.

The first concept we should consider is consent. Salk tested his vaccine on himself before large-scale tests of others. Mengele, by contrast, performed experiments on unwilling subjects confined in concentration camps. Informed consent always makes human experimentation more ethical. In some cases, obtaining informed consent is not feasible. For example, if we perform experiments about which outdoor billboard designs are most effective, we can't obtain informed consent from every possible human research subject, since any person in the world could conceivably see a public billboard, and we don't have a way to contact every living human.

Other cases form a large gray area. For example, a website that performs A/B tests may have a Terms and Conditions section, with small print and legalese that claims that every website visitor provides consent to be experimented on (via A/B tests of user-interface features) whenever they navigate to the site. This may technically meet the definition of informed consent, but only a tiny percentage of any website's visitors likely visit and understand these conditions. In gray-area cases, it helps to consider other ethical concepts.

Another important ethical consideration related to A/B testing is risk. Risk itself involves two considerations: potential downsides to participation as a human subject and the probability of experiencing those downsides. Salk's vaccine had a large potential downside—contracting polio—but because of Salk's preparation and knowledge, the probability of subjects experiencing it was remarkably low. A/B testing for marketing campaigns usually has potential downsides that are minuscule or smaller, as it's hard to even imagine any downside that could occur because (for example) someone was exposed to blue rather than black text in one marketing email. Experiments with low risks to subjects are more ethical than risky experiments.

We should also consider the potential benefits that could result from our experimentation. Salk's vaccine experiments had the potential (later realized) of eradicating polio from most of the Earth. A/B tests are designed to improve profits, not cure diseases, so your judgment of their benefits will have to depend on your opinion of the moral status of corporate profits. The only other benefit likely to come from a corporation's marketing experiment would be an advance in understanding of human psychology. Indeed, corporate marketing practitioners occasionally publish the results of marketing experiments in psychology journals, so this isn't unheard of.

Ethical and philosophical questions can never reach a definitive, final conclusion that everyone agrees on. You can make up your own mind about whether you feel that A/B testing is fundamentally good, like Salk's vaccine experiments, or fundamentally abhorrent, like Mengele's horrors. Most people agree that the extremely low risks of most online A/B testing, and the fact that people rarely refuse consent to benign A/B tests, mean that A/B testing is an ethically justifiable activity when performed properly. Regardless, you should think carefully through your own situation and come to your own conclusion.

Summary

In this chapter, we discussed A/B testing. We started with a simple t-test, and then looked at the need for random, non-confounded data collection as part of the A/B testing process. We covered some nuances of A/B testing, including the champion/challenger framework and Twyman's law, as well as ethical concerns. In the next chapter, we'll discuss binary classification, an essential skill for any data scientist.

5

BINARY CLASSIFICATION

Many difficult questions can be phrased simply as yes/no questions: To buy the stock or not? To take the job or not? To hire the applicant or not? This chapter is about *binary classification*, the technical term for answering yes/no questions, or deciding between true and false, 1 and 0.

We'll start by introducing a common business scenario that depends on binary classification. We'll continue by discussing linear probability models, a simple but powerful binary classification approach based on linear regression. We'll also cover logistic regression, a more advanced classification method that improves on some of the shortcomings of linear probability models. We'll conclude by going over some of the many applications of binary classification methods, including risk analysis and forecasting.

Minimizing Customer Attrition

Imagine you're running a big tech company with about 10,000 large clients. Each client has a long-term contract with you, promising that they'll pay you regularly to use your company's software. However, all your clients are free to exit their contracts at any time and stop paying you if they decide they don't want to use your software anymore. You want to have as many clients as you can, so you do your best to do two things: one, grow the company by signing new contracts with new clients and, two, prevent attrition by ensuring that your existing clients don't exit their contracts.

In this chapter, we'll focus on your second goal: preventing client attrition. This is an extremely common concern for businesses in every industry, and one that every company struggles with. It's especially important since acquiring new customers is well known to be much more costly than retaining existing ones.

To prevent attrition, you have a team of client managers who stay in touch with clients, make sure they're happy, resolve any problems that come up, and in general ensure that they're satisfied enough to continue renewing their contracts indefinitely. Your client management team is small, however—only a few people who together have to try to keep 10,000 clients happy. It's impossible for them to be in constant contact with all 10,000 clients, and inevitably some clients will have concerns and problems that your client management team isn't able to find out about or resolve.

As the leader of your company, you have to decide how to direct the efforts of the client managers to minimize attrition. Every hour they spend working with a client who's at high risk of attrition is probably worthwhile, but their time is wasted when they spend too much time on a client who is not at risk of attrition. The best use of the client managers' time will be to focus on the clients who have the highest likelihood of canceling their contracts. All the managers need is a list of all the high-risk clients to contact, and then they can use their time with maximum efficiency to minimize attrition.

Getting an accurate list of high-attrition-risk clients is not an easy task, since you can't read the minds of all your clients and immediately know which ones are in danger of canceling their contracts and which ones are happy as clams. Many companies rely on intuition or guessing to decide which clients have the highest attrition risk. But intuition and guessing rarely lead to the most accurate possible results. We'll get better accuracy, and therefore better cost savings, by using data science tools to decide whether each client is high risk or low risk.

Deciding whether a client is high risk or low risk for attrition is a binary classification problem; it consists of answering a yes-or-no question: Is this client at high risk for attrition? What started as a daunting business problem (how to increase revenue growth with limited resources) has been reduced to a much simpler data analysis problem (how to perform a binary classification of attrition risk). We'll approach this problem by reading in historical data related to past attrition, analyzing that data to find useful patterns in it, and applying our knowledge of those patterns to more recent data to perform our binary classification and make useful business recommendations.

Using Linear Probability Models to Find High-Risk Customers

We can choose from several data analysis methods to do binary classification. But before we explore these methods, we should read some data into Python. We'll use fabricated data about hypothetical clients of our imaginary firm. You can load it into your Python session directly from its online home by using the following snippet:

```
import pandas as pd
attrition_past=pd.read_csv('https://bradfordtuckfield.com/attrition_past.csv')
```

In this snippet, we import pandas and read the file for our data. This time, we read the file directly from a website where it's being stored. The file is in *.csv* format, which you've already encountered in previous chapters. You can print the top five rows of our data as follows:

```
print(attrition_past.head())
```

You should see the following output:

	corporation	lastmonth_activity	...	number_of_employees	exited
0	abcd	78	...	12	1
1	asdf	14	...	20	0
2	xyzz	182	...	35	0
3	acme	101	...	2	1
4	qwer	0	...	42	1

The last line of the output tells us that the dataset has five columns. Suppose that the first four columns of the data were generated about six months ago. The first column is a four-character code for every client. The second column is lastmonth_activity, a measurement of the number of times someone at that client company accessed our software in the last month before this data was generated (between 6 and 7 months ago). The third column is lastyear_activity, the same measurement for the entire year before the data was generated (between 6 and 18 months ago). The lastyear_activity column is not visible in the preceding snippet, where we can see only ellipses between the second and fourth columns. The reason for this is that the pandas package has default display settings that ensure its output will be small enough to fit easily onscreen. If you'd like to change the maximum number of columns that pandas prints out, you can run the following line in Python:

```
pd.set_option('display.max_columns', 6)
```

Here, we use the pandas option display.max_columns to change the maximum number of columns pandas will display to 6. This change ensures that if we ever print the attrition_past dataset again, we'll see all five of its columns, and when we add one more column to the dataset, we'll then be able to see all six of its columns. If you want to display all columns of every dataset, no matter how many, you can change the 6 to None, which will mean that there's no maximum limit on the number of columns for pandas to display.

Besides columns recording activity levels, we also have a record of the number of employees each company had six months ago in the number_of _employees column. Finally, suppose that the final column, exited, was generated today. This column records whether a given corporation exited its contract at any time in the six-month period between when the first four columns were generated and today. This column is recorded in a binary format: 1 for a client that exited in the last six months and 0 for a client that didn't exit. The exited column is our binary measurement of attrition, and it's the column that interests us most because it's what we're going to learn to predict.

Having four columns that are six months old and one column that's new may seem like a bug or an unnecessary complication. However, this temporal difference between our columns enables us to find patterns relating the past and the future. We'll find patterns in the data that show how activity levels and employee numbers at one particular time can be used to predict attrition levels later. Eventually, the patterns we'll find in this data will enable us to use a client's activity as measured today to predict their attrition likelihood during the next six months. If we can predict a client's attrition risk in the next six months, we can take action during those six months to change their minds and keep them around. Convincing clients to stay will be the client manager's role—the contribution of data science will be to make the attrition prediction itself.

Plotting Attrition Risk

Before we jump into finding all these patterns, let's check how often attrition occurs in our data:

```
print(attrition_past['exited'].mean())
```

The result we get is about 0.58, meaning that about 58 percent of the clients in the data exited their contracts in the last six months. This shows us that attrition is a big problem for the business.

Next, we should make plots of our data. Doing this early and often is a good idea in any data analysis scenario. We're interested in how each of our variables will relate to the binary exited variable, so we can start with a plot of the relationship of lastmonth_activity and exited:

```
from matplotlib import pyplot as plt
plt.scatter(attrition_past['lastmonth_activity'],attrition_past['exited'])
plt.title('Historical Attrition')
plt.xlabel('Last Month\'s Activity')
plt.ylabel('Attrition')
plt.show()
```

We can see the result in Figure 5-1.

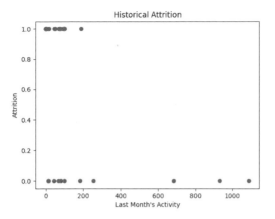

Figure 5-1: Historical attrition of clients of a hypothetical company

On the x-axis, we see last month's activity, although since the data was recorded six months ago, it's really activity from six to seven months ago. The y-axis shows attrition from our exited variable, and that's why all values are 0 (did not exit) or 1 (exited) in the most recent six months. Eyeballing this figure can give us a basic idea of the relationship between past activity and future attrition. In particular, the clients with the most activity (> 600) did not exit their contracts in the six months after their high activity was recorded. High activity seems to be a predictor of client loyalty, and if it is, low activity will be a predictor of client attrition.

Confirming Relationships with Linear Regression

We'll want to confirm our initial visual impression by performing a more rigorous quantitative test. In particular, we can use linear regression. Remember that in Chapter 2, we had a cloud of points and used linear regression to find a line that was the best fit to the cloud. Here, our points don't look very cloud-like because of the limited range of the y variable: our "cloud" is two scattered lines at $y = 0$ and $y = 1$. However, linear regression is a mathematical method from linear algebra, and it doesn't care how cloud-like our plot looks. We can perform linear regression on our attrition data with code that's almost identical to the code we used before:

```
x = attrition_past['lastmonth_activity'].values.reshape(-1,1)
y = attrition_past['exited'].values.reshape(-1,1)

from sklearn.linear_model import LinearRegression
regressor = LinearRegression()
regressor.fit(x, y)
```

In this snippet, we create a variable called regressor, which we then fit to our data. After fitting our regressor, we can plot our regression line going through our "cloud" of data, just as we did in Chapter 2:

```
from matplotlib import pyplot as plt            '
plt.scatter(attrition_past['lastmonth_activity'],attrition_past['exited'])
prediction = [regressor.coef_[0]*x+regressor.intercept_[0] for x in \
list(attrition_past['lastmonth_activity'])]
plt.plot(attrition_past['lastmonth_activity'],  prediction, color='red')
plt.title('Historical Attrition')
plt.xlabel('Last Month\'s Activity')
plt.ylabel('Attrition')
plt.show()
```

Figure 5-2 shows the result of this code.

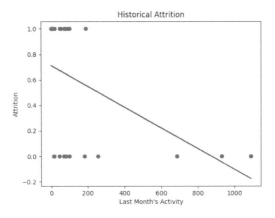

Figure 5-2: A linear regression predicting a 0–1 attrition outcome

You can compare this plot with Figure 2-2 in Chapter 2. Just as we did in Figure 2-2, we have a collection of points, and we've added a regression line that we know is the line of best fit to those points. Remember that we interpret the value of a regression line as an expected value. In Figure 2-2, we saw that our regression line went approximately through the point $x = 109$, $y = 17,000$, and we interpreted that to mean that in month 109, we expect about 17,000 car sales.

In Figure 5-2, the way to interpret our expected values may not seem immediately obvious. For example, at $x = 400$, the y value of the regression line is about 0.4. This means that our expected value of exited is 0.4, but that's not a cogent statement because exited can be only 0 or 1 (either you exit or you don't, with no middle ground). So, what could it mean to expect 0.4 "exiteds," or 0.4 units of exiting at that activity level?

The way we interpret an expected value of *0.4 units of exiting* is as a probability: we conclude that clients with an activity level of about 400 in the most recent month have about a 40 percent probability of exiting their contracts. Since our exited data consists of six months of exits after the activity levels were recorded, we interpret the value of the regression line as a 40 percent probability of attrition over the next six months after the activity level was recorded. Another way we can phrase our estimated 40 percent attrition probability is to say that we estimate a 40 percent attrition risk for clients with an activity level of 400.

The regression in Figure 5-2 is a standard linear regression, exactly like the linear regression model we created in Chapter 2 and plotted in Figure 2-2. However, when we perform a standard linear regression on binary data (data consisting of only two values like 0 and 1), we have a special name for it: we call it a *linear probability model (LPM)*. These models are simple and easy to implement, but they can be useful whenever we want to know a predicted probability of something that's hard to predict.

After performing our regression and interpreting its values, the last important step is to make a business decision based on everything we've learned. Figure 5-2 shows a simple relationship between activity and exit probability: lower activity is associated with higher exit probability, and higher activity is associated with lower exit probability. What we call *exit probability*, we can also call *attrition risk*, so we can also say that last month's activity is negatively correlated with the next six months' attrition risk. This negative correlation makes sense from a business point of view: if a client uses your product very actively, we expect them to be unlikely to exit their contract, and if a client is very inactive, we expect them to be more likely to exit.

Knowing that a general negative correlation exists between activity and attrition risk is helpful. But we can be even more specific in our reasoning and decision-making if we calculate the exact predicted attrition risk for each client. This will enable us to make individualized decisions for each client based on their predicted risk. The following code calculates the attrition risk for each client (the predicted value from our regression) and stores its value in a new column called predicted:

```
attrition_past['predicted']=regressor.predict(x)
```

If you run print(attrition_past.head()), you can see that our attrition dataset now has six columns. Its new sixth column is the predicted attrition probability for each client based on our regression. Of course, this is not very useful to us; we don't need predicted attrition probabilities, since this is a record of past attrition and we already know with certainty whether each of these clients exited.

Altogether, attrition prediction has two steps. First, we learn the relationships between features and target variables by using data from the past. Second, we use the relationships we learned from past data to make predictions for the future. So far, we've done only the first step: we've fit a regression that captures the relationship between customer attributes and attrition risk. Next, we need to make predictions for the future.

Predicting the Future

Let's download and open more fabricated data. This time, suppose that all the data was generated today, so its lastmonthactivity column refers to the previous month, and its lastyearactivity column refers to the 12-month period ending today. We can read in our data as follows:

```
attrition_future=pd.read_csv('http://bradfordtuckfield.com/attrition2.csv')
```

The attrition_past dataset that we worked with before used old data (more than six months old) to predict attrition that happened in the recent past (any time in the last six months). By contrast, with this dataset, we'll use new data (generated today) to predict attrition that we expect to happen in the near future (in the next six months). That's why we're calling it attrition_future. If you run print(attrition_future.head()), you can see the first five rows of this data:

	corporation	lastmonth_activity	lastyear_activity	number_of_employees
0	hhtn	166	1393	91
1	slfm	824	16920	288
2	pryr	68	549	12
3	ahva	121	1491	16
4	dmai	4	94	2

You can see that this dataset's first four columns have the same names and interpretations as the first four columns of attrition_past. However, this dataset doesn't have a fifth, exited column. The dataset lacks this column because the exited column is supposed to record whether a client exited their contract in the six-month period after the other columns were generated. But that six-month period hasn't happened yet; it's the six months that start today. We need to use what we've learned from the attrition dataset to predict the probabilities of attrition for this new set of clients. When we do, we'll be making a prediction about the future rather than the past.

All of the four-character corporation codes in the first column of attrition_future are new—they didn't appear in the original attrition dataset. We can't use anything from the original attrition dataset to learn directly about this new dataset. However, we can use the regressor we fit to make attrition probability predictions for this new dataset. In other words, we don't use the actual data from attrition_past to learn about attrition_future, but we do use the patterns we found in attrition_past, which we encoded in a linear regression, to make predictions about attrition_future.

We can predict attrition probabilities for the attrition_future dataset in exactly the same way we predicted attrition probabilities for the attrition_past dataset, as follows:

```
x = attrition_future['lastmonth_activity'].values.reshape(-1,1)
attrition_future['predicted']=regressor.predict(x)
```

This snippet adds a new column called predicted to the attrition_future dataset. We can run print(attrition_future.head()) to see the top five rows after the change:

	corporation	lastmonth_activity	...	number_of_employees	predicted
0	hhtn	166	...	91	0.576641
1	slfm	824	...	288	0.040352
2	pryr	68	...	12	0.656514
3	ahva	121	...	16	0.613317
4	dmai	4	...	2	0.708676

You can see that the pattern of low predicted exit probability for high-activity clients matches the pattern we observed for the attrition_past dataset. This is because our predicted probabilities were generated using the same regressor that was trained on the attrition_past dataset.

Making Business Recommendations

After calculating these predicted probabilities, we want to translate them to business recommendations for our client management team. The simplest way to direct the team members' efforts would be to provide them with a list of high-risk clients to focus their efforts on. We can specify a number of clients *n* that we think they have the time and bandwidth to focus on, and create a list of the top *n* highest-risk clients. We can do this for *n* = 5 as follows:

```
print(attrition_future.nlargest(5,'predicted'))
```

When we run this line, we get the following output:

	corporation	lastmonth_activity	...	number_of_employees	predicted
8	whsh	0	...	52	0.711936
12	mike	0	...	49	0.711936
24	pian	0	...	19	0.711936
21	bass	2	...	1400	0.710306
4	dmai	4	...	2	0.708676

```
[5 rows x 5 columns]
```

You can see that our top five highest-risk clients have predicted probabilities over 0.7 (70 percent), quite a high attrition probability.

Now, suppose your client managers are unsure of the number of clients they can focus on. Instead of asking for the top *n* clients for some *n*, they may simply want a ranked list of every client from highest to lowest attrition probability. The client managers can start at the beginning of the list and work their way through it as far as they can get. You can print this list easily as follows:

```
print(list(attrition_future.sort_values(by='predicted',ascending=False).loc[:,'corporation']))
```

The output is a list of all corporations in the `attrition_future` dataset, ranked from highest to lowest attrition probability:

```
['whsh', 'pian', 'mike', 'bass', 'pevc', 'dmai', 'ynus', 'kdic', 'hlpd',\
 'angl', 'erin', 'oscr', 'grce', 'zamk', 'hlly', 'xkcd', 'dwgt', 'pryr',\
 'skct', 'frgv', 'ejdc', 'ahva', 'wlcj', 'hhtn', 'slfm', 'cred']
```

The first three corporations in this list—whsh, pian, and mike—are estimated to have the highest attrition risk (highest probability of exiting their contracts). In this case, the data shows a three-way tie for highest risk, since all three of these corporations have the same predicted high risk, and all the other corporations have lower predicted attrition risk.

Finally, you may decide that you're interested in any clients whose predicted probabilities are higher than a certain threshold x. We can do this as follows for $x = 0.7$:

```
print(list(attrition_future.loc[attrition_future['predicted']>0.7,'corporation']))
```

You'll see a full list of all corporations that are predicted to have a greater than 70 percent attrition risk over the next six months. This could be a useful priority list for your client managers.

Measuring Prediction Accuracy

In the previous section, we went through all the steps necessary to send a list of at-risk corporations to our client managers. Having reported our attrition risk predictions, we may feel that our task is complete and we can move on to the next one. But we're not finished yet. As soon as we deliver our predictions to client managers, they'll likely immediately ask us how accurate we expect our predictions to be. They'll want to know how much they can trust our predictions before they put in great effort acting on them.

In Chapter 2, we went over two common ways to measure the accuracy of linear regressions: root mean squared error (RMSE) and mean absolute error (MAE). Our LPM is technically a linear regression, so it's possible to use these metrics again. However, for classification problems, the common convention is to use a different set of metrics that express classification accuracy in a more easily interpretable way. The first thing we'll need to do is create lists of our predictions and actual values, respectively:

```
themedian=attrition_past['predicted'].median()
prediction=list(1*(attrition_past['predicted']>themedian))
actual=list(attrition_past['exited'])
```

In this snippet, we calculate the median value of our `predicted` column. Then we create `prediction`, which will be 0 when our LPM predicts below-median probability, and 1 when our LPM predicts above-median probability. We're doing this because when we measure accuracy for classification tasks, we'll use metrics that count exact matches like predicted = 1, actual = 1 and predicted = 0, actual = 0. Typical classification accuracy metrics don't give "partial credit" for predicting 0.99 probability when the actual value is 1, so we convert our probabilities to 1s and 0s so we can get "full credit" where possible. We also convert our list of actual values (from the exited column) to a Python list.

Now that our data is in the right format, we can create a *confusion matrix*, a standard way to measure accuracy in classification models:

```
from sklearn.metrics import confusion_matrix
print(confusion_matrix(prediction,actual))
```

The confusion matrix that is output shows the number of true positives, true negatives, false positives, and false negatives we get when making predictions on our dataset. Our confusion matrix looks like this:

```
>>> print(confusion_matrix(prediction,actual))
[[7 6]
 [4 9]]
```

Every confusion matrix has the following structure:

```
[[true positives     false positives]
 [false negatives    true negatives]]
```

So, when we look at our confusion matrix, we find that our model made seven true-positive classifications: for seven corporations, our model predicted above-median exit probability (high attrition risk), and those seven corporations did exit. Our false positives are six cases in which we predicted above-median exit probability but the corporation didn't exit. Our false negatives are four cases in which we predicted below-median exit probability but the corporation did exit. Finally, our true negatives are nine cases in which we predicted below-median exit probability for clients that didn't exit.

We're always happy about true positives and true negatives, and we always want both (the values on the main diagonal of the confusion matrix) to be high. We're never happy about false positives or false negatives, and we always want both (the values off the main diagonal) to be as low as possible.

The confusion matrix contains all possible information about the classifications we've made and their correctness. However, data scientists can never get enough new ways to slice and dice and re-represent data. We can calculate a huge number of derived metrics from our little confusion matrix.

Two of the most popular metrics we can derive are precision and recall. *Precision* is defined as *true positives / (true positives + false positives)*. *Recall* is also called *sensitivity* and is defined as *true positives / (true positives + false negatives)*. Precision is answering the question, Out of everything we thought was positive, how many times was it actually positive? (In our case, *positive* refers to attrition—out of all the times we thought a client was at high risk of leaving, how many times did they actually leave?) Recall is answering the slightly different question, Out of all the actually positive cases, how many did we think were positive? (In other words, out of all the clients who actually exited their contracts, how many did we predict were at high attrition risk?) If false positives are high, precision will be low. If false negatives are high, recall will be low. Ideally, both will be as high as possible.

We can calculate both precision and recall as follows:

```
conf_mat = confusion_matrix(prediction,actual)
precision = conf_mat[0][0]/(conf_mat[0][0]+conf_mat[0][1])
recall = conf_mat[0][0]/(conf_mat[0][0]+conf_mat[1][0])
```

You'll see that our precision is about 0.54, and our recall is about 0.64. These are not extremely encouraging values. Precision and recall are always between 0 and 1, and they're supposed to be as close to 1 as possible. Our results are higher than 0, which is good news, but we have plenty of room for improvement. Let's do our best to get better precision and recall by making some improvements in the next sections.

Using Multivariate LPMs

So far, all of our results have been simple: the clients with the lowest activity levels are also the clients with the highest predicted attrition probabilities. These models are so simple that they may hardly seem worthwhile. You may think that the relationship between low activity and attrition risk is both intuitive and visually evident in Figure 5-2, so fitting a regression to confirm it is superfluous. This is reasonable, although it's wise to seek rigorous confirmation from a regression even in cases that seem intuitively obvious.

Regressions begin to become more useful when we have no clear intuitive relationship and no simple plots that can show them instantly. For example, we can use three predictors to predict attrition risk: last month's activity, last year's activity, and a client's number of employees. If we wanted to plot the relationship of all three variables with attrition simultaneously, we would need to create a four-dimensional plot, which would be hard to read and think about. If we didn't want to create a four-dimensional plot, we could create separate plots for the relationship between each individual variable and attrition. But each of these plots would show only one variable's relationship with attrition, thus failing to capture the whole story told by the whole dataset together.

Instead of trying to discover attrition risk through plotting and intuition, we can run a multivariate regression with the predictors we're interested in:

```
x3 = attrition_past.loc[:,['lastmonth_activity', 'lastyear_activity',\
 'number_of_employees']].values.reshape(-1,3)
y = attrition_past['exited'].values.reshape(-1,1)
regressor_multi = LinearRegression()
regressor_multi.fit(x3, y)
```

This is a multivariate linear regression, just like the multivariate linear regressions we introduced in Chapter 2. Since we're running it to predict 0–1 data, it's a *multivariate linear probability model*. Just as we've done for previous regressions we've created, we can use this new multivariate regressor to predict probabilities for the attrition_future dataset:

```
attrition_future['predicted_multi']=regressor_multi.predict(x3)
```

When we run print(attrition_future.nlargest(5,'predicted_multi')), we can see the five corporations with the highest predicted attrition risk, based on this new multivariate regressor. The output looks like this:

	corporation	lastmonth_activity	lastyear_activity	number_of_employees \
11	ejdc	95	1005	61
12	mike	0	0	49
13	pevc	4	6	1686
4	dmai	4	94	2
22	ynus	9	90	12

	predicted	predicted_multi
11	0.634508	0.870000
12	0.711936	0.815677
13	0.708676	0.788110
4	0.708676	0.755625
22	0.704600	0.715362

```
[5 rows x 5 columns]
```

Since we're using three variables to predict attrition probability instead of one, it's not as obvious which corporations will have the highest and lowest estimated attrition risk. The regression's ability to predict for us will be helpful in this more complex scenario.

Let's look at a list of all corporations, sorted by highest attrition risk to lowest risk based on this most recent regression:

```
print(list(attrition_future.sort_values(by='predicted_multi',\
ascending=False).loc[:,'corporation']))
```

You'll see the following list of corporations:

```
['ejdc', 'mike', 'pevc', 'dmai', 'ynus', 'wlcj', 'angl', 'pian', 'slfm',\
 'hlpd', 'frgv', 'hlly', 'oscr', 'cred', 'dwgt', 'hhtn', 'whsh', 'grce',\
 'pryr', 'xkcd', 'bass', 'ahva', 'erin', 'zamk', 'skct', 'kdic']
```

These are the same corporations we saw before, but they're in a different order, since their attrition risk was predicted using regressor_multi instead of regressor. You can see that in some cases, the order is similar. For example, the dmai corporation was ranked sixth by regressor and ranked fourth by regressor_multi. In other cases, the order is quite different. For example, the whsh corporation was ranked first (tied with two other corporations) by regressor, but it's seventeenth in the prediction by regressor_multi. The order changes because the distinct regressors take into account different information and find different patterns.

Creating New Metrics

After running a regression that uses all the numeric predictors in the dataset, you may think that we've done all the regression that's possible. But we can do more, because we're not strictly limited to creating LPMs based on the columns of our attrition dataset in their raw form. We can also create a *derived feature*, or engineered feature—a feature or metric created by transforming and combining existing variables. The following is an example of a derived feature:

```
attrition_future['activity_per_employee']=attrition_future.loc[:,\
'lastmonth_activity']/attrition_future.loc[:,'number_of_employees']
```

Here, we create a new metric called activity_per_employee. This is simply the last month's activity for the whole corporation divided by the number of employees at the corporation. This new derived metric could be a better predictor of attrition risk than the raw activity level or the raw number of employees alone.

For example, two companies may both have high activity levels at exactly 10,000 each. However, if one of those companies has 10,000 employees, and the other has 10 employees, we might have very different expectations about their attrition risk. The average employee at the smaller company is accessing our tool 1,000 times per month, while the average employee at the larger company is accessing it only 1 time per month. Even though both companies have the same level of activity according to our raw measurement, the smaller company seems to have a lower likelihood of attrition because our tool appears to be much more important to the work of each of its employees, on average. We can use this new activity_per_employee metric in a regression that's just like all the regressions we've done before:

```
attrition_past['activity_per_employee']=attrition_past.loc[:,\
'lastmonth_activity']/attrition_past.loc[:,'number_of_employees']
x = attrition_past.loc[:,['activity_per_employee','lastmonth_activity',\
 'lastyear_activity', 'number_of_employees']].values.reshape(-1,4)
y = attrition_past['exited'].values.reshape(-1,1)

regressor_derived= LinearRegression()
regressor_derived.fit(x, y)
attrition_past['predicted3']=regressor_derived.predict(x)

x = attrition_future.loc[:,['activity_per_employee','lastmonth_activity',\
 'lastyear_activity', 'number_of_employees']].values.reshape(-1,4)
attrition_future['predicted3']=regressor_derived.predict(x)
```

This snippet contains a lot of code, but everything it does is something you've done before. First, we define the activity_per_employee metric, our new derived feature. Then, we define our x and y variables. The x variable will be our features: the four variables we'll use to predict attrition. The y variable will be our target: the one variable we're trying to predict. We create and fit a linear regression that uses x to predict y, and then we create predicted3, a new column that contains predictions of attrition risk made by this new regression. We create a predicted3 column both for our past data and our present data.

As we did before, we can look at the predictions made by this model:

```
print(list(attrition_future.sort_values(by='predicted3',ascending=False).loc[:,'corporation']))
```

Again, you'll see that the order is different from the order given by the previous regressors we tried:

```
['pevc', 'bass', 'frgv', 'hlpd', 'angl', 'oscr', 'zamk', 'whsh', 'mike',\
 'hhtn', 'ejdc', 'grce', 'pian', 'ynus', 'dmai', 'kdic', 'erin', 'slfm',\
 'dwgt', 'pryr', 'hlly', 'xkcd', 'skct', 'ahva', 'wlcj', 'cred']
```

Just as we did before, we can check the confusion matrix for our latest model. First, we'll put our predictions and actual values in the correct 0–1 format:

```
themedian=attrition_past['predicted3'].median()
prediction=list(1*(attrition_past['predicted3']>themedian))
actual=list(attrition_past['exited'])
```

Now we can calculate our latest confusion matrix:

```
>>> print(confusion_matrix(prediction,actual))
[[9 4]
 [2 11]]
```

This confusion matrix should immediately look better to you than our previous confusion matrix. If you need more evidence that our latest model is better, look at the precision and recall values for this model:

```
conf_mat = confusion_matrix(prediction,actual)
precision = conf_mat[0][0]/(conf_mat[0][0]+conf_mat[0][1])
recall = conf_mat[0][0]/(conf_mat[0][0]+conf_mat[1][0])
```

You'll see that our precision is about 0.69, and our recall is about 0.82—still not perfect, but big improvements on our previous, lower values.

Considering the Weaknesses of LPMs

LPMs have good points: it's easy to interpret their values, it's easy to estimate them with centuries-old methods and many useful Python modules, and they're simple in a way only a straight line can be. However, LPMs also have weaknesses. One is that they don't fit the points of a dataset well: they pass through the middle of the points and get close to only a few points.

The biggest weakness of LPMs is apparent if you look at the right side of Figure 5-2. There, you can see that the regression line dips below $y = 0$. If we try to interpret the value of the regression line at that part of the plot, we reach an absurd conclusion: we predict approximately a –20 percent probability of attrition for corporations with about 1,200 logins. There's no reasonable way to interpret a negative probability; it's just nonsense that our model has output. Unfortunately, this kind of nonsense is inevitable with every LPM that isn't a horizontal line. Any non-horizontal regression line will make predictions that are below 0 percent or above 100 percent for certain values. The inevitability of these nonsensical predictions is the major weakness of LPMs and the reason you should learn alternative binary classification methods.

Predicting Binary Outcomes with Logistic Regression

We need a method for binary classification that is not subject to the weaknesses of LPMs. If you think about Figure 5-2, you'll realize that whatever method we use can't rely on fitting straight lines to points, since any straight line besides a perfectly flat horizontal line will inevitably make predictions that are higher than 100 percent or lower than 0 percent. Any straight line will also be far from many of the points it's trying to fit. If we're going to fit a line to points to do binary classification, it will have to be a curve that doesn't go below 0 or above 1, and that also gets close to many of the points (which are all at $y = 0$ or $y = 1$).

One important curve that fits these criteria is called the *logistic curve.* Mathematically, the logistic curve can be described by the following function:

$$logistic\ (x) = \frac{1}{1 + e^{-(\beta_0 + \beta_1 x)}}$$

The logistic function is used to model populations, epidemics, chemical reactions, and linguistic shifts, among other things. If you look closely at the denominator of this function, you'll see $\beta_0 + \beta_1 \cdot x$. If that reminds you of the type of expression that we used when we were doing linear regression in Chapter 2, it should—it's exactly the same expression as we find in a standard regression formula (one with an intercept, a slope, and an x variable).

Soon, we'll go over a new type of regression using this logistic function. We'll be working with many of the same elements that we've used before, so much of what we'll do should feel familiar. We'll use the logistic function to model attrition risk, and the way we'll use it can be applied to any situation where you need a model of the probability of a yes/no or 0/1 answer.

Drawing Logistic Curves

We can draw a simple logistic curve in Python as follows:

```
from matplotlib import pyplot as plt
import numpy as np
```

```
import math
x = np.arange(-5, 5, 0.05)
y = (1/(1+np.exp(-1-2*x)))
plt.plot(x,y)
plt.xlabel("X")
plt.ylabel("Value of Logistic Function")
plt.title('A Logistic Curve')
plt.show()
```

We can see the output of this code in Figure 5-3.

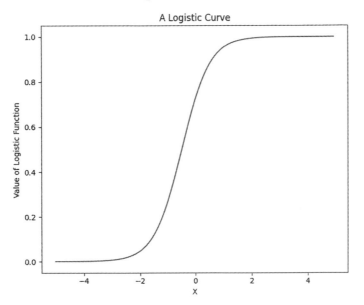

Figure 5-3: An example of a logistic curve

The logistic curve has an S-like shape, so it stays close to $y = 0$ and $y = 1$ over most of its domain. Also, it never goes above 1 and never goes below 0, so it resolves the weaknesses of LPMs.

If we change the coefficients in our logistic equation to be positive instead of negative, we reverse the direction of the logistic curve, so it's a backward S instead of a standard S:

```
from matplotlib import pyplot as plt
import numpy as np
import math
x = np.arange(-5, 5, 0.05)
y = (1/(1+np.exp(1+2*x)))
plt.plot(x,y)
plt.xlabel("X")
plt.ylabel("Value of Logistic Function")
plt.title('A Logistic Curve')
plt.show()
```

This code snippet is the same as the previous code snippet, except for the change of two numbers from negative to positive (shown in bold). We can see the final plot in Figure 5-4.

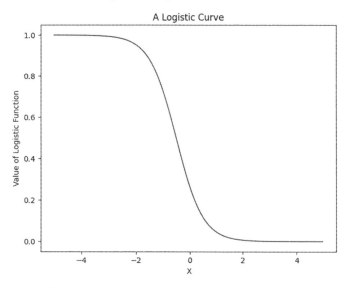

Figure 5-4: Another example of a logistic curve, showing a backward S shape

Now let's use logistic curves with our data.

Fitting the Logistic Function to Our Data

We can fit a logistic curve to binary data in much the same way that we fit a straight line to binary data when we created our LPM. Fitting a logistic curve to binary data is also called performing *logistic regression*, and it's a common, standard alternative to linear regression for binary classification. We can choose from several useful Python modules to perform logistic regression:

```
from sklearn.linear_model import LogisticRegression
model = LogisticRegression(solver='liblinear', random_state=0)
x = attrition_past['lastmonth_activity'].values.reshape(-1,1)
y = attrition_past['exited']
model.fit(x, y)
```

After we fit the model, we can access predicted probabilities for each element as follows:

```
attrition_past['logisticprediction']=model.predict_proba(x)[:,1]
```

We can then plot the results:

```
fig = plt.scatter(attrition_past['lastmonth_activity'],attrition_past['exited'], color='blue')
attrition_past.sort_values('lastmonth_activity').plot('lastmonth_activity',\
'logisticprediction',ls='--', ax=fig.axes,color='red')
```

```
plt.title('Logistic Regression for Attrition Predictions')
plt.xlabel('Last Month\'s Activity')
plt.ylabel('Attrition (1=Exited)')
plt.show()
```

You can see in the output plot in Figure 5-5 that we have exactly what we wanted: a regression that never predicts above 100 percent or below 0 percent probability and gets very close to some of the points in our strange "cloud." We've resolved the weaknesses of LPMs with this new method.

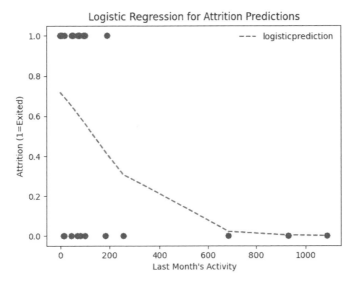

Figure 5-5: A logistic regression predicting attrition risk

You may object that we introduced logistic regression as something that produces an S-shaped curve like the curves in Figures 5-3 and 5-4, and there's no S-shaped curve in Figure 5-5. But Figure 5-5 shows only a portion of the full S; it's like Figure 5-5 is zoomed in on the lower-right side of Figure 5-4, so we see only the right side of the backward S. If we zoomed out the plot and considered hypothetical activity levels that were negative, we would see a fuller backward S, including predicted attrition probabilities close to 1. Since negative activity levels are impossible, we see only a portion of the full S that the logistic equation specifies.

Just as we did with other regressions, we can look at the predictions our logistic regression makes. In particular, we can predict the probabilities of attrition for every company in our attrition2 dataset and print them out in order from highest to lowest attrition risk:

```
x = attrition_future['lastmonth_activity'].values.reshape(-1,1)
attrition_future['logisticprediction']=model.predict_proba(x)[:,1]
print(list(attrition_future.sort_values(by='logisticprediction',\
ascending=False).loc[:,'corporation']))
```

We can see that the output consists of every corporation in `attrition2`, sorted in order of highest to lowest predicted attrition probability based on the results of our logistic regression:

```
['whsh', 'pian', 'mike', 'bass', 'pevc', 'dmai', 'ynus', 'kdic', 'hlpd',\
'angl', 'erin', 'oscr', 'grce', 'zamk', 'hlly', 'xkcd', 'dwgt', 'pryr',\
'skct', 'frgv', 'ejdc', 'ahva', 'wlcj', 'hhtn', 'slfm', 'cred']
```

You can look at these results and compare them to the predictions from our other regressions. Taking into account different information and using different functions to model the data can lead to different results each time we perform regression. In this case, since our logistic regression used the same predictor (last month's activity) as our first LPM, it ranks corporations from highest to lowest risk in the same order.

Applications of Binary Classification

Logistic regressions and LPMs are commonly used to predict binary outcomes. We can use them not only for attrition prediction but also for predicting whether a stock will go up, whether an applicant will be successful in a job, whether a project will be profitable, whether a team will win a game, or any other binary classification that can be expressed in a true/false, 0/1 framework.

The LPMs and logistic regressions you learned about in this chapter are statistical tools that can tell us the probability of attrition. But knowing the probability of attrition does not fully solve the business problem that attrition represents. A business leader needs to communicate these attrition predictions and make sure that client managers act on them effectively. A host of business considerations could alter the strategy a leader implements to manage an attrition problem. For example, attrition probability is not the only thing that could determine the priority assigned to a client. That priority will also depend on the relative importance of the client, probably including the revenue the company expects to gain from the client, the size of the client, and other strategic considerations. Data science is always part of a larger business process, every step of which is difficult and important.

LPMs and logistic regressions have one important thing in common: they're *monotonic*: they express a trend that moves in only one direction. In Figures 5-1, 5-2, and 5-5, less activity is always associated with higher attrition risk, and vice versa. However, imagine a more complex situation, in which low activity is especially associated with high attrition risk, medium activity is associated with low attrition risk, and high activity again is associated with high attrition risk. A monotonic function like the ones examined in this chapter wouldn't be able to capture this pattern, and we would have to turn to more complex models. The next chapter describes methods for machine learning—including methods to capture non-monotonic trends in complex, multivariate data—to make predictions and perform classifications even more accurately.

Summary

In this chapter, we discussed binary classification. We started with a simple business scenario and showed how linear regression can enable us to predict probabilities that help solve a business problem. We considered the weaknesses of those linear probability models and introduced logistic regression as a more complex model that overcomes those weaknesses. Binary classification may seem like an unimportant topic, but we can use it for analyzing risk, predicting the future, and making difficult yes/no decisions. In our discussion of machine learning in the next chapter, we'll discuss prediction and classification methods that go beyond regressions.

SUPERVISED LEARNING

Computer scientists use the term *supervised learning* to refer to a broad range of quantitative methods that predict and classify. In fact, you've already done supervised learning: the linear regression you did in Chapter 2 and the LPMs and logistic regression from Chapter 5 are all instances of supervised learning. By learning those methods, you've already become familiar with the basic ideas of supervised learning. This chapter introduces some advanced supervised learning methods and discusses the idea of supervised learning in general. We're dwelling on this topic so much because it's such a crucial component of data science.

We'll start by introducing yet another business challenge and describing how supervised learning can help us resolve it. We'll talk about linear regression as an imperfect solution and discuss supervised learning in general. Then we'll introduce k-NN, a simple but elegant supervised learning method. We'll also briefly introduce decision trees, random forests, and neural networks, and discuss how to use them for prediction and classification. We'll close with a discussion of how to measure accuracy and what unites each of these disparate methods.

Predicting Website Traffic

Imagine that you're running a website. Your website's business model is simple: you post articles on interesting topics, and you earn money from the people who view your website's articles. Whether your revenue comes from ad sales, subscriptions, or donations, you earn money in proportion to the number of people who visit your site: the more visitors, the higher your revenue.

Amateur writers submit articles to you with the hope that you'll publish them on your site. You receive an enormous number of submissions and can't possibly read, much less publish, everything you receive. So you have to do some curation. You may consider many factors as you're deciding what to publish. Of course, you'll try to consider the quality of submitted articles. You'll also want to consider which articles fit with the "brand" of your site. But in the end, you're trying to run a business, and maximizing your site's revenue will be crucial to ensuring your business's long-term survival. Since you earn revenue in proportion to the number of visitors to your site, maximizing revenue will depend on selecting articles to publish that are likely to get many visitors.

You could try to rely on intuition to decide which articles are likely to receive many visitors. This would require either you or your team to read every submission and make difficult judgments about which articles are likely to attract visitors. This would be extremely time-consuming, and even after spending all that time reading articles, it's far from certain that your team would have the right judgment about which articles will attract the most visitors.

A faster and potentially more accurate approach to this problem is through supervised learning. Imagine that you could write code to read articles for you as soon as they arrived in your inbox and could then use information that the code gleans from each submitted article to accurately predict the number of visitors it will attract, before you publish it. If you had code like that, you could even fully automate your publishing process: a bot could read submissions from emails, predict the likely revenue expected from every submitted article, and publish every article that had an expected revenue above a particular threshold.

The hardest part of that process would be predicting an article's expected revenue; that's the part we need to rely on supervised learning to accomplish. In the rest of the chapter, we'll go through the steps required for the supervised learning that would enable this kind of automated system to predict the number of visitors a given article will attract.

Reading and Plotting News Article Data

Like most data science scenarios, supervised learning requires us to read in data. We'll read in a dataset that's available for free from the University of California, Irvine (UCI) Machine Learning Repository (*https://archive-beta .ics.uci.edu/*). This repository contains hundreds of datasets that machine learning researchers and enthusiasts can use for research and fun.

The particular dataset we'll use contains detailed information about news articles published on Mashable (*https://mashable.com*) in 2013 and 2014. This Online News Popularity dataset has a web page at *https://archive-beta .ics.uci.edu/dataset/332/online+news+popularity* that presents more information about the data, including its source, the information it contains, and papers that have been published containing analyses of it.

You can obtain a ZIP file of the data from *https://archive.ics.uci.edu/ml/ machine-learning-databases/00332/OnlineNewsPopularity.zip*. After you download the ZIP archive, you must extract it on your computer. You'll then see the *OnlineNewsPopularity.csv* file, which is the dataset itself. After extracting that *.csv*, you can read it into your Python session as follows:

```
import pandas as pd
news=pd.read_csv('OnlineNewsPopularity.csv')
```

We import our old friend the pandas package and read the news dataset into a variable called news. Each row of news contains detailed information about one particular article published on Mashable. The first column, url, contains the URL of the original article. If you visit the URL of a particular article, you can see the text and images associated with it.

In total, our news dataset has 61 columns. Each column after the first contains a numeric measurement of something about the article. For example, the third column is called n_tokens_title. This is a count of the *tokens* in the title, which in this case just means the number of words in the title. Many of the columns in the news dataset have names that refer to advanced methods in *natural language processing (NLP)*. NLP is a relatively new field concerned with using computer science and mathematical algorithms to analyze, generate, and translate natural human language in a way that's quick and automatic and doesn't require human effort.

Consider the 46th column, global_sentiment_polarity. This column contains a measure of each article's overall *sentiment*, ranging from –1 (highly negative) to 0 (neutral) to 1 (highly positive). The ability to automatically measure the sentiment of text written in natural human language is one of the recent, exciting developments in the world of NLP. The most advanced sentiment analysis algorithms are able to closely match humans' sentiment ratings, so an article about death, horror, and sadness will be ranked by both humans and NLP algorithms as having a highly negative sentiment (close to –1), while an article about joy, freedom, and data analysis will be universally agreed to have a highly positive sentiment (close to 1). The creators of our dataset have already run a sentiment analysis algorithm to measure the sentiment of each article in the dataset, and the result is stored in global_sentiment_polarity. Other columns have other measurements, including simple things like article length as well as other advanced NLP results.

The final column, shares, records the number of times each article was shared on social media platforms. Our true goal is to increase revenue by increasing the number of visitors. But our dataset doesn't contain any direct measurement of either revenue or visitors! This is a common occurrence in the practice of data science: we want to analyze something, but our data contains only other things. In this case, it's reasonable to suppose that the number of social media shares is correlated with the number of visitors to an article, both because highly visited articles will be shared often and because highly shared articles will be visited often. And, as we mentioned before, our revenue is directly related to the number of website visits. So, we can reasonably suppose that the number of social media shares of an article is closely related to the revenue obtained from the article. This means that we'll use shares as a *proxy* for visits and revenue.

It will help our analysis if we can determine which features of an article are positively related to shares. For example, we might guess that articles with high sentiment scores will also get shared frequently, if we believe that people like to share happy things. If that's true, knowing the sentiment of an article will help us predict the number of times an article will be shared. By learning how to predict shares, we suppose that we'll be simultaneously learning how to predict both visitors and revenue as well. And, if we know the features of a highly shared article, we'll know how to design future articles to maximize our revenue.

As we've done before (especially in Chapter 1), we can start with simple exploration. We'll start by drawing a graph. Let's consider a graph of the relationship between sentiment and shares:

```
from matplotlib import pyplot as plt
plt.scatter(news[' global_sentiment_polarity'],news[' shares'])
plt.title('Popularity by Sentiment')
plt.xlabel('Sentiment Polarity')
plt.ylabel('Shares')
plt.show()
```

You may notice that when we access our dataset's columns in this Python snippet, we put a space at the beginning of every column name. For example, we write news[' shares'] instead of news['shares'] to refer to the column recording the number of shares. We do this because that's the way the column names are recorded in the original data file. For whatever reason, that file contains a space before every column name instead of the column name alone, so we need to include that space when we tell Python to access each column by name. You'll see these spaces throughout the chapter; every dataset has its own quirks, and part of being a successful data scientist is being able to understand and adapt to quirks like this one.

Figure 6-1 shows the relationship between sentiment polarity and shares.

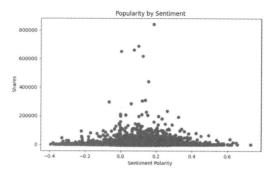

Figure 6-1: The relationship between sentiment and shares for every article in our dataset

One thing we can notice about this plot is that, at least to the naked eye, no clear linear relationship exists between polarity and shares. High-sentiment articles don't seem to be shared much more than low-sentiment articles, or vice versa. If anything, articles close to the middle of the polarity scale (articles that have close to neutral sentiment) seem to earn the most shares.

Using Linear Regression as a Prediction Method

We can do a more rigorous test for this (lack of a) linear relationship by performing a linear regression, just as we did in Chapters 2 and 5:

```
from sklearn.linear_model import LinearRegression
x = news[' global_sentiment_polarity'].values.reshape(-1,1)
y = news[' shares'].values.reshape(-1,1)
regressor = LinearRegression()
regressor.fit(x, y)
print(regressor.coef_)
print(regressor.intercept_)
```

This snippet performs a linear regression predicting shares using sentiment polarity. It does so in the same way we outlined in Chapter 2. We start by importing from the module `sklearn.linear_model`, which contains the `LinearRegression()` function we want to use. Then, we reshape the data so that the module we're importing can work with it. We create a variable called `regressor`, and we fit the regressor to our data. Finally, we print out the coefficient and intercept obtained by fitting the regression: 499.3 and 3,335.8.

You'll remember from Chapter 2 that we can interpret these numbers as the slope and intercept of the regression line, respectively. In other words, our linear regression estimates the relationship between sentiment and shares as follows:

$$shares = 3335.8 + 499.3 \cdot sentiment$$

We can plot this regression line together with our data as follows:

```
regline=regressor.predict(x)
plt.scatter(news[' global_sentiment_polarity'],news[' shares'],color='blue')
plt.plot(sorted(news[' global_sentiment_polarity'].tolist()),regline,'r')
plt.title('Shares by Sentiment')
plt.xlabel('Sentiment')
plt.ylabel('Shares')
plt.show()
```

The output should look like Figure 6-2.

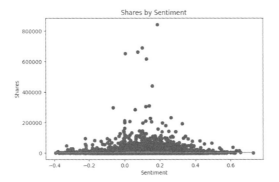

Figure 6-2: A regression line showing the estimated
relationship between sentiment and shares

Our regression line, which should be red if you create the plot at home, appears quite flat, showing only a weak relationship between sentiment and shares. Using this regression line to predict shares probably wouldn't help us much, since it predicts nearly identical numbers of shares for every sentiment value. We'll want to explore other supervised learning methods that can lead to better, more accurate predictions. But first, let's think about supervised learning in general, including what it is about linear regression that makes it a type of supervised learning, and what other types of supervised learning could also be applicable to our business scenario.

Understanding Supervised Learning

The linear regression we just did is an example of supervised learning. We've mentioned supervised learning several times in this chapter, without precisely defining it. We can define it as the process of learning a function that maps feature variables to target variables. This may not sound immediately obvious or clear. To understand what we mean, consider Figure 6-3.

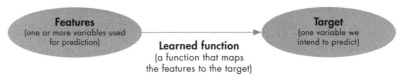

Figure 6-3: The supervised learning process

Think about how this figure applies to the linear regression we completed earlier in the chapter. We used sentiment as our only feature (the oval on the left). Our target variable was shares (the oval on the right). The following equation shows our *learned function* (the arrow in the middle):

$$shares = 3{,}335.8 + 499.3 \cdot sentiment$$

This function does what every learned function is supposed to do in supervised learning: it takes a feature (or multiple features) as its input, and it outputs a prediction of the value of a target variable. In our code, we imported capabilities from the sklearn module that determined the coefficients, or learned the function, for us. (For its part, sklearn learned the function by relying on linear algebra equations that are guaranteed to find the coefficients that minimize the mean squared error on our target variable, as we discussed in Chapter 2.)

The term *supervised learning* refers to the process of determining (learning) this function. The target variable is what supervises the process, because as we're determining the learned function, we check whether it leads to accurate predictions of the target. Without a target variable, we would have no way to learn the function, because we'd have no way to determine which coefficients led to high accuracy and which led to low accuracy.

Every supervised learning method you'll ever use can be described by Figure 6-3. In some cases, we can do *feature engineering*, in which we carefully select which variables in our dataset will lead to the most accurate possible predictions. In other cases, we'll adjust our target variable—for example, by using a proxy or a transformation of the original variable. But the most important part of any supervised learning method is the learned function that maps the features to the target. Mastering new supervised learning methods consists of mastering new ways to determine these learned functions.

When we use linear regression as our chosen supervised learning method, the learned function we get is always in the form shown in Equation 6-1:

$$target = intercept + coefficient_1 \cdot feature_1 + coefficient_2 \cdot feature_2 + \ldots + coefficient_n \cdot feature_n$$

Equation 6-1: The general form of every linear regression's learned function

For someone who has taken lots of algebra classes, this may seem like a natural form for a function to take. Coefficients are multiplied by features and added up. When we do this in two dimensions, we get a line, like the line in Figure 6-2.

However, this is not the only possible form for a learned function. If we think more deeply about this form, we can realize that the function for linear regression is implicitly expressing an assumed view, or *model*, of the world. In particular, linear regression is implicitly assuming that the world can be described by lines: that anytime we have two variables x and y, there's a way to relate them accurately as the line $y = a + bx$, for some a and b. Many things in the world can be described by lines, but not everything. The universe is a big place, and there are many models of the world, many learned functions, and many supervised learning methods that can give us more accurate predictions by abandoning this assumption of linearity.

If the world isn't described by lines and linear relationships, what model of the world is the correct one, or the most accurate or useful one? Many answers are possible. For example, instead of a world made up of lines, we could think of the world as composed of unique little neighborhoods around points. Instead of using a line to make predictions, we could measure characteristics of neighborhoods around points, and use those neighborhoods to make predictions. (This approach will become clearer in the next section.)

If everything we observe in the world is related by lines and linear relationships, linear regression is the right model for studying it. If the world is instead made up of neighborhoods, another supervised learning model is more suitable: k-nearest neighbors. We'll examine this method next.

k-Nearest Neighbors

Suppose that you have an intern who has never studied statistics, linear regression, supervised learning, or data science at any level. You just received a new article from an author who wants to be published on your website. You give the intern the newly submitted article as well as the news dataset and some NLP software. You assign the intern to predict the number of times the new article will be shared. If your intern predicts a high number of shares, you'll publish the article. Otherwise, you won't.

Your intern uses NLP software to determine that this article has global _sentiment_polarity equal to 0.42. Your intern doesn't know how to do the linear regression that we did at the beginning of the chapter. Instead, they have a simple idea of how they'll predict shares. Their simple idea is to look through the news dataset until they find an article that closely resembles this new article. If an existing article in the dataset closely resembles the newly submitted article, it's reasonable to suppose that the new article's number of shares will resemble the existing article's number of shares.

For example, suppose they find an existing article in the dataset that has global_sentiment_polarity equal to 0.4199. They'll conclude, reasonably, that the existing article is similar to our new article, because their sentiment ratings are nearly identical. If the existing article achieved 1,200 shares, we can expect that our new article, with a nearly identical global_sentiment_polarity, should have a similar number of shares. "Similar articles get similar numbers of shares" is one way to sum up this simple thought process. In the context of supervised learning, we can rephrase this as "similar feature values lead to similar target values," though of course your intern has never heard of supervised learning.

Since we're working with numeric data, we don't need to speak merely qualitatively about articles *resembling* each other. We can directly measure the *distance* between any two observations in our dataset. The existing article that resembles our new article has global_sentiment_polarity equal to 0.4199, which is 0.0001 different from our new article's global_sentiment_polarity of 0.42. Since global_sentiment_polarity is the only variable we've considered so far, we can say that these two articles have a *distance* of 0.0001 between them.

You may think that distance is something that has one nonnegotiable definition. But in data science and machine learning, we often find ourselves measuring distances that don't match what we mean by the term in everyday life. In this example, we're using a difference between sentiment scores as our distance, even though it's not a distance that can be walked or measured with a ruler. In other cases, we may find ourselves expressing a distance between true and false values, especially if we're doing a classification as in Chapter 5. When we talk about distance, we're often using the term as a loose analogy rather than a literal physical measurement.

Observations that have a small distance between them can be called *neighbors*, and in this case we've found two close neighbors. Another article with sentiment 0.41 would have distance 0.1 from our new article: still a neighbor, but a little further down the "street." For any two articles, we can measure the distance between them on all variables that interest us and use this as a measurement of the extent to which any two articles are neighbors.

Instead of considering just one neighbor article, we can consider the entire neighborhood surrounding the new article we want to make predictions about. We might find the 15 nearest neighbors to our new article—the 15 points in our dataset with global_sentiment_polarity closest to 0.42. We can consider the number of shares associated with each of those 15 articles. The mean of the number of shares achieved by these 15 nearest neighbors is a reasonable prediction for the number of shares we can expect our new article to get.

Your intern didn't think their prediction method was anything special. It just seemed like a natural, simple way to make a prediction without using any calculus or computer science. However, their simple process is actually a powerful supervised learning algorithm called *k-nearest neighbors (k-NN)*. We can describe the whole method in four simple steps; truly, it is simplicity itself:

1. Choose a point p you want to make a prediction about for a target variable.
2. Choose a natural number, k.
3. Find the k nearest neighbors to point p in your dataset.
4. The mean target value of the k nearest neighbors is the prediction for the target value of p.

You may have noticed that the k-NN process doesn't require any matrix multiplication or calculus or really any math at all. Though it's usually taught in only postgraduate-level computer science classes, k-NN is nothing more than a simple idea that children and even interns already intuitively grasp: that if things resemble each other in some ways, they're likely to resemble each other in other ways. If things live in the same neighborhood, they might be similar to each other.

Implementing k-NN

Writing code for k-NN supervised learning is straightforward. We'll start by defining k, the number of neighbors we'll look at, and newsentiment, which will hold the global_sentiment_polarity of the hypothetical new article we want to make a prediction about. In this case, let's suppose that we receive another new article, and this one has a sentiment score of 0.5:

```
k=15
newsentiment=0.5
```

So, we'll be predicting the number of shares that will be achieved by a new article with a sentiment score of 0.5. We'll look at the 15 nearest neighbors of our new article to make these predictions. It will be convenient to convert our polarity and shares data to lists, as follows:

```
allsentiment=news[' global_sentiment_polarity'].tolist()
allshares=news[' shares'].tolist()
```

Next, we can calculate the distance between every article in our dataset and the hypothetical new article:

```
distances=[abs(x-newsentiment) for x in allsentiment]
```

This snippet uses a list comprehension to calculate the absolute value of the difference between the sentiment of each existing article and the sentiment of our new article.

Now that we have all these distances, we need to find which are the smallest. Remember, the articles with the smallest distance to the new article are the nearest neighbors, and we'll use them to make our final prediction. A useful function in Python's NumPy package enables us to easily find the nearest neighbors:

```
import numpy as np
idx = np.argsort(distances)
```

In this snippet, we import NumPy and then define a variable called idx, which is short for *index*. If you run **print(idx[0:k])**, you can see what this variable consists of:

```
[30230, 30670, 13035, 7284, 36029, 19361, 29598, 22546, 25556, 6744, 26473,\
7211, 9200, 15198, 31496]
```

These 15 numbers are the index numbers of the nearest neighbors. The 30,230th article in our dataset has the global_sentiment_polarity that is closest to 0.5 out of all articles in the data. The 30,670th article has the global_sentiment_polarity that's second closest, and so on. The argsort() method we use is a convenient method that sorts the distances list from smallest to largest, then provides the indices of the k smallest distances (the indices of the nearest neighbors) to us.

After we know the indices of the nearest neighbors, we can create a list of the number of shares associated with each neighbor:

```
nearbyshares=[allshares[i] for i in idx[0:k]]
```

Our final prediction is just the mean of this list:

```
print(np.mean(nearbyshares))
```

You should get the output 7344.466666666666, indicating that past articles with sentiment equal to about 0.5 get about 7,344 social media shares, on average. If we trust the logic of k-NN, we should expect that any future article that has sentiment about equal to 0.5 will also get about 7,344 social media shares.

Performing k-NN with Python's sklearn

We don't have to go through that whole process every time we want to use k-NN for prediction. Certain Python packages can perform k-NN for us, including the sklearn package, whose relevant module we can import into Python as follows:

```
from sklearn.neighbors import KNeighborsRegressor
```

You may be surprised that the module we import here is called KNeighborsRegressor. We just finished describing how k-NN is very different from linear regression, so why would a k-NN module be using the word *regressor* just like a linear regression module does?

The k-NN method is certainly not linear regression, and it doesn't use any of the matrix algebra that linear regression relies on, and it doesn't output regression lines like linear regression. However, since it's a supervised learning method, it's accomplishing the same goal as linear regression: determining a function that maps features to targets. Since regression was the dominant supervised learning method for well over a century, people began to think of *regression* as synonymous with *supervised learning*. So people started to call k-NN functions *k-NN regressors* because they accomplish the same goal as regression, though without doing any actual linear regression.

Today, the words *regression* and *regressors* are used for all supervised learning methods that make predictions about continuous, numeric target variables, regardless of whether they're actually related to linear regression. Since supervised learning and data science are relatively new fields (compared to mathematics, which has been around for millennia), many instances of confusing or redundant terminology like these remain that haven't been cleaned up; part of learning data science is getting used to these confusing names.

Just as we've done with linear regression, we need to reshape our sentiment list so that it's in the format this package expects:

```
x=np.array(allsentiment).reshape(-1,1)
y=np.array(allshares)
```

Now, instead of calculating distances and indices, we can simply create a "regressor" and fit it to our data:

```
knnregressor = KNeighborsRegressor(n_neighbors=15)
knnregressor.fit(x,y)
```

Now we can find the prediction our classifier makes for any sentiment, as long as it's properly reshaped:

```
print(knnregressor.predict(np.array([newsentiment]).reshape(1,-1)))
```

This k-NN regressor has predicted that the new article will receive 7,344.46666667 shares. This exactly matches the number we got before, when doing the k-NN process manually. You should be pleased that the numbers match: it means that you know how to write code for k-NN at least as well as the authors of the respected and popular sklearn package.

Now that you've learned a new supervised learning method, think about how it's similar to and different from linear regression. Both linear regression and k-NN rely on feature variables and a target variable, as shown in Figure 6-3. Both create a learned function that maps feature variables to the target variable. In the case of linear regression, the learned function is a linear sum of variables multiplied by coefficients, in the form shown in Equation 6-1. In the case of k-NN, the learned function is a function that finds the mean target value for *k* nearest neighbors in the relevant dataset.

While linear regression implicitly expresses a model of the world in which all variables can be related to each other by lines, k-NN implicitly expresses a model of the world in which neighborhoods of points are all similar to each other. These models of the world, and the learned functions they imply, are quite different. Because the learned functions are different, they could make different predictions about numbers of article shares or anything else we want to predict. But the goal of accurately predicting a target variable is the same in both cases, and so both are commonly used supervised learning methods.

Using Other Supervised Learning Algorithms

Linear regression and k-NN are only two of many supervised learning algorithms that can be used for our prediction scenario. The same sklearn package that allowed us to easily do k-NN regression can also enable us to use these other supervised learning algorithms. Listing 6-1 shows how to do supervised learning with five methods, each using the same features and target variables, but with different supervised learning algorithms (different learned functions):

```
#linear regression
from sklearn.linear_model import LinearRegression
regressor = LinearRegression()
regressor.fit(np.array(allsentiment).reshape(-1,1), np.array(allshares))
print(regressor.predict(np.array([newsentiment]).reshape(1,-1)))
```

```
#knn
from sklearn.neighbors import KNeighborsRegressor
knnregressor = KNeighborsRegressor(n_neighbors=15)
knnregressor.fit(np.array(allsentiment).reshape(-1,1), np.array(allshares))
print(knnregressor.predict(np.array([newsentiment]).reshape(1,-1)))

#decision tree
from sklearn.tree import DecisionTreeRegressor
dtregressor = DecisionTreeRegressor(max_depth=3)
dtregressor.fit(np.array(allsentiment).reshape(-1,1), np.array(allshares))
print(dtregressor.predict(np.array([newsentiment]).reshape(1,-1)))

#random forest
from sklearn.ensemble import RandomForestRegressor
rfregressor = RandomForestRegressor()
rfregressor.fit(np.array(allsentiment).reshape(-1,1), np.array(allshares))
print(rfregressor.predict(np.array([newsentiment]).reshape(1,-1)))

#neural network
from sklearn.neural_network import MLPRegressor
nnregressor = MLPRegressor()
nnregressor.fit(np.array(allsentiment).reshape(-1,1), np.array(allshares))
print(nnregressor.predict(np.array([newsentiment]).reshape(1,-1)))
```

Listing 6-1: A collection of five supervised learning methods

This snippet contains five sections of four code lines each. The first two sections are for linear regression and k-NN; they're the same code we ran previously to use sklearn's prebuilt packages to easily get linear regression and k-NN predictions. The other three sections have the exact same structure as the first two sections:

1. Import the package.
2. Define a "regressor."
3. Fit the regressor to our data.
4. Use the fitted regressor to print a prediction.

The difference is that each of the five sections uses a different kind of regressor. The third section uses a decision tree regressor, the fourth uses a random forest regressor, and the fifth uses a neural network regressor. You may not know what any of these types of regressors are, but you can think of that as a convenient thing: supervised learning is so easy that you can write code to build models and make predictions before you even know what the models are! (That's not to say this is a good practice—it's always better to have a solid theoretical understanding of every algorithm you use.)

Describing every detail of all these supervised learning algorithms goes beyond the scope of this book. But we can provide a sketch of the main ideas. Each approach accomplishes the same goal (prediction of a target variable), but does it using different learned functions. In turn, these learned functions implicitly express different assumptions and different math or, in other words, different models of the world.

Decision Trees

Let's begin by looking at decision trees, the first type of model in our code after our k-NN section. Instead of assuming that variables are related by lines (like linear regression) or by membership in neighborhoods (like k-NN), *decision trees* assume that the relationships among variables can be best expressed as a tree that consists of binary splits. Don't worry if that description doesn't sound immediately clear; we'll use sklearn's decision tree–plotting function to create a plot of the decision tree regressor called dtregressor that was created by the code in Listing 6-1:

```
from sklearn.tree import plot_tree
import matplotlib.pyplot as plt
plt.figure(figsize=(16,5))
plot_tree(dtregressor, filled=True, fontsize=8)
plt.savefig('decisiontree.png')
```

We can see the result in Figure 6-4.

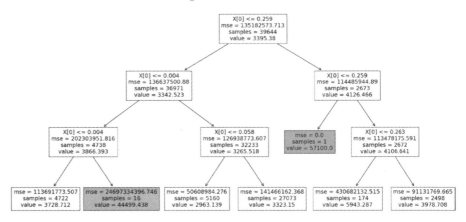

Figure 6-4: A decision tree for predicting article shares based on sentiment

We can follow this flowchart to make predictions about shares, given any global_sentiment_polarity. Since the flowchart has a branching structure that resembles a tree's branches, and since it enables decision-making, we call it a *decision tree.*

We start at the box at the top of the tree. The first line of the box expresses a condition: X[0] <= 0.259. Here, X[0] is referring to the global_sentiment_polarity variable, which is the only feature in our dataset. If that condition is true, we proceed along the leftward arrow to a box on the next lowest level. Otherwise, we proceed along the rightward arrow to the other side of the tree. We continue to check the conditions in each box until we arrive at a box that specifies no condition and has no arrows pointing to other, lower boxes. We then check the value specified there and use that as our prediction.

For the sentiment value we've been working with in our example (0.5), we go right from the first box because 0.5 > 0.259, then we go right at the second box for the same reason, and then we go right yet again at our third box because 0.5 > 0.263. Finally, we arrive at the fourth box, which doesn't have any condition to check, and we get our prediction: about 3,979 shares for an article with sentiment polarity 0.5.

If you create this decision tree at home, you'll see that some of the boxes are shaded or colored. This shading is done automatically, and the level of shading applied is proportional to the value predicted by the decision tree. For example, you can see that one box in Figure 6-4 indicates a prediction of 57,100 shares, and it has the darkest shading. Boxes that predict lower numbers of shares will have lighter shading or no shading at all. This automatic shading is done to highlight especially high predicted values.

You can find the details of how sklearn creates the decision tree in Figure 6-4 in advanced machine learning textbooks. For most standard business use cases, the details and math of optimizing decision trees is not as important as the much easier task of writing a few simple Python lines to create one and then read its plot.

The decision tree in Figure 6-4 can be generated with only a few lines of code and can be interpreted without any special training. This means that decision trees are well suited to business applications. You can quickly generate a decision tree and show it to clients or company leaders, and explain it without needing to go into any math, computer science, or other difficult topics. Because of this, data scientists often say that decision trees are *interpretable models*, in contrast to other models like neural networks that are more opaque and difficult to quickly understand or explain. A decision tree can be a natural, quick addition to any presentation or report that can provide visual interest and can help others understand a dataset or prediction problem. These are important advantages of decision trees in business applications. On the other hand, decision trees tend to have lower accuracy than other, more complex methods like random forests (see the next section).

Just like linear regression and k-NN, a decision tree uses a feature of data (in this case, sentiment) to make a prediction about a target (in this case, shares). The difference is that decision trees don't rely on an assumption that the variables are related by a line (the assumption of linear regression) or that the variables are related by small neighborhoods around points (the assumption of k-NN). Instead, decision trees are built with the assumption that the branching structure shown in Figure 6-4 is the appropriate model of the world.

Random Forests

The fourth section of Listing 6-1 uses *random forests* for prediction. Random forests are a type of *ensemble method*. Ensemble methods got their name because they consist of a collection of many simpler methods. As you might surmise from the name, random forests consist of a collection of simpler decision trees. Every time you use a random forest regressor for prediction, the sklearn code creates many decision tree regressors. Each of the individual decision tree regressors is created with a different subset of the training data and a different subset of the training features. The final random forest prediction is the mean of the predictions made by each of the many individual decision trees.

In the context of Figure 6-3, random forests learn a complicated function: one that consists of a mean of many learned functions from multiple randomly selected decision trees. Nevertheless, because random forests learn a function that maps features to a target variable, they are a standard supervised learning method, just like linear regression, k-NN, and all the rest.

Random forests have become popular because their code is relatively easy to write and they often have much better accuracy than decision trees or linear regressions. These are their main advantages. On the other hand, while we can draw an easily interpretable representation of a decision tree, like Figure 6-4, random forests often consist of hundreds of unique decision trees averaged together, and it's not easy to draw a representation of a random forest in a way a human can understand. Choosing a random forest as your supervised learning method will probably increase your accuracy, but at the cost of interpretability and explainability. Every supervised learning method has advantages and disadvantages, and choosing the right trade-offs that are appropriate for your situation is important for any data scientist who wants to succeed at supervised learning.

Neural Networks

Neural networks have become extremely popular in recent years as our computer hardware has matured to the point of being able to handle their computational complexity. The complexity of neural networks also makes them hard to describe succinctly, except to say that we can use them for supervised learning. We can start by showing a diagram of one particular neural network (Figure 6-5).

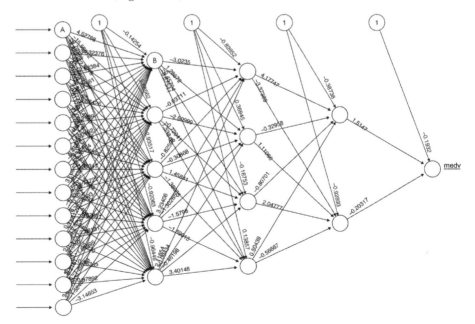

Figure 6-5: A diagram of a neural network

This plot is a representation of a neural network's learned function. In this plot, you can see a column of 13 circles, called *nodes*, on the left side. These 13 nodes are collectively called the *input layer* of the neural network. Each node of the input layer represents one feature of the training data. The single node on the far right represents the neural network's final prediction of a target variable. All of the lines and nodes between the left and right represent a complex learned function that maps feature inputs to the final target prediction.

For example, you can see that the topmost node in the leftmost column (labeled *A*) has an arrow pointing to another node (labeled *B*), with the number 4.52768 written near it. This number is a *weight*, and we're supposed to multiply this weight by the value of the feature corresponding to node A. We then add the result of that multiplication to a running total that corresponds to node B. You can see that node B has 13 arrows pointing to it, one for each node in the input layer. Each feature will be multiplied by a different weight, and the product of the feature value and the weight will be added to the running total for node B. Then, the number −0.14254 will be added to the result; this is the number drawn on an arrow between a blue node with a 1 inside it and node B. (This blue node is also called a *bias node*.)

After all this multiplication and addition, we'll have a running total for node B, and we'll apply a new function called an *activation function* to it. Many possible activation functions exist, one of which is the logistic function you met in Chapter 5. After we apply our activation function, we'll have a final numeric value for node B. We've only barely begun the process of calculating the neural network's learned function. You can see that node B has four arrows emanating from it, each pointing to other nodes further to the right. For each of those arrows, we'll have to follow the same steps of multiplying weights by node values, adding to running totals for every node, and applying activation functions. After we do this for all the nodes and all the arrows in the diagram, we'll have a final value for the rightmost node: this will be our prediction of the target value.

Neural networks are designed in such a way that this whole process, including repeated multiplication and addition and activation functions, should give us a highly accurate prediction as its final output. The complexity of neural networks can be a challenge, but it's also what enables them to accurately model our complex nonlinear world.

These networks are called *neural* because the nodes and arrows in Figure 6-5 resemble the neurons and synapses in a brain. This resemblance is mostly superficial. You could depict neural networks in a way that didn't look like a brain, or you could write down other methods like linear regression in a way that did look like a brain.

To really master neural networks, you need to learn a lot more. Some of the interesting advances in neural networks have come from experimenting with different structures, or *architectures*, of the nodes. For example, *deep neural networks* have many layers between the leftmost input nodes and the rightmost output. *Convolutional neural networks* add an extra type of layer that performs a special operation called *convolution* to the network structure. *Recurrent neural networks* allow connections to flow in multiple directions, instead of just from left to right.

Researchers have found remarkable applications for neural networks in computer vision (like recognizing a dog or a cat or a car or a person), language processing (like machine translation and speech recognition), and much more. On the other hand, neural networks are hard to interpret, hard to understand, and hard to train properly, and they sometimes require specialized hardware. These downsides sometimes make neural networks an unattractive option in business applications despite their power.

Measuring Prediction Accuracy

Whichever supervised learning model we choose, after we fit it, we'll want to measure its prediction accuracy. Here is how we do it for our scenario of predicting shares of articles:

```
allprediction=regressor.predict(np.array([allsentiment]).reshape(-1,1))
predictionerror=abs(allprediction-allsentiment)
print(np.mean(predictionerror))
```

This simple snippet calculates the MAE, as we've done before. In the first line, we use our regressor's predict() method to predict the number of shares for each article in our dataset. (Remember, this regressor is the linear regression model we created near the beginning of the chapter. If you'd like, you can replace regressor with rfregressor or nnregressor to measure the accuracy of our random forest or our neural network, respectively.) In the second line, we calculate the prediction error of these predictions: this is simply the absolute value of the difference between predicted and actual. The mean of our prediction error, calculated in the third line, is a measurement of how well our particular supervised learning method performed, where 0 is the best-possible value, and higher values are worse. We can use this process to calculate prediction accuracy for many supervised learning algorithms, and then choose the algorithm that leads to the highest accuracy (the lowest mean absolute error) as the best method for our scenario.

The only problem with this approach is that it doesn't resemble a true prediction scenario. In real life, we'd have to make predictions for articles that were not in our training dataset—articles that our regressor had never seen during its training process. In contrast, we've taken a dataset of articles from 2013 and 2014, fit a regressor to that whole dataset, and then judged our accuracy based on the same 2013–14 dataset that was used to fit our regressor. Since we judged our accuracy based on the same data that was used to fit our regressor, what we've done isn't truly prediction. It's *postdiction*—saying what happened after it happened instead of before. When we do postdiction, we're liable to be guilty of overfitting, the dastardly peril that we already encountered in Chapter 2.

To avoid the problems of postdiction and overfitting, we can take the same approach we took in Chapter 2: split our dataset into two mutually exclusive subsets, a training set and a test set. We use the training set to train the data or, in other words, to allow our supervised learning model to learn its learned function. After we train the data using only the training dataset, we test it using the test data. The test data, since it wasn't used in the training process, is "as if" from the future, since our regressor hasn't used it for learning, even if it's actually from the past.

The sklearn package has a convenient function we can use to split our data into training and test sets:

```
from sklearn.model_selection import train_test_split
x=np.array([allsentiment]).reshape(-1,1)
y=np.array(allshares)
trainingx,testx,trainingy,testy=train_test_split(x,y,random_state=1)
```

The four outputs of this snippet are trainingx and trainingy—the *x* and *y* components of our training data—and testx and testy—the *x* and *y* components of our test data. Let's check the length of each of these outputs:

```
>>> print(len(trainingx))
29733
>>> print(len(trainingy))
29733
>>> print(len(testx))
9911
>>> print(len(testy))
9911
```

You can see that our training data consists of trainingx (the sentiment scores of the training examples) and trainingy (the share statistics of the training examples). Both of these training datasets consist of 29,733 observations, or 75 percent of the data. The test datasets (testx and testy) consist of 9,911 observations, or the other 25 percent. This type of split follows the same approach that we took in Chapter 2: training our model with the majority of the data and testing our model with a smaller minority of the data.

One important difference between the training/test split we did here and the training/test split we did in Chapter 2 is that, in Chapter 2, we used earlier data (the first years of our dataset) as training data and later data (the last years of our dataset) as test data. Here, we don't do a before/after split for our training and test data. Instead, the train_test_split() function we used performs a random split: randomly choosing training and test sets, instead of neatly selecting from earlier and later times. This is an important distinction to remember: for time-series data (data recorded at regular, ordered intervals), we choose training and test sets based on a split between earlier and later data, but for all other datasets, we select training and test sets randomly.

Next, we need to train our models by using these training sets, and we need to calculate prediction error by using these test sets:

```
rfregressor = RandomForestRegressor(random_state=1)
rfregressor.fit(trainingx, trainingy)
predicted = rfregressor.predict(testx)
predictionerror = abs(predicted-testy)
```

You can see in this snippet that we fit the regressor by using only the training data. Then we calculate the prediction error by using only the test data. Even though all of our data comes from the past, by making predictions for data that weren't included in our training, we're making sure that our process resembles a true prediction process instead of postdiction.

We can see the error on the test set by running print(np.mean(prediction error)). You'll see that the mean prediction error on our test set is about 3,816 when using our random forest regressor.

We can also do the same with our other regressors. For example, this is how we can check the prediction error of our k-NN regressor:

```
knnregressor = KNeighborsRegressor(n_neighbors=15)
knnregressor.fit(trainingx, trainingy)
predicted = knnregressor.predict(testx)
predictionerror = abs(predicted-testy)
```

Again, we can use print(np.mean(predictionerror)) to find out whether this method seems to perform better than our other supervised learning methods. When we do, we find that our k-NN regressor has a mean prediction error equal to about 3,292 on the test set. In this case, k-NN has better performance than random forests, as measured by prediction error on the test set. When we want to choose the best supervised learning method for a particular scenario, the simplest way to do it is to choose the one with the lowest prediction error *on a test set*.

Working with Multivariate Models

So far in this chapter, we've worked with only univariate supervised learning, meaning that we've used only one feature (sentiment) to predict shares. Once you know how to do univariate supervised learning, jumping to *multivariate supervised learning*, where we use multiple features to predict a target, is completely straightforward. All we need to do is specify more features in our *x* variable, as follows:

```
x=news[[' global_sentiment_polarity',' n_unique_tokens',' n_non_stop_words']]
y=np.array(allshares)
trainingx,testx,trainingy,testy=train_test_split(x,y,random_state=1)
from sklearn.ensemble import RandomForestRegressor
rfregressor = RandomForestRegressor(random_state=1)
rfregressor.fit(trainingx, trainingy)
predicted = rfregressor.predict(testx)
predictionerror = abs(predicted-testy)
```

Here, we specify an x variable that contains not only the sentiment of an article but also two other features from other columns in our dataset. After that, the process is the same as we've followed before: splitting into a training and test set, creating and fitting a regressor using a training set, and calculating prediction error on a test set. When we run print(np.mean(predictionerror)) now, we see that our multivariate model has a mean prediction error equal to about 3,474, indicating that our multivariate random forest model performs better than our univariate random forest model on our test set.

Using Classification Instead of Regression

So far, this whole chapter has presented various ways to predict shares, given different features of an article. The shares variable can take any integer value from 0 to infinity. For data like that (continuous, numeric variables), it's appropriate to use regression to predict the values it will take. We used linear regression, k-NN regression, decision tree regression, random forest regression, and neural network regression: five supervised learning methods, all of them used to predict targets that can take a wide range of values.

Instead of doing prediction and regression, we may want to do categorical classification, as we did in Chapter 5. In our business scenario, we might not be interested in predicting a precise number of shares. Instead, we may be interested only in whether an article will reach a number of shares that's higher than the median number. Deciding whether something is above or below a median is a classification scenario, since it consists of deciding true/false to a question with only two possible answers.

We can create a variable that enables us to do classification as follows:

```
themedian=np.median(news[' shares'])
news['abovemedianshares']=1*(news[' shares']>themedian)
```

Here, we create a themedian variable that represents the median value of shares in our dataset. Then we add a new column to the news dataset called abovemedianshares. This new column is 1 when an article's share count is above the median, and it's 0 otherwise. This new measurement is derived from a numeric measurement (number of shares), but we can think of it as a categorical measurement: one that expresses a true/false proposition of whether an article is in the high-share category. Since our business goal is to publish high-share articles and not publish low-share articles, being able to accurately classify new articles as likely high-share articles or likely low-share articles would be useful to us.

To perform classification instead of regression, we need to change our supervised learning code. But luckily, the changes we have to make are minor. In the following snippet, we use classifiers instead of regressors for our new categorical target variable:

```
x=news[[' global_sentiment_polarity',' n_unique_tokens',' n_non_stop_words']]
y=np.array(news['abovemedianshares'])
from sklearn.neighbors import KNeighborsClassifier
knnclassifier = KNeighborsClassifier(n_neighbors=15)
trainingx,testx,trainingy,testy=train_test_split(x,y,random_state=1)
knnclassifier.fit(trainingx, trainingy)
predicted = knnclassifier.predict(testx)
```

You can see that the difference between the regression we were doing before and the classification we're doing here is quite minor. The only changes are shown in bold. In particular, instead of importing the KNeighborsRegressor module, we import the KNeighborsClassifier module. Both modules use k-NN, but one is designed for regression and the other for classification. We name our variable knnclassifier instead of knnregressor, but beyond that, the supervised learning process is just the same: importing a supervised learning module, splitting data into training and test sets, fitting the model to a training dataset, and finally using the fit model for predictions on a test set.

You should remember from Chapter 5 that we usually measure accuracy differently in classification scenarios than we do in regression scenarios. The following snippet creates a confusion matrix, just like the ones we made in Chapter 5:

```
from sklearn.metrics import confusion_matrix
print(confusion_matrix(testy,predicted))
```

Remember that the output of this code is a confusion matrix that shows the number of true positives, true negatives, false positives, and false negatives on our test set. The confusion matrix looks like this:

```
[[2703 2280]
 [2370 2558]]
```

Remember that every confusion matrix has the following structure:

```
[[true positives      false positives]
 [false negatives     true negatives]]
```

So, when we look at our confusion matrix, we find that our model made 2,703 true-positive classifications: our model predicted above-median shares for 2,703 articles, and those articles did have above-median shares. We have 2,280 false positives: predictions of above-median shares for articles that instead had below-median shares. We have 2,370 false negatives: predictions for below-median shares for articles that instead had above-median shares. Finally, we have 2,558 true negatives: predictions of below-median shares for articles that did have below-median shares.

We can calculate our precision and recall as follows:

```
from sklearn.metrics import precision_score
from sklearn.metrics import recall_score

precision = precision_score(testy,predicted)
recall = recall_score(testy,predicted)
```

You'll see that our precision is equal to about 0.53, and our recall is equal to about 0.52. These are not extremely encouraging values; precision and recall are supposed to be as close to 1 as possible. One reason these values are so low is that we're trying to make difficult predictions. It's inherently hard to know the number of shares an article will get, no matter how good your algorithms are.

It's important to remember that even though supervised learning is a sophisticated set of methods based on ingenious ideas and executed on powerful hardware, it's not magic. Many things in the universe are inherently difficult to predict, even when using the best-possible methods. But just because perfect prediction may be impossible doesn't mean we shouldn't try to make predictions at all. In this case, a model that helps us even a little bit is better than nothing.

Summary

In this chapter, we explored supervised learning. We started with a business scenario related to prediction. We reviewed linear regression, including its shortcomings. We then talked about supervised learning in general and introduced several other supervised learning methods. We went on to discuss some finer points of supervised learning, including multivariate supervised learning and classification.

In the next chapter, we'll discuss supervised learning's less popular younger sibling: unsupervised learning. Unsupervised learning gives us powerful ways to explore and understand hidden relationships in data, without even using a target variable for supervision. Supervised learning and unsupervised learning together make up the bulk of machine learning, one of the most essential data science skills.

7

UNSUPERVISED LEARNING

We'll start this chapter with an introduction to the concept of unsupervised learning, comparing it to supervised learning. Then we'll generate data for clustering, the most common task associated with unsupervised learning. We'll first focus on a sophisticated method called E-M clustering. Finally, we'll round out the chapter by looking at how other clustering methods relate to the rest of unsupervised learning.

Unsupervised Learning vs. Supervised Learning

The easiest way to understand unsupervised learning is by comparing it to supervised learning. Remember from Chapter 6 that the supervised learning process is captured by Figure 7-1.

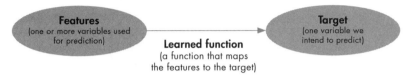

Figure 7-1: The conceptual map of all supervised learning methods

The *target* that Figure 7-1 refers to is the special variable in our dataset that we want to predict. The *features* are the variables in our dataset that we'll use to predict the target. The *learned function* is a function that maps the features to the target. We can check the accuracy of the learned function by comparing our predictions to actual target values. If the predictions are very far from the target values, we know that we should try to find a better learned function. It's like the target values are supervising our process by telling us how accurate our function is and enabling us to push toward the highest possible accuracy.

Unsupervised learning doesn't have this supervision because it doesn't have a target variable. Figure 7-2 depicts the process of unsupervised learning.

Figure 7-2: The conceptual map of the unsupervised learning process

Instead of trying to map features to a target variable, unsupervised learning is concerned with creating a model of the features themselves; it does this by finding relationships between observations and natural groups in the features. In general, it's a way of exploring the features. Finding relationships among observations in our data can help us understand them better; it will also help us find anomalies and make the dataset a little less unwieldy.

The arrow in Figure 7-2 connects the features to themselves. This arrow indicates that we are finding ways that features relate to one another, such as the natural groups they form; it does not indicate a cycle or repeating process. This probably sounds rather abstract, so let's make it clearer by looking at a concrete example.

Generating and Exploring Data

Let's start by looking at some data. Instead of reading in existing data as we've done in previous chapters, we'll generate new data by using Python's random number generation capabilities. Randomly generated data tends to be simpler and easier to work with than data from real life; this will help us as we're trying to discuss the complexities of unsupervised learning.

More importantly, one of the main goals of unsupervised learning is to understand how subsets of data relate to one another. Generating data ourselves will mean that we can judge whether our unsupervised learning methods have found the right relationships among subsets of our data, since we'll know exactly where those subsets came from and how they relate.

Rolling the Dice

We'll start by generating simple example data with some dice rolls:

```
from random import choices,seed
numberofrolls=1800
seed(9)
dice1=choices([1,2,3,4,5,6], k=numberofrolls)
dice2=choices([1,2,3,4,5,6], k=numberofrolls)
```

In this snippet, we import the choices() and seed() functions from the random module. These are the functions we'll use to do random number generation. We define a variable called numberofrolls, which is storing the value 1800, the number of simulated dice rolls we want Python to generate for us. We call the seed() function, which isn't necessary but will ensure you get the same results as the ones presented here in the book.

Next, we create two lists, dice1 and dice2, using the choices() function. We pass two arguments to this function: the list [1,2,3,4,5,6], which tells the choices() function that we want it to make random selections from the integers between 1 and 6, and k=numberofrolls, which tells the choices() function that we want it to make 1,800 such selections. The dice1 list represents 1,800 rolls of one die, and the dice2 variable likewise represents 1,800 rolls of a second, separate die.

You can look at the first 10 elements of dice1 as follows:

```
print(dice1[0:10])
```

You should see the following output (if you ran seed(9) in the preceding snippet):

```
[3, 3, 1, 6, 1, 4, 6, 1, 4, 4]
```

This list looks plausible as a record of 10 rolls of a fair die. After generating lists of 1,800 random rolls from two dice, we can find the sums of each of the 1,800 rolls:

```
dicesum=[dice1[n]+dice2[n] for n in range(numberofrolls)]
```

Here we create the dicesum variable by using a list comprehension. The first element of dicesum is the sum of the first element of dice1 and the first element of dice2, the second element of dicesum is the sum of the second element of dice1 and the second element of dice2, and so on. All of this code simulates a common scenario: rolling two dice together and looking at the sum of the numbers that are face up after rolling. But instead of rolling the dice ourselves, we have Python simulate all 1,800 rolls for us.

Once we have the summed dice rolls, we can draw a histogram of all of them:

```
from matplotlib import pyplot as plt
import numpy as np
fig, ax = plt.subplots(figsize =(10, 7))
ax.hist(dicesum,bins=[2,3,4,5,6,7,8,9,10,11,12,13],align='left')
plt.show()
```

Figure 7-3 shows the result.

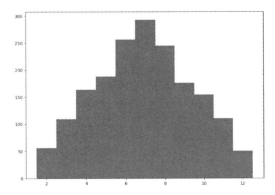

Figure 7-3: The outcomes of 1,800 simulated dice rolls

This is a histogram just like the ones we've seen in Chapters 1 and 3. Each vertical bar represents a frequency of a particular dice outcome. For example, the leftmost bar indicates that of our 1,800 rolls, about 50 summed to 2. The tallest bar in the middle indicates that around 300 of our dice rolls summed to 7.

Histograms like this one show us the *distribution* of our data—the relative frequency of different observations occurring. Our distribution shows that the highest and lowest values, like 2 and 12, are relatively uncommon, while the middle values, like 7, are much more common. We can also interpret a distribution in terms of probabilities: if we roll two fair dice, 7 is a highly likely outcome, and 2 and 12 are not likely outcomes. We can know the approximate likelihood of each outcome by looking at the height of each bar of our histogram.

We can see that this histogram takes a shape that resembles a bell. The more times we roll our dice, the more bell-like our histogram will become. For large numbers of dice rolls, the histogram of outcomes is closely approximated by a special distribution called the *normal distribution*, or *Gaussian distribution*. You also met this distribution in Chapter 3, although in that chapter we called it by one of its other names: the bell curve. The normal distribution is a common pattern we observe when we measure the relative frequencies of certain things, like differences between means in Chapter 3, or sums of dice rolls here.

Every bell curve is fully described by just two numbers: a *mean*, describing the center and highest point of the bell curve, and a *variance*, describing how widely spread out the bell curve is. The square root of the variance is the *standard deviation*, another measure of how widely spread out a bell curve is. We can calculate the mean and standard deviation of our dice roll data with the following simple function:

```
def getcenter(allpoints):
    center=np.mean(allpoints)
    stdev=np.sqrt(np.cov(allpoints))
    return(center,stdev)

print(getcenter(dicesum))
```

This function takes a list of observations as its input. It uses the np.mean() function to get the mean of the list and store it in the variable called center. Then, it uses the np.cov() method. This method's name, cov, is short for *covariance*, another measurement of the way data varies. When we calculate a covariance of two separate lists of observations, it tells us how much those datasets vary together. When we calculate a covariance of one list of observations alone, it's simply called the variance, and the square root of the variance is the standard deviation.

If we run the preceding snippet, we should get the mean and standard deviation of our dice rolls:

```
(6.9511111111111115, 2.468219092930105)
```

This output tells us that the mean of our observed dice rolls is about 7 and the standard deviation is about 2.5. Now that we know these numbers, we can plot a bell curve as an overlay on our histogram as follows:

```
fig, ax = plt.subplots(figsize =(10, 7))
ax.hist(dicesum,bins=range(2,14),align='left')
import scipy.stats as stats
import math
mu=7
sigma=2.5
x = np.linspace(mu - 2*sigma, mu + 2*sigma, 100)*1
```

```
plt.plot(x, stats.norm.pdf(x, mu, sigma)*numberofrolls,linewidth=5)
plt.show()
```

Figure 7-4 shows our output.

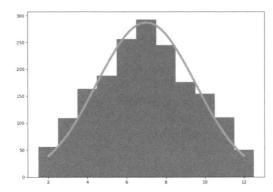

Figure 7-4: A bell curve overlaid on a histogram of dice rolls

You can see that the bell curve is a continuous curve that we've plotted over our histogram. Its value represents relative probability: since it has a relatively high value at 7, and a relatively low value at 2 and 12, we interpret that to mean that we are more likely to roll a 7 than to roll a 2 or 12. We can see that these theoretical probabilities match our observed dice rolls pretty closely, since the height of the bell curve is close to the height of each histogram bar. We can easily check the number of rolls predicted by the bell curve as follows:

```
stats.norm.pdf(2, mu, sigma)*numberofrolls
# output: 38.8734958894954

stats.norm.pdf(7, mu, sigma)*numberofrolls
# output: 287.23844188903155

stats.norm.pdf(12, mu, sigma)*numberofrolls
# output: 38.8734958894954
```

Here, we use the stats.norm.pdf() function to calculate the expected number of dice rolls for 2, 7, and 12. This function is from the stats module, and its name, norm.pdf, is short for *normal probability density function*, which is yet another name for our familiar bell curve. The snippet uses stats.norm.pdf() to calculate how high the bell curve is at $x = 2$, $x = 7$, and $x = 12$ (in other words, how likely rolling a 2, rolling a 7, and rolling a 12 are based on the mean and standard deviation we calculated before). Then, it multiplies these likelihoods by the number of times we want to roll the dice (1,800 in this case) to get the total number of expected rolls of 2, 7, and 12, respectively.

Using Another Kind of Die

We've calculated probabilities for the hypothetical scenario of rolling two 6-sided dice together because dice rolls give us an easy, familiar way to think about important data science ideas like probabilities and distributions. But of course this is not the only possible type of data we could analyze, or even the only type of dice roll we could analyze.

Imagine rolling a pair of nonstandard 12-sided dice, whose sides are marked with the numbers 4, 5, 6, . . . , 14, 15. When these dice are rolled together, their sum could be any integer between 8 and 30. We can randomly generate 1,800 hypothetical rolls again and draw a histogram of those rolls by using the same type of code we used before, with a few small changes:

```
seed(913)
dice1=choices([4,5,6,7,8,9,10,11,12,13,14,15], k=numberofrolls)
dice2=choices([4,5,6,7,8,9,10,11,12,13,14,15], k=numberofrolls)
dicesum12=[dice1[n]+dice2[n] for n in range(numberofrolls)]
fig, ax = plt.subplots(figsize =(10, 7))
ax.hist(dicesum12,bins=range(8,32),align='left')
mu=np.mean(dicesum12)
sigma=np.std(dicesum12)
x = np.linspace(mu - 2*sigma, mu + 2*sigma, 100)*1
plt.plot(x, stats.norm.pdf(x, mu, sigma)*numberofrolls,linewidth=5)
plt.show()
```

Figure 7-5 shows the resulting histogram.

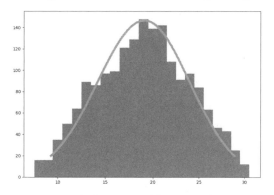

Figure 7-5: A bell curve and histogram for dice rolls using a pair of custom 12-sided dice

The bell shape is roughly the same as in Figure 7-4, but in this case, 19 is the most likely outcome, not 7, and the range goes from 8 to 30 instead of from 2 to 12. So we have a normal distribution or bell curve again, but with a different mean and standard deviation.

We can plot both of our histograms (Figures 7-4 and 7-5) together as follows:

```
dicesumboth=dicesum+dicesum12
fig, ax = plt.subplots(figsize =(10, 7))
ax.hist(dicesumboth,bins=range(2,32),align='left')
import scipy.stats as stats
import math
mu=np.mean(dicesum12)
sigma=np.std(dicesum12)
x = np.linspace(mu - 2*sigma, mu + 2*sigma, 100)*1
plt.plot(x, stats.norm.pdf(x, mu, sigma)*numberofrolls,linewidth=5)
mu=np.mean(dicesum)
sigma=np.std(dicesum)
x = np.linspace(mu - 2*sigma, mu + 2*sigma, 100)*1
plt.plot(x, stats.norm.pdf(x, mu, sigma)*numberofrolls,linewidth=5)
plt.show()
```

Figure 7-6 shows the result.

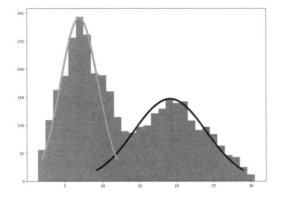

Figure 7-6: A combined histogram showing outcomes from 6-sided and 12-sided dice pairs

This is technically one histogram, though we know that it was generated by combining the data from two separate histograms. Remember that for the pair of 6-sided dice, 7 is the most common outcome, and for the pair of 12-sided dice, 19 is the most common outcome. We see this reflected in a local peak at 7 and another local peak at 19 in our histogram. These two local peaks are called *modes*. Since we have two modes, this is what we call a *bimodal* histogram.

When you look at Figure 7-6, it should help you start to understand what the conceptual diagram in Figure 7-2 is trying to illustrate. We're not predicting or classifying dice rolls as we've done in previous chapters on supervised learning. Instead, we're making simple theoretical models—in this case, our bell curves—that express our understanding of the data and the way observations relate to one another. In the next section, we'll use these bell curve models to reason about the data and understand it better.

The Origin of Observations with Clustering

Imagine that we randomly select one dice roll out of all the rolls that we plotted in Figure 7-6:

```
seed(494)
randomselection=choices(dicesumboth, k=1)
print(randomselection)
```

You should see the output [12], indicating that we randomly selected one instance in our data in which we rolled a sum of 12. Without giving you any other information, imagine that I ask you to make an educated guess about which pair of dice was responsible for rolling this particular 12. It could have been either pair: the 6-sided die could have come up as a pair of 6s, or the 12-sided die could have come up in various combinations, like 8 and 4. How can you make an educated guess about which pair of dice is most likely to be the origin of this observation?

You may have strong intuition already that the 12 was not likely to have been rolled by the 6-sided dice. After all, 12 is the least likely roll for 6-sided dice (tied with 2), but 12 is closer to the middle of Figure 7-5, indicating that it's a more common roll for the 12-sided dice.

Your educated guess need not be based merely on intuition. We can look at the heights of the histogram bars in Figures 7-4 and 7-5 to see that when we rolled both pairs of dice 1,800 times, we got about 50 instances of 12s from the 6-sided dice and more than 60 instances of 12s from the 12-sided dice. And from a theoretical perspective, the heights of the bell curves in Figure 7-6 enable us to directly compare the relative probabilities of each outcome for each pair of dice, since we roll both pairs equally often.

We can do this same type of reasoning to think about dice rolls other than 12. For example, we know that 8 is more likely for the 6-sided dice, not only because of our intuition but also because the left bell curve in Figure 7-6 is higher than the right bell curve when the x value is 8. In case we don't have Figure 7-6 in front of us, we can calculate the heights of each bell curve as follows:

```
stats.norm.pdf(8, np.mean(dicesum), np.std(dicesum))*numberofrolls
# output: 265.87855493973007

stats.norm.pdf(8, np.mean(dicesum12), np.std(dicesum12))*numberofrolls
# output: 11.2892030357587252
```

Here we see that the 6-sided dice are more likely to be the origin of the observed 8 roll: it's expected about 266 times out of 1,800 rolls of the 6-sided dice, while we expect to roll 8 only about 11 or 12 times out of 1,800 rolls of the 12-sided dice. We can follow exactly the same process to determine that the 12-sided pair is more likely to be the origin of the observed 12 roll:

```
stats.norm.pdf(12, np.mean(dicesum), np.std(dicesum))*numberofrolls
# results in 35.87586208537935

stats.norm.pdf(12, np.mean(dicesum12), np.std(dicesum12))*numberofrolls
# results in 51.42993240324318
```

If we use this method of comparing the heights of bell curves, then for any observed dice roll, we can say which dice pair is most likely to be its origin.

Now that we can make educated guesses about the origin of any dice rolls, we're ready to tackle *clustering*, one of the most important, most common tasks in unsupervised learning. The goal of clustering is to answer a global version of the question we considered previously: Which pair of dice is the origin of every observation in our data?

Clustering begins with a reasoning process that's similar to the reasoning in our previous section. But instead of reasoning about a single dice roll, we try to determine which dice pair is the origin of every observation in our data. This is a simple process that we can go through as follows:

- For all rolls of 2, dice pair 1's bell curve is higher than dice pair 2's, so, without knowing anything else, we suppose that all rolls of 2 came from dice pair 1.

- For all rolls of 3, dice pair 1's bell curve is higher than dice pair 2's, so, without knowing anything else, we suppose that all rolls of 3 came from dice pair 1.

- . . .

- For all rolls of 12, dice pair 2's bell curve is higher than dice pair 1's, so, without knowing anything else, we suppose that all rolls of 12 came from dice pair 2.

- . . .

- For all rolls of 30, dice pair 2's bell curve is higher than dice pair 1's, so, without knowing anything else, we suppose that all rolls of 30 came from dice pair 2.

By considering each of the 29 possible dice roll outcomes individually, we can make good guesses about the respective origins of every observation in our data. We can also write code to accomplish this:

```
from scipy.stats import multivariate_normal
def classify(allpts,allmns,allvar):
    vars=[]
    for n in range(len(allmns)):
        vars.append(multivariate_normal(mean=allmns[n], cov=allvar[n]))
    classification=[]
    for point in allpts:
        this_classification=-1
        this_pdf=0
        for n in range(len(allmns)):
```

```
        if vars[n].pdf(point)>this_pdf:
            this_pdf=vars[n].pdf(point)
            this_classification=n+1
    classification.append(this_classification)
return classification
```

Let's look at the classify() function. It takes three arguments. The first argument it requires is allpts, which represents a list of every observation in our data. The other two arguments the function requires are allmns and allvar. These two arguments represent the means and variances, respectively, of every group (that is, every dice pair) in our data.

The function needs to accomplish what we did visually when we looked at Figure 7-6 to find which dice pairs were the origin of each roll. We consider the bell curves for each dice pair, and whichever bell curve has a higher value for a particular dice roll is assumed to be the dice pair it came from. In our function, instead of looking visually at bell curves, we need to calculate the values of bell curves and see which one is higher. This is why we create a list called vars. This list starts out empty, but then we append our bell curves to it with the multivariate_normal() function.

After we have our collection of bell curves, we consider every point in our data. If the first bell curve is higher than the other bell curves at that point, we say that the point is associated with the first dice pair. If the second bell curve is the highest at that point, we say the point belongs to the second dice pair. If we have more than two bell curves, we can compare all of them, classifying every point according to which bell curve is highest. We find the highest bell curve the same way we did when we were looking at Figure 7-6 previously, but now we're doing it with code instead of with our eyes. Every time we classify a point, we append its dice pair number to a list called classification. When the function finishes running, it has filled up the list with a dice pair classification for every point in our data, and it returns this as its final value.

Let's try out our new classify() function. First, let's define some points, means, and variances:

```
allpoints = [2,8,12,15,25]
allmeans = [7, 19]
allvar = [np.cov(dicesum),np.cov(dicesum12)]
```

Our allpoints list is a collection of hypothetical dice rolls that we want to classify. Our allmeans list consists of two numbers: 7, the mean dice roll expected from our 6-sided dice pair, and 19, the mean dice roll expected from our 12-sided dice pair. Our allvar list consists of the respective variances of the two dice pairs. Now that we have the three required arguments, we can call our classify() function:

```
print(classify(allpoints,allmeans,allvar))
```

We see the following output:

```
[1, 1, 2, 2, 2]
```

This list is telling us that the first two dice rolls in our `allpoints` list, 2 and 8, are more likely to be associated with the 6-sided dice pair. The other dice rolls in our `allpoints` list—12, 15, and 25—are more likely to be associated with the 12-sided dice pair.

What we've just done is take a list of very different dice rolls and classify them into two distinct groups. You might want to call this classification or grouping, but in the world of machine learning, it's called *clustering*. If you look at Figure 7-6, you can begin to see why. Dice rolls from the 6-sided dice appear to cluster around their most common value, 7, while dice rolls from the 12-sided dice appear to cluster around their most common value, 19. They form little mountains of observations, or groups, that we're going to call clusters regardless of their shape or size.

It's common in practice for data to have this type of clustered structure, in which a small number of subsets (clusters) are apparent, with most observations in each subset appearing close to the subset's mean, and only a small minority of observations between subsets or far away from the mean. By forming a conclusion about the clusters that exist in our data, and assigning each observation to one of our clusters, we've accomplished a simple version of clustering, the main task of this chapter.

Clustering in Business Applications

Dice rolls have probabilities that are easy to understand and reason about. But not many situations in business require being directly interested in dice rolls. Nevertheless, clustering is commonly used in business, especially by marketers.

Imagine that Figure 7-6 is not a record of dice rolls but rather a record of transaction sizes at a retail store you're running. The lower cluster around 7 indicates that people in one group are spending about $7 at your store, and the higher cluster around 19 indicates that people in another group are spending around $19 at your store. You can say that you have a cluster of low-spending customers and a cluster of high-spending customers.

Now that you know that you have two distinct groups of customers and you know who they are, you can act on this information. For example, instead of using the same advertising strategy for all your customers, you may want to advertise or market differently to each group. Maybe advertisements emphasizing bargains and utility are persuasive to low spenders, while advertisements emphasizing premium quality and social prestige are more appealing to high spenders. Once you have a firm grasp of the boundary between your two groups of customers, the size of each group, and their most common spending habits, you have most of what you need to enact a sophisticated two-pronged advertisement strategy.

On the other hand, after discovering the clusters in your data, you might want to eliminate them rather than cater to them. For example, you may believe that your low-spending customers are not budget conscious but rather simply unaware of some of your more expensive, useful products. You may focus on more aggressive and informative advertising strictly for them, to encourage all of your customers to be in the high-spending group. Your exact approach will depend on many other details of your business, your products, and your strategy. A cluster analysis can give you important input to your strategic decisions by showing you the salient groups of customers and their characteristics, but it won't go all the way to providing a clear business strategy from scratch.

Instead of transaction size, we could imagine that the x-axis of the histogram in Figure 7-6 refers to another variable, like customer age. Then, our clustering analysis would be telling us that two distinct groups patronize our business: a younger group and an older group. You could do clustering on any numeric variable that you measure related to your customers and potentially find interesting customer groups.

Corporate marketers had been splitting customers into groups for many years before the term *data science* was common or even before most of today's clustering methods were invented. Before the age of data science and clustering, marketers called the practice of splitting customers into groups *customer segmentation*.

In practice, marketers often perform segmentation in a nonscientific way, not by finding clusters and boundaries from data but by picking round numbers from guesses or intuition. For example, a television producer might commission surveys of viewers and analyze the data in a way that seems natural, by looking at results from all viewers younger than age 30, then looking at viewers age 30 and up separately. Using the nice, round number 30 provides a potentially natural-seeming boundary between younger and older viewers. However, maybe the producer's show has scarcely any viewers above age 30, so analyzing responses from this group separately would be a distraction from the much larger group of viewers under 30. A simple cluster analysis might instead reveal a large cluster of viewers around age 18 and a large cluster around age 28, with a boundary between these groups at age 23. Analyzing segments based on this clustering analysis, rather than the round-sounding but ultimately misguided under-30 and over-30 segments, would be more useful to understand the show's viewers and their opinions.

Segmentation predates clustering, but clustering is a great way to do segmentation because it enables us to find more accurate and useful segments, and precise boundaries between them. In this case, you could say that the clustering approach is giving us objective, data-driven insights, as compared to the intuition-based or experience-based approach associated with round-number segmentation. Improving from intuition to objective, data-driven insights is one of the main contributions of data science to business.

So far, we've discussed segmentation on only one variable at a time: dice rolls, spending, or age analyzed individually. Instead of clustering and segmenting on only one variable at a time, we can start thinking in multiple dimensions. For example, if we're running a retail company in the United States, we might find a cluster of young, high spenders in the west; a group of older, low spenders in the southeast; and a cluster of middle-aged, moderately high spenders in the north. To discover this, we would have to perform clustering in multiple dimensions at once. Data science clustering methods have this capability, giving them another advantage over traditional segmentation methods.

Analyzing Multiple Dimensions

In our dice roll data, each observation consists of just one number: the sum of the face-up numbers on the dice we rolled. We don't record the temperature or color of the dice, the length or width of their edges, or anything else except for exactly one raw number per roll. Our dice roll dataset is *one-dimensional*. Here a *dimension* doesn't necessarily refer to a dimension in space but rather to any measurement that can vary between low and high. Dice rolls can vary a great deal between a low roll like 2 and a high roll like 12 (or more, depending on the dice we're using), but we measure only their highs and lows on one metric: the sum of the numbers that are face up after we roll them.

In business scenarios, we're almost always interested in more than one dimension. When we're analyzing customer clusters, for example, we want to know customers' ages, locations, incomes, genders, years of education, and as much more as we can so we can successfully market to them. When we're working with many dimensions, some things will look different. For example, the bell curves we've seen in Figures 7-3 through 7-6 will gain an extra dimension, as in the right side of Figure 7-7.

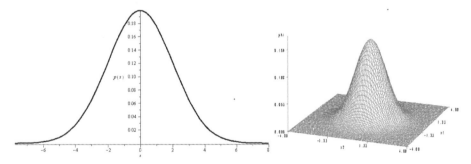

Figure 7-7: A univariate bell curve (left) and a bivariate bell curve (right)

The left side of this diagram shows a *univariate bell curve*, called *univariate* because it shows relative probabilities for only one variable (the x-axis). The right side shows a *bivariate bell curve*, one that shows relative probabilities varying along two dimensions: the x- and y-axes. We can imagine that the x- and y-axes in the plot on the right side of Figure 7-7 could be age and average transaction size, for example.

A univariate Gaussian curve has a mean that's represented by just one number, like $x = 0$ in the left side of Figure 7-7. A bivariate Gaussian curve has a mean that's represented by two numbers: an ordered pair consisting of an x-coordinate and a y-coordinate, like (0, 0). The number of dimensions increases, but the idea of using the mean of each dimension to find the highest point of the bell is the same. Finding the means of each dimension will tell us where to find the center and highest point of the bell, around which the other observations tend to cluster. In both the univariate and bivariate cases, we can interpret the height of the bell curve as a probability: points where the bell curve is higher correspond to observations that are more likely.

Going from one to two dimensions also affects the way we express how spread out our bell curve is. In one dimension, we use the variance (or standard deviation) as a single number that expresses the degree of spread of our curve. In two or more dimensions, we use a matrix, or a rectangular array of numbers, to express the degree of the bell curve's spread. The matrix we use, called a *covariance matrix*, records not only how spread out each dimension is on its own but also the extent to which different dimensions vary together. We don't need to worry about the details of the covariance matrix; we mostly just need to calculate it with the `np.cov()` function and use it as an input in our clustering methods.

When you increase the number of dimensions in your clustering analysis from two to three or more, the adjustment is straightforward. Instead of a univariate or bivariate bell curve, we'll have a *multivariate bell curve*. In three dimensions, a mean will have three coordinates; in n dimensions, it will have n coordinates. The covariance matrix will also get bigger every time you increase the dimension of your problem. But no matter how many dimensions you have, the features of the bell curve are always the same: it has a mean, which most observations are near, and it has a measure of covariance, which shows how spread out the bell curve is.

In the rest of the chapter, we'll look at a two-dimensional example, which will show the idea and process of clustering while still enabling us to draw simple, interpretable plots. This example will show all the essential features of clustering and unsupervised learning that you can apply in any number of dimensions.

E-M Clustering

We now have all the ingredients required to perform *E-M clustering*, a powerful unsupervised learning approach that enables us to intelligently find natural groups in multidimensional data. This technique is also called *Gaussian mixture modeling*, because it uses bell curves (Gaussian distributions) to model how groups mix together. Whatever you call it, it's useful and relatively straightforward.

We'll start by looking at new two-dimensional data that we want to perform clustering on. We can read the data from its online home as follows:

```
import ast
import requests
link = "https://bradfordtuckfield.com/emdata.txt"
f = requests.get(link)
allpoints = ast.literal_eval(f.text)
```

This snippet uses two modules: ast and requests. The requests package allows Python to request a file or dataset from a website—in this case, the website where the clustering data lives. The data is stored in a file as a Python list. Python reads *.txt* files as strings by default, but we want to read the data into a Python list instead of a string. The ast module contains a literal_eval() method that enables us to read list data from files that would otherwise be treated as strings. We read our list into a variable called allpoints.

Now that we've read the data into Python, we can plot it to see what it looks like:

```
allxs=[point[0] for point in allpoints]
allys=[point[1] for point in allpoints]
plt.plot(allxs, allys, 'x')
plt.axis('equal')
plt.show()
```

Figure 7-8 shows the results.

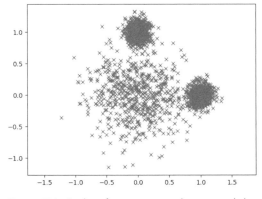

Figure 7-8: A plot of our new two-dimensional data

One thing you might notice is that these axes have no labels. This is not an accident: we're going to work with this data as an unlabeled example and then talk about how it can be applied to many scenarios. You could imagine many possible labels for the axes in this example: maybe the points represent cities, the x-axis is percent population growth, and the y-axis is percent economic growth. If so, performing clustering will identify clusters of cities whose growth has been comparable recently. Maybe this could be useful if you're a CEO and you're trying to decide where to open a new franchise of your business. But the axes don't have to represent the cities' growth: they could represent anything at all, and our clustering algorithms will work in the same way regardless.

A few other things are immediately apparent in Figure 7-8. Two particularly dense clusters of observations appear at the top and right of the plot, respectively. In the center of the plot, another cluster appears to be much less dense than the other two. We seem to have three clusters in different locations, with different sizes and densities.

Instead of relying only on our eyes for this clustering exercise, let's use a powerful clustering algorithm: the E-M algorithm. *E-M* is short for *expectation-maximization*. We can describe this algorithm in four steps:

1. Guessing: Make guesses for the means and covariances of every cluster.

2. Expectation: Classify every observation in our data according to which cluster it's most likely to be a member of, according to the most recent estimates of means and covariances. (This is called the *E*, or *Expectation*, step because we're classifying based on our expectation of how likely each point is to be in each cluster.)

3. Maximization: Use the classifications obtained in the Expectation step to calculate new estimates for the means and covariances of each cluster. (This is called the *M*, or *Maximization*, step because we find the means and variances that maximize the probability of matching our data.)

4. Convergence: Repeat the Expectation and Maximization steps until reaching a stopping condition.

If this algorithm seems intimidating, don't worry; you've already done all the hard parts earlier in the chapter. Let's proceed through each step in turn to understand them better.

The Guessing Step

The first step is the easiest, since we can make any guess whatsoever for the means and covariances of our clusters. Let's make some initial guesses:

```
#initial guesses
mean1=[-1,0]
mean2=[0.5,-1]
mean3=[0.5,0.5]

allmeans=[mean1,mean2,mean3]

cov1=[[1,0],[0,1]]
cov2=[[1,0],[0,1]]
cov3=[[1,0],[0,1]]

allvar=[cov1,cov2,cov3]
```

In this snippet, we first make guesses for mean1, mean2, and mean3. These guesses are two-dimensional points that are supposed to be the respective centers of our three clusters. We then make guesses for the covariance of each cluster. We make the easiest-possible guess for covariance: we guess a special, simple matrix called the *identity matrix* as the covariance matrix for each cluster. (The details of the identity matrix aren't important right now; we use it because it's simple and tends to work well enough as an initial guess.) We can draw a plot to see what these guesses look like:

```
plt.plot(allxs, allys, 'x')
plt.plot(mean1[0],mean1[1],'r*', markersize=15)
plt.plot(mean2[0],mean2[1],'r*', markersize=15)
plt.plot(mean3[0],mean3[1],'r*', markersize=15)
plt.axis('equal')
plt.show()
```

The plot looks like Figure 7-9.

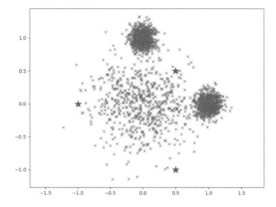

Figure 7-9: Our data with some guesses at cluster centers shown as stars

You can see the points plotted again, with stars representing the guesses we made for cluster centers. (The stars will be red if you're plotting at home.) Our guesses clearly were not very good. In particular, none of our guesses are in the center of the two dense clusters we see at the top and right of the plot, and none are close to the center of the main cloud of points. In this case, starting with inaccurate guesses is good, because it will enable us to see how powerful the E-M clustering algorithm is: it can find the right cluster centers even if our initial guesses in the Guessing step are quite poor.

The Expectation Step

We've completed the Guessing step of the algorithm. For the next step, we need to classify all of our points according to which cluster we believe they're in. Luckily, we already have our classify() function for this:

```
def classify(allpts,allmns,allvar):
    vars=[]
    for n in range(len(allmns)):
        vars.append(multivariate_normal(mean=allmns[n], cov=allvar[n]))
    classification=[]
    for point in allpts:
        this_classification=-1
        this_pdf=0
        for n in range(len(allmns)):
```

```
        if vars[n].pdf(point)>this_pdf:
            this_pdf=vars[n].pdf(point)
            this_classification=n+1
        classification.append(this_classification)
    return classification
```

Remember what this function does. Earlier in the chapter, we used it to classify dice rolls. We took a set of dice roll observations and found which dice pair each dice roll was likely to come from by comparing the heights of two bell curves. Here, we will use the function for a similar task, but we'll use our new unlabeled data instead of dice roll data. For each observation in our new data, this function finds which group it's likely to belong to by comparing the heights of the bell curve associated with each group. Let's call this function on our points, means, and variances:

```
theclass=classify(allpoints,allmeans,allvar)
```

Now we have a list called theclass, which contains a classification of every point in our data. We can look at the first 10 elements of theclass by running print(theclass[:10]). We see the following output:

```
[1, 1, 1, 1, 3, 1, 3, 3, 1, 3]
```

This output is telling us that the first point in our data seems to be in cluster 1, the fifth point is in cluster 3, and so on. We've accomplished the Guessing step and the Expectation step: we have some values for means and variances of our clusters, and we've classified every data point into one of our clusters. Before we move on, let's create a function that will plot our data and clusters:

```
def makeplot(allpoints,theclass,allmeans):
    thecolors=['black']*len(allpoints)
    for idx in range(len(thecolors)):
        if theclass[idx]==2:
            thecolors[idx]='green'
        if theclass[idx]==3:
            thecolors[idx]='yellow'
    allxs=[point[0] for point in allpoints]
    allys=[point[1] for point in allpoints]
    for i in range(len(allpoints)):
        plt.scatter(allxs[i], allys[i],color=thecolors[i])
    for i in range(len(allmeans)):
        plt.plot(allmeans[i][0],allmeans[i][1],'b*', markersize=15)
    plt.axis('equal')
    plt.show()
```

This function takes our data (allpoints), our cluster classifications (theclass), and our cluster means (allmeans) as inputs. Then it assigns colors to each cluster: points in the first cluster are black, points in the second cluster are green, and points in the third cluster are yellow. The plt.scatter() function draws all our points in their colors. Finally, it draws red stars for each of our cluster centers. Note this book is printed in black-and-white, so you will see these colors only if you try this code on your own computer.

We can call this function by running makeplot(allpoints,theclass,allmeans), and we should see Figure 7-10.

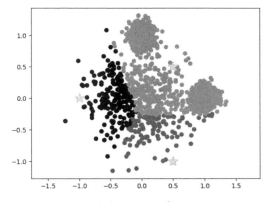

Figure 7-10: Initial cluster classifications

This is a two-dimensional plot. But to understand how it performed classification into clusters, you should imagine three bivariate bell curves (like the one on the right side of Figure 7-7) jutting out of the page, each one centered on one of the star-shaped cluster centers. The covariance we've estimated will determine how widely spread out each bell curve is. The cluster classifications are determined by which of these three bell curves is highest for each point in our data. You can imagine that if we moved the centers or changed the covariance estimates, our bivariate bell curves would look different, and we could get different classifications. (This will happen very soon.)

It's clear from Figure 7-10 that we haven't finished our clustering task. For one thing, the cluster shapes don't match the shapes we think we see in Figure 7-8. But even more obviously, the points that we've called *cluster centers*, shown as stars on this plot, are clearly not in the center of their respective clusters; they're more or less on the edge of their data. This is why we need to do the Maximization step of the E-M clustering algorithm, in which we'll recalculate the means and variances of each cluster (and thereby move cluster centers to more appropriate locations).

The Maximization Step

This step is pretty simple: we just need to take the points in each of our clusters and calculate their means and variances. We can update the getcenters() function we used previously to accomplish this:

```
def getcenters(allpoints,theclass,k):
    centers=[]
    thevars=[]
    for n in range(k):
        pointsn=[allpoints[i] for i in range(0,len(allpoints)) if theclass[i]==(n+1)]
        xpointsn=[points[0] for points in pointsn]
```

```
    ypointsn=[points[1] for points in pointsn]
    xcenter=np.mean(xpointsn)
    ycenter=np.mean(ypointsn)
    centers.append([xcenter,ycenter])
    thevars.append(np.cov(xpointsn,ypointsn))
return centers,thevars
```

Our updated getcenters() function is simple. We pass a number k to the function as an argument; this number indicates the number of clusters in our data. We also pass the data and the cluster classifications to the function. The function calculates the mean and variance of every cluster and then returns a list of means (which we call centers) and a list of variances (which we call thevars).

Let's call our updated getcenters() function to find the actual means and variances of our three clusters:

```
allmeans,allvar=getcenters(allpoints,theclass,3)
```

Now that we have newly calculated means and variances, let's plot our clusters again by running makeplot(allpoints,theclass,allmeans). The result should look like Figure 7-11.

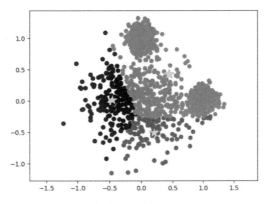

Figure 7-11: Recalculated cluster centers

You can see that our cluster centers, the star shapes, have moved since we recalculated them in the Expectation step. But now that the cluster centers have moved, some of our previous cluster classifications are probably incorrect. If you run this on your computer, you'll see some yellow points that are quite far from the center of the yellow cluster (the cluster at the top right of the plot), and quite close to the centers of the other clusters. Since the centers have moved and we've recalculated covariances, we need to rerun our classification function to reclassify all the points into their correct clusters (meaning, we need to run our Expectation step again):

```
theclass=classify(allpoints,allmeans,allvar)
```

Again, to think about how this classification is accomplished, you can imagine three bivariate bell curves jutting out of the page, with bell curve centers determined by the positions of the stars, and widths determined by the bell curve covariances we've calculated. Whichever bell curve is highest at each point will determine that point's cluster classification.

Let's make another plot that will reflect these newly recalculated cluster classifications by running `makeplot(allpoints,theclass,allmeans)` yet again. The result is Figure 7-12.

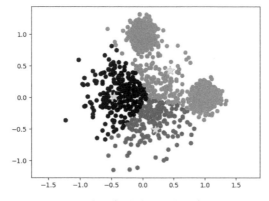

Figure 7-12: Reclassified cluster classifications

Here, you can see that the stars (cluster centers) are in the same locations as in Figure 7-11. But we've accomplished reclassification of the points: based on comparing the bell curves for each cluster, we've found the cluster that's most likely to contain every point, and we've changed the coloring accordingly. You can compare this to Figure 7-10 to see the progress we've made since we started: we've changed our estimates of where the cluster centers are as well as our estimates of which points belong in which clusters.

The Convergence Step

You can see that two clusters have grown (the lower cluster and the cluster on the left), while one cluster has shrunk (the cluster at the top right). But now we're in the same situation we were in before: after reclassifying the clusters, the centers are not correct, so we need to recalculate them too.

Hopefully, you can see the pattern in this process by now: every time we reclassify our clusters, we have to recalculate the clusters' centers, but every time we recalculate the centers, we have to reclassify the clusters. Stated another way, every time we perform the Expectation step, we have to perform the Maximization step, but every time we perform the Maximization step, we have to perform the Expectation step again.

That's why the next, final step of E-M clustering is to repeat the Expectation and Maximization steps: both steps create a need for the other one. We can write a short loop that will accomplish this for us:

```
for n in range(0,100):
    theclass=classify(allpoints,allmeans,allvar)
    allmeans,allvar=getcenters(allpoints,theclass,3)
```

The first line of the loop's body (starting with theclass=) accomplishes the Expectation step, and the next line accomplishes the Maximization step. You may wonder whether we'll get caught in an infinite loop, in which we have to constantly recalculate centers and reclassify clusters again and again forever, never reaching a final answer. We're lucky because E-M clustering is mathematically guaranteed to *converge*, meaning that eventually we'll reach a step where we recalculate the centers and find the same centers we calculated in the previous step, and we reclassify the clusters and find the same clusters we classified in the previous step. At that point, we can stop running our clustering because continuing will just give us a repetition of the same answers over and over.

In the previous snippet, instead of checking for convergence, we set a limit at 100 iterations. For a dataset as small and simple as ours, this will certainly be more than enough iterations. If you have a complex dataset that doesn't seem to converge after 100 iterations, you can increase to 1,000 or more until your E-M clustering reaches convergence.

Let's think about what we've done. We did the Guessing step, guessing means and variances of our clusters. We did the Expectation step, classifying clusters based on means and variances. We did the Maximization step, calculating means and variances based on clusters. And we did the Convergence step, repeating the Expectation and Maximization steps until reaching a stopping condition.

We've completed E-M clustering! Now that we've finished, let's look at a plot of the final estimated clusters and centers by running makeplot(allpoints, theclass,allmeans) one final time; see Figure 7-13.

When we look at this plot, we can see that our clustering succeeded. One of our cluster centers (stars) appears close to the center of the large, spread-out cluster. The other two cluster centers appear near the center of the smaller, more compact clusters. Importantly, we can see observations that are closer (in absolute distance) to the small clusters but are classified as being part of the large cluster. This is because E-M clustering takes variance into account; since it sees that the center cluster is more spread out, it assigns a higher variance to it, and therefore it's able to include more points. Remember that we started with some atrocious guesses for cluster centers, but we got a result that exactly matches what looks perfect to us. Starting from our bad guesses in Figure 7-10, we've arrived at reasonable-looking results in Figure 7-13. This shows the strength of E-M clustering.

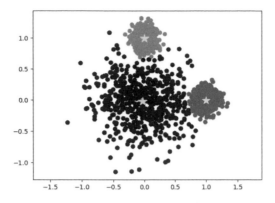

Figure 7-13: Final E-M clustering results

Our E-M clustering process has identified clusters in our data. We've completed the clustering algorithm, but we haven't applied it to any business scenario yet. The way we apply it to business will depend on what the data represents. This was just example data generated for the book, but we could perform exactly the same E-M clustering process on any other data from any field. For example, we might imagine, as we described before, that the points of Figure 7-13 represent cities, and the x- and y-axes represent types of urban growth. Or, the points of Figure 7-13 could represent customers, and the x- and y-axes represent customer attributes like total spending, age, location, or anything else.

What you do with your clusters will depend on the data you're working with and your goals. But in every situation, knowing the clusters that exist in your data can help you craft different marketing approaches or different products for different clusters, or different strategies for interacting with each of them.

Other Clustering Methods

E-M clustering is a powerful clustering method, but it's not the only one. Another method, *k-means clustering*, is more popular because it's easier. If you can do E-M clustering, k-means clustering is easy after some straightforward changes to our code. The following are the steps of k-means clustering:

1. Guessing: Make guesses for the means of every cluster.
2. Classification: Classify every observation in our data according to which cluster it's most likely to be a member of, according to which mean it's closest to.
3. Adjustment: Use the classifications obtained in the Classification step to calculate new estimates for the means of each cluster.
4. Convergence: Repeat the Classification and Adjustment steps until reaching a stopping condition.

You can see that k-means clustering consists of four steps, just like E-M clustering. The first and last steps (Guessing and Convergence) are identical: we make guesses at the beginning of both processes, and we repeat steps until convergence in both processes. The only differences are in the second and third steps.

In both algorithms, the second step (Expectation for E-M clustering, Classification for k-means clustering) determines which observations belong to which clusters. The difference is in the way we determine which observations belong to which cluster. For E-M clustering, we determine an observation's cluster based on comparing the heights of bell curves, as illustrated in Figure 7-6. With k-means clustering, we determine an observation's cluster more simply: by measuring the distance between the observation and each cluster center, and finding which cluster center it's closest to. So, when we see a dice roll equal to 12, E-M clustering will tell us that it was rolled by the 12-sided dice, because of the heights of bell curves in Figure 7-6. However, k-means clustering will tell us that it was rolled by the 6-sided dice, because 12 is closer to 7 (the mean roll of 6-sided dice) than it is to 19 (the mean roll of our 12-sided dice).

The other difference between E-M clustering and k-means clustering is in the third step (Maximization for E-M clustering and Adjustment for k-means clustering). In E-M clustering, we need to calculate the means and covariance matrices for every cluster. But in k-means clustering, we need to calculate only the means of each cluster—we don't use covariance estimates at all in k-means clustering. You can see that E-M clustering and k-means clustering both have the same general outline, and differ in only a few particulars of the way classification and adjustment are performed.

Actually, we can easily implement k-means clustering in Python if we import the right modules:

```
from sklearn.cluster import KMeans
kmeans = KMeans(init="random", n_clusters=3, n_init=10, max_iter=300, random_state=42)
kmeans.fit(allpoints)
newclass=[label+1 for label in kmeans.labels_]
makeplot(allpoints,newclass,kmeans.cluster_centers_)
```

Here, we import `KMeans()` from the same sklearn module we've used before. Then, we create an object called `kmeans`; this is the object we can use to do k-means clustering on our data. You can see that when we call the `KMeans()` function, we need to specify a few important parameters, including the number of clusters we're looking for (`n_clusters`). After we've created our `kmeans` object, we can call its `fit()` method to find the clusters in our `allpoints` data (the same data we used before). When we call the `fit()` method, this determines what cluster every point is in, and we can access the classification of each cluster in the `kmeans.labels_` object. We can also access the cluster centers in the `kmeans.cluster_centers_` object. Finally, we can call our `makeplot()` function, to plot our data and the clusters we found using k-means. Figure 7-14 has the result.

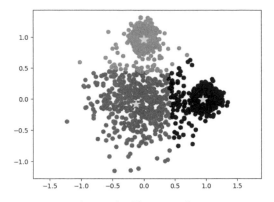

Figure 7-14: The result of k-means clustering

You can see in this plot that the results of k-means clustering are not very different from the results of E-M clustering: we've identified the two dense clusters at the top and right of the plot, and we've identified the looser cluster in the rest of the plot. One difference is that the cluster boundaries are not the same: in k-means clustering, the top and right clusters include some observations that look more like members of the less dense cluster. This is not a coincidence; k-means clustering is designed to find clusters that are approximately the same sizes, and it doesn't have the flexibility that E-M clustering has to find different cluster sizes with different densities.

Many other clustering methods exist besides E-M and k-means, so many that they are too numerous to write about in detail here. Every clustering method is suited to a particular type of data and a particular application. For example, one powerful yet underappreciated clustering method is called *density-based spatial clustering of applications with noise (DBSCAN)*. Unlike E-M and k-means clustering, DBSCAN can detect clusters that have unique, nonspherical, non-bell-like shapes, like the shapes shown in Figure 7-15.

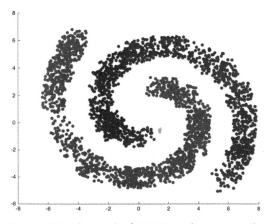

Figure 7-15: The result of DBSCAN clustering, with nonspherical clusters

You can see two distinct groups, or clusters, of data. But since they swirl around each other, using bell curves to classify them wouldn't work well. Bell curves can't easily find the complex boundaries that these clusters have. DBSCAN doesn't rely on bell curves, but rather relies on careful considerations of the distances between each of the points within and between clusters.

Another important kind of clustering is called *hierarchical clustering*. Instead of simply classifying observations into groups, hierarchical clustering yields a nested hierarchy that shows groups of observations in closely related, then successively more distant groups. Every type of clustering has different assumptions and methods associated with it. But all of them are accomplishing the same goal: classifying points into groups without any labels or supervision.

Other Unsupervised Learning Methods

Clustering is the most popular application of unsupervised learning, but a variety of algorithms besides clustering fall under the broad umbrella of unsupervised learning. Several unsupervised learning methods accomplish *anomaly detection*: finding observations that don't fit with the general pattern of a dataset. Some anomaly detection methods are broadly similar to clustering methods, because they sometimes include identifying dense groups of near neighbors (like clusters) and measuring distances between observations and their closest clusters.

Another group of unsupervised learning methods are called *latent variable models*. These models try to express the observations in a dataset as a function of hypothetical hidden, or *latent*, variables. For example, a dataset may consist of student scores in eight classes. We might have a hypothesis that two main types of intelligence exist: analytic and creative. We can check whether students' scores in quantitative, analytic classes like math and science tend to correlate, and whether students' scores in more creative classes like language and music tend to correlate. In other words, we hypothesize that there are two hidden, or latent, variables that we haven't directly measured, analytic intelligence and creative intelligence, and these two latent variables determine the values of all the variables we do observe, all the students' grades, to a large extent.

This isn't the only possible hypothesis. We could also hypothesize that student grades are determined by only one latent variable, general intelligence, or we could hypothesize that student grades are determined by three or any other number of latent variables that we could then try to measure and analyze.

The E-M clustering we accomplished in this chapter can also be thought of as a type of latent variable model. In the case of clustering dice rolls, the latent variables we're interested in finding are the mean and standard deviations of the bell curves that indicate cluster locations and sizes. Many of these latent variable models rely on linear algebra and matrix algebra, so if you're interested in unsupervised learning, you should study those topics diligently.

Remember that all of these methods are unsupervised, meaning we have no labels that we can rigorously test our hypotheses against. In the case of Figure 7-13 and Figure 7-14, we can see that the cluster classifications we've found look right and make sense in certain ways, but we can't say with certainty whether they're correct. Nor can we say whether E-M clustering (whose results are shown in Figure 7-13) or k-means clustering (whose results are shown in Figure 7-14) is more correct than the other—because there are no "ground truth" group labels that we can use to judge correctness. This is why unsupervised learning methods are often used for data exploration but aren't often used to get final answers about predictions or classifications.

Since it's not possible to definitively say whether any unsupervised learning method has delivered correct results, unsupervised learning requires good judgment to do well. Instead of giving us final answers, it tends to give us insight into data that in turn helps us get ideas for other analyses, including supervised learning. But that doesn't mean it's not worthwhile; unsupervised learning can provide invaluable insights and ideas.

Summary

In this chapter, we covered unsupervised learning, with a focus on E-M clustering. We discussed the concept of unsupervised learning, the details of E-M clustering, and the differences between E-M clustering and other clustering methods like k-means clustering. We finished with a discussion of other unsupervised learning methods. In the next chapter, we'll discuss web scraping and how to get data quickly and easily from websites for analysis and business applications.

8

WEB SCRAPING

You need data to do data science, and when you don't have a dataset on hand, you can try *web scraping*, a set of techniques for reading information directly from public websites and converting it to usable datasets. In this chapter, we'll cover some common web-scraping techniques.

We'll start with the simplest possible kind of scraping: downloading a web page's code and looking for relevant text. We'll then discuss regular expressions, a set of methods for searching logically through text, and Beautiful Soup, a free Python library that can help you parse websites more easily by directly accessing HyperText Markup Language (HTML) elements and attributes. We'll explore tables and conclude by going over some advanced topics related to scraping. Let's start by looking at how websites work.

Understanding How Websites Work

Suppose you want to see the website of No Starch Press, the publisher of this book. You open a browser like Mozilla Firefox, Google Chrome, or Apple Safari. You enter the URL of No Starch's home page, *https://nostarch.com*. Then your browser shows you the page, which, at the time of writing, looks like Figure 8-1.

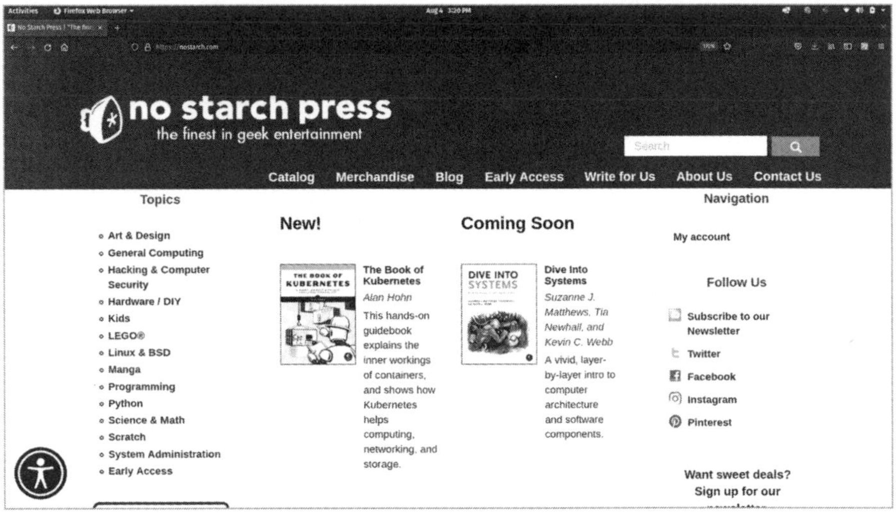

Figure 8-1: The home page of the publisher of this book, accessible at https://nostarch.com

You can see a lot on this page, including text, images, and links, all arranged and formatted carefully so that the page is easy for humans to read and understand. This careful formatting doesn't happen by accident. Every web page has source code that specifies the page's text and images, as well as its formatting and arrangement. When you visit a website, you see a browser's *interpretation* of this code.

If you're interested in seeing the actual code of a website, rather than the browser's visual interpretation of it, you can use special commands. In Chrome and Firefox, you can see the source code for *https://nostarch.com* by opening the page, right-clicking (in Windows, or CTRL+clicking in macOS) on blank space on the page, and then clicking View Page Source. When you do that, you'll see a tab that looks like Figure 8-2.

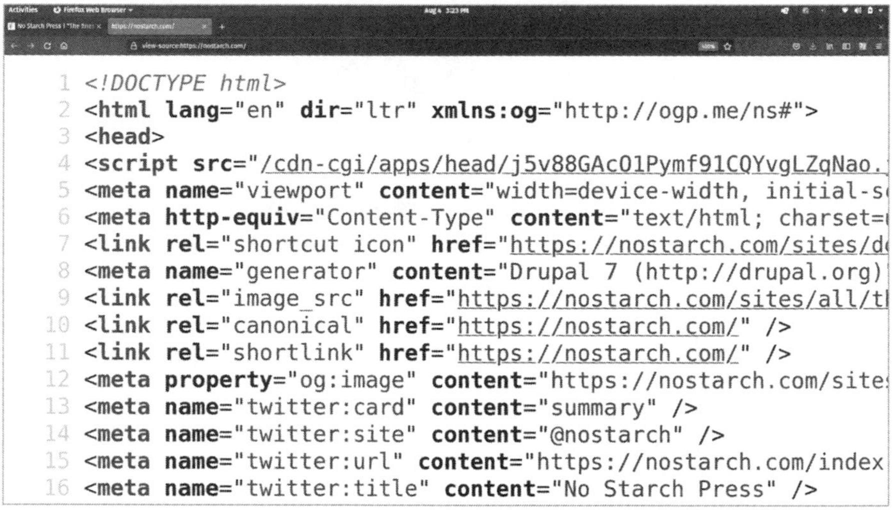

Figure 8-2: The HTML source code of the No Starch Press home page

This tab contains the code that specifies all the content on the No Starch Press home page. It's in the form of raw text, without the visual interpretation that browsers usually provide. Code for web pages is usually written in the HTML and JavaScript languages.

In this chapter, we're interested in this raw data. We're going to write Python scripts that automatically scan through HTML code, like the code shown in Figure 8-2, to find useful information that can be used for data science projects.

Creating Your First Web Scraper

Let's start with the simplest possible scraper. This scraper will take a URL, get the source code of the page associated with that URL, and print out the first part of the source code it got:

```
import requests
urltoget = 'https://bradfordtuckfield.com/indexarchive20210903.html'
pagecode = requests.get(urltoget)
print(pagecode.text[0:600])
```

This snippet starts by importing the requests package, which we used in Chapter 7; here we'll use it to get a page's source code. Next, we specify the urltoget variable, which will be the URL of the web page whose code we want to request. In this case, we're requesting an archived page from my personal website. Finally, we use the requests.get() method to get the code of our web page. We store this code in the pagecode variable.

The `pagecode` variable has a `text` attribute that contains all of the web page's code. If you run `print(pagecode.text)`, you should be able to see all the HTML code of the page, stored as one long text string. Some pages have a huge amount of code, so printing out all the code at once may be unwieldy. If so, you can specify that you want to print only part of the code. That's why we specify that we want only the first 600 characters of the page's code by running `print(pagecode.text[0:600])` in the preceding snippet.

The output looks like this:

```
<?xml version="1.0" encoding="utf-8"?>
<!DOCTYPE html PUBLIC "-//W3C//DTD XHTML 1.0 Strict//EN" "http://www.w3.org/TR/xhtml1/DTD/
xhtml1-strict.dtd">
<html xmlns="http://www.w3.org/1999/xhtml" xml:lang="en-US" lang="en-US">
  <head><meta http-equiv="Content-Type" content="text/html; charset=utf-8">

    <title>Bradford Tuckfield</title>
    <meta name="description" content="Bradford Tuckfield" />
    <meta name="keywords" content="Bradford Tuckfield" />
    <meta name="google-site-verification" content="eNw-LEFxVf71e-ZlYnv5tGSxTZ7V32coMCV9bxS3MGY"
/>
<link rel="stylesheet" type="text/css" href=
```

This output is HTML, which consists largely of *elements* that are marked with angle brackets (< and >). Each element gives a browser like Firefox or Chrome information about how to display the website to visitors. For example, you can see a `<title>` tag in the output; also called a *start tag*, this marks the beginning of the title element. At the end of the seventh line, `</title>` is another tag, this time called an *end tag*, which marks the end of the title element. The actual title of the site is the text that appears between the beginning and ending tags; in this case, it's `Bradford Tuckfield`. When a browser visits the site, it will interpret the meaning of the start and end tags of the title element and then display the title text `Bradford Tuckfield` at the top of the browser tab. This isn't an HTML book, so we're not going to go over every detail of the code we see here. We can be successful at scraping even without deep HTML expertise.

Now that we've scraped a web page, you may feel like you have all the scraping skills you need. However, you have much more to learn. Most web pages have a great deal of HTML code and content, but a data scientist rarely needs a web page's entire source code. In business scenarios, you'll more likely need only one specific piece of information or data on a web page. To find the specific information you need, it will be useful to be able to quickly and automatically search through long strings of HTML code. In other words, you will need to *parse* the HTML code. Let's look at how to do this.

Parsing HTML Code

In the previous section, we went over how to download any public web page's code to a Python session. Now let's talk about how to parse the downloaded code to get the exact data you need.

Scraping an Email Address

Suppose you're interested in automatically harvesting email addresses to create a marketing list. You might use the scraper we introduced previously to download the source code for many web pages. But you won't need all the information in the long strings that represent the full code for each page. Instead, you will want only the small substrings that represent the email addresses that appear on the pages you scraped. So you will want to search through each page you scrape to find these smaller substrings.

Suppose that one of the pages whose code you've downloaded is *https:// bradfordtuckfield.com/contactscrape.html*. If you visit this web page, you'll see that a browser displays its content, as in Figure 8-3.

Company: Demo Company
Phone: +1 879-890-9767
Email: demo@bradfordtuckfield.com
Website: www.bradfordtuckfield.com

Figure 8-3: The content of a demo page that can be scraped easily

This page displays only one email address, which is not hard to find after glancing at the page content for a moment. If we want to write a script that finds the email address on pages that are formatted like this one, we could search for the text Email: and look at the characters immediately following that text. Let's do this, with a simple text search through the page's code:

```
urltoget = 'https://bradfordtuckfield.com/contactscrape.html'
pagecode = requests.get(urltoget)

mail_beginning=pagecode.text.find('Email:')
print(mail_beginning)
```

The first two lines of this snippet follow the same scraping process used in the previous section: we specify a URL, download the page code for that URL, and store the code in the pagecode variable. After that, we use find() to search for the email text. This method takes a string of text as its input and returns the location of that text as its output. In this case, we use the Email: string as the input to the find() method, and we store the location of this text in the mail_beginning variable. The final output is 511, indicating that the text Email: begins at the 511th character in the page's code.

After we know the location of the Email: text, we can try to get the actual email address by looking at characters just after that text:

```
print(pagecode.text[(mail_beginning):(mail_beginning+80)])
```

Here, we print out the 80 characters that immediately follow the beginning of the Email: text (which starts at the 511th character). The output looks like this:

```
Email:    <label class="email" href="#">demo@bradfordtuckfield.com</label>
</div>
```

You can see that the code contains more than just the text visible in Figure 8-3. In particular, an HTML element called label appears between the Email: text and the actual email address. If you want the email address alone, you have to skip the characters associated with the <label> tag, and you also have to remove the characters that appear after the email address:

```
print(pagecode.text[(mail_beginning+38):(mail_beginning+64)])
```

This snippet will print out demo@bradfordtuckfield.com, exactly the text we wanted to find on the page, since it skips the 38 characters of the Email: text and the <label> tag, and it trims off the final characters after the email address, which ends at 64 characters after the Email: text.

Searching for Addresses Directly

We were able to find the email address in the page's HTML code by looking for the 38th through 64th characters after the Email: text. The problem with this approach is that it's not likely to work automatically when we try it on a different web page. If other pages don't have the same <label> tag we found, looking at the 38th character after Email: won't work. Or if the email address has a different length, stopping our search at the 64th character after Email: won't work. Since scraping is usually supposed to be performed on many websites in rapid, automatic succession, it probably won't be feasible to manually check for which characters we should look at instead of the 38th and 64th characters. So this technique probably won't work for a scraper in an actual business scenario.

Instead of searching for the text Email: and looking at the following characters, we could try searching for the at sign (@) itself. Every email address should contain an @, so if we find this, we're likely to have found an email address. There won't be any HTML tags in the middle of an email address, so we won't have to worry about skipping HTML tags to find the address. We can search for the @ in the same way we searched for the Email: text:

```
urltoget = 'https://bradfordtuckfield.com/contactscrape.html'
pagecode = requests.get(urltoget)

at_beginning=pagecode.text.find('@')
print(at_beginning)
```

This is the same scraping code we used before. The only difference is that we are searching for @ instead of Email:. The final output shows that @ appears as the 553rd character in the code. We can print out the characters immediately before and after the @ to get the email address itself:

```
print(pagecode.text[(at_beginning-4):(at_beginning+22)])
```

There were no HTML tags to skip over. But we still have a problem: to get the email address without other extra characters, we have to know the number of characters before and after the @ (4 and 22, respectively). Again, this wouldn't work if we tried to repeat it to automatically scrape multiple email addresses from many websites.

Our searches would be more successful and easier to automate if we had a way to do intelligent searches. For example, imagine that we could search for text that matches the following pattern:

```
<characters matching the beginning of an email address>
                          @
<characters matching the end of an email address>
```

In fact, there is a way to perform automated searches through text in a way that can recognize patterns like the one described here. We'll introduce this approach now.

Performing Searches with Regular Expressions

Regular expressions are special strings that enable advanced, flexible, custom searches of patterns in text. In Python, we can do regular expression searches by using the re module, which is part of the Python standard library that comes preinstalled with Python. The following is an example of a regular expression search that uses the re module:

```
import re

print(re.search(r'recommend','irrelevant text I recommend irrelevant text').span())
```

In this snippet, we import the re module. As its abbreviation indicates, this module is used for regular expressions. This module provides a search() method that can be used to search for text in any string. In this case, we specify two arguments: the string recommend and a string of text that contains the word *recommend*. We're asking the method to search for the substring recommend within the larger string that also has some irrelevant text. Note that we add a single r character before the recommend string. This r tells Python to treat the recommend string as a *raw* string, meaning that Python won't process or adjust it before using it in a search. The span() method will give us the beginning and end locations of this substring.

The output, (18,27), indicates that recommend exists in the second string, starting at index 18 in the string and ending at index 27. This search() method is similar to the find() method that we used in the previous section; both are finding the locations of substrings within longer strings.

But suppose you are searching a web page written by someone who has a tendency to misspell words. By default, the re.search() method looks for exact matches, so if you're searching a web page that contains recommend spelled incorrectly, you won't find any matches. In this case, we may want to ask Python to look for recommend, but to look for different spellings of it. The following is one way to accomplish this with regular expressions:

```
import re
print(re.search('rec+om+end', 'irrelevant text I recommend irrelevant text').span())
```

Here, we change the argument of our code: instead of searching for recommend spelled correctly, we search for rec+om+end. This works because the re module interprets the plus sign (+) as a *metacharacter*. When this special type of character is used in a search, it has a special logical interpretation that can help you do flexible searches instead of requiring exact matches. The + metacharacter indicates repetition: it specifies that Python should search for one or more repetitions of the preceding character. So when we write c+, Python knows that it should search for one or more repetitions of the letter c, and when we write m+, Python knows that it should search for one or more repetitions of the letter m.

A string that uses a metacharacter like + with a special, logical meaning is called a *regular expression*. Regular expressions are used in every major programming language and are extremely important in all code applications that deal with text.

You should try to experiment with the + metacharacter to get more comfortable with the way it works. For example, you could try to search for various misspellings of recommend as follows:

```
import re
print(re.search('rec+om+end','irrelevant text I recomend irrelevant text').span())
print(re.search('rec+om+end','irrelevant text I reccommend irrelevant text').span())
print(re.search('rec+om+end','irrelevant text I reommend irrelevant text').span())
print(re.search('rec+om+end','irrelevant text I recomment irrelevant text').span())
```

This snippet contains four regular expression searches. The output of the first search is (18,26), indicating that the misspelled word recomend matches the regular expression rec+om+end that we searched for. Remember that the + metacharacter searches for one or more repetitions of the preceding character, so it will match the single c and single m in the misspelled recomend. The output of the second search is (18,28), indicating that the misspelling reccommend also matches the regular expression rec+om+end, again because the + metacharacter specifies one or more repetitions of a character, and c and m are both repeated twice here. In this case, our regular expression using + has provided flexibility to our search so it can match multiple alternative spellings of a word.

But the flexibility of regular expressions is not absolute. Our third and fourth searches return errors when you run them in Python, because the regular expression rec+om+end doesn't match any part of the specified strings (reommend and recomment). The third search doesn't return any matches because c+ specifies one or more repetitions of c, and there are zero repetitions of c in reommend. The fourth search doesn't return any matches because, even though the number of c and m characters is correct, searching for rec+om+end requires a d character at the end, and recomment doesn't have a match for the d. When you use regular expressions, you need to be careful to make sure that they're expressing precisely what you want, with the exact amount of flexibility you want.

Using Metacharacters for Flexible Searches

In addition to +, several other important metacharacters can be used in Python regular expressions. Several metacharacters, like +, are used to specify repetitions. For example, the asterisk (*) specifies that the preceding character is repeated *zero* or more times. Notice that this is different from +, which represents a character repeated *one* or more times. We can use * in a regular expression as follows:

```
re.search('10*','My bank balance is 100').span()
```

This regular expression would find the location of a bank balance in a string that specifies 1, 10, 100, 1,000, or indeed any number of 0s (even zero 0s). Here are examples of using * as a metacharacter:

```
import re
print(re.search('10*','My bank balance is 1').span())
print(re.search('10*','My bank balance is 1000').span())
print(re.search('10*','My bank balance is 9000').span())
print(re.search('10*','My bank balance is 1000000').span())
```

In this snippet, we again perform searches for the regular expression 10* in four strings. We find matches for the first, second, and fourth strings, because, though all specify different amounts of money, each contains the character 1 followed by zero or more repetitions of the character 0. The third string also contains repetitions of the 0 character, but no match occurs because the string doesn't contain a 1 character adjacent to the 0s.

In practice, having characters in plaintext that repeat more than twice is uncommon, so the * may not always be useful to you. If you don't want to allow more than one repetition of a character, the question mark (?) is useful as a metacharacter. The ?, when used as a metacharacter, specifies that the preceding character appears either zero or one times:

```
print(re.search('Clarke?','Please refer questions to Mr. Clark').span())
```

In this case, we use the ? because we want to search for either Clark or Clarke, but not for Clarkee or Clarkeee or Clark with more *e*'s.

Fine-Tuning Searches with Escape Sequences

Metacharacters enable you to perform useful, flexible text searches, allowing for many spellings and formats. However, they can also lead to confusion. For example, suppose that you want to search some text for a particular math equation, like 99 + 12 = 111. You could try to search for it as follows:

```
re.search('99+12=111','Example addition: 99+12=111').span()
```

When you run this code, you'll get an error, because Python doesn't find any matches for the search string. This may surprise you, since it's easy to see an exact match for the equation we specified in the string we searched. This search returns no results because the default interpretation of + is as a metacharacter, not a literal addition sign. Remember that + specifies that the preceding character is repeated one or more times. We would find a match if we did a search like this one:

```
re.search('99+12=111','Incorrect fact: 999912=111').span()
```

In this case, Python finds an exact match by interpreting the + sign as a metacharacter, since 9 is repeated in the string on the right. If you want to search for an actual addition sign rather than using + as a metacharacter, you need to use yet another metacharacter to specify this preference. You can do it as follows:

```
re.search('99\+12=111','Example addition: 99+12=111').span()
```

Here, we use the backslash (\) as a special metacharacter. The \ is called an *escape character*. It allows the + addition sign to "escape" from its metacharacter status and be interpreted literally instead. We call the \+ string an *escape sequence*. In the preceding snippet, we find a match for our math equation because we escape the + addition sign, so Python looks for a literal addition sign instead of interpreting + as a metacharacter and looking for repetitions of the 9 character.

You can do a literal search for any metacharacter by using an escape sequence. For example, imagine that you want to look for a question mark, instead of doing a search with a question mark as a metacharacter. You could do the following:

```
re.search('Clarke\?','Is anyone here named Clarke?').span()
```

This finds a match for Clarke?, but it won't find a match for Clark? Because we escape the question mark, Python searches for a literal question mark instead of interpreting it as a metacharacter.

If you ever need to search for a backslash, you'll need two backslashes—one to escape from metacharacter interpretation and another to tell Python which literal character to search for:

```
re.search(r'\\',r'The escape character is \\').span()
```

In this snippet, we use the r character again to specify that we want to interpret the strings as raw text and to make sure Python doesn't do any adjustment or processing before our search. Escape sequences are common and useful in regular expressions. Some escape sequences give special meaning to standard characters (not metacharacters). For example, \d will search for any digit (numbers 0 to 9) in a string, as follows:

```
re.search('\d','The loneliest number is 1').span()
```

This snippet finds the location of the character 1 because the \d escape sequence refers to any digit. The following are other useful escape sequences using non-metacharacters:

\D   Searches for anything that's not a digit

\s   Searches for whitespace (spaces, tabs, and newlines)

\w   Searches for any alphabetic characters (letters, numbers, or underscores)

Other important metacharacters are the square brackets [and]. These can be used as a pair in regular expressions to represent types of characters. For example, we can look for any lowercase alphabetic character as follows:

```
re.search('[a-z]','My Twitter is @fake; my email is abc@def.com').span()
```

This snippet is specifying that we want to find any characters that are in the "class" of characters between a and z. This returns the output (1,2), which consists of only the character y, since this is the first lowercase character in the string. We could search for any uppercase characters similarly:

```
re.search('[A-Z]','My Twitter is @fake; my email is abc@def.com').span()
```

This search outputs (0,1), because the first uppercase character it finds is the M at the beginning of the string.

Another important metacharacter is the pipe (|), which can be used as an *or* logical expression. This can be especially useful if you're not sure which of two ways is the correct way to spell something. For example:

```
re.search('Manchac[a|k]','Lets drive on Manchaca.').span()
```

Here, we specify that we want the string Manchac with either an a or a k at the end. It would also return a match if we searched Lets drive on Manchack.

Combining Metacharacters for Advanced Searches

The following are other metacharacters you should know:

$ For the end of a line or string

^   For the beginning of a line or string

.   For a wildcard, meaning any character except the end of a line (\n)

You can combine text and metacharacters for advanced searches. For example, suppose you have a list of all the files on your computer. You want to search through all the filenames to find a certain *.pdf* file. Maybe you remember that the name of your *.pdf* has something to do with *school*, but you can't remember anything else about the name. You could use this flexible search to find the file:

```
re.search('school.*\.pdf$','schoolforgottenname.pdf').span()
```

Let's look at the regular expression in this snippet. It starts with school since you remember that the filename contains that word. Then, it has two metacharacters together: .*. The . is a wildcard metacharacter, and the * refers to any amount of repetition. So, .* specifies any number of any other characters coming after school. Next, we have an escaped period (full stop): \., which refers to an actual period sign rather than a wildcard. Next, we search for the string pdf, but only if it appears at the end of the filename (specified by $). In summation, this regular expression specifies a filename that starts with school, ends with .pdf, and may have any other characters in between.

Let's search different strings for this regular expression to make sure you're comfortable with the patterns it's searching for:

```
import re
print(re.search('school.*\.pdf$','schoolforgottenname.pdf').span())
print(re.search('school.*\.pdf$','school.pdf').span())
print(re.search('school.*\.pdf$','schoolothername.pdf').span())
print(re.search('school.*\.pdf$','othername.pdf').span())
print(re.search('school.*\.pdf$','schoolothernamepdf').span())
print(re.search('school.*\.pdf$','schoolforgottenname.pdf.exe').span())
```

Some of these searches will find matches, and some will throw errors because they don't find matches. Look closely at the searches that throw errors to make sure you understand why they're not finding matches. As you get more comfortable with regular expressions and the metacharacters they use, you'll be able to quickly grasp the logic of any regular expression you see instead of seeing it as a meaningless jumble of punctuation.

You can use regular expressions for many kinds of searches. For example, you can specify a regular expression that searches for street addresses, URLs, particular types of filenames, or email addresses. As long as a logical pattern occurs in the text you're searching for, you can specify that pattern in a regular expression.

To learn more about regular expressions, you can check out the official Python documentation at *https://docs.python.org/3/howto/regex.html*. But really, the best way to get comfortable with regular expressions is to simply practice them on your own.

Using Regular Expressions to Search for Email Addresses

Regular expressions enable you to search flexibly and intelligently for many types of patterns. Let's return to our initial example of searching for email addresses and see how we can use regular expressions there. Remember that we want to search for text that matches the following pattern:

<some text> @ *<some more text>*

Here's a regular expression that will accomplish this search:

```
re.search('[a-zA-Z]+@[a-zA-Z]+\.[a-zA-Z]+',\
'My Twitter is @fake; my email is abc@def.com').span()
```

Let's look closely at the elements of this snippet:

1. It starts with [a-zA-Z]. This includes the square bracket metacharacters, which specify a class of characters. In this case, it will look for the characters represented by a-zA-Z, which refers to any lowercase or uppercase alphabetic character.
2. The [a-zA-Z] is followed by +, specifying one or more instances of any alphabetic character.
3. The @ is next. This is not a metacharacter but rather searches for the literal at sign (@).
4. Next, we have [a-zA-Z]+ again, specifying that after the @, any number of alphabetic characters should appear. This should be the first part of an email domain, like the *protonmail* in *protonmail.com*.
5. The \. specifies a period or full-stop character, to search for this character in *.com* or *.org* or any other top-level domain.
6. Finally, we have [a-zA-Z]+ again, specifying that some alphabetic characters should come after the full stop. This is the *com* in *.com* or the *org* in *.org* addresses.

Together, these six elements specify the general pattern of an email address. If you weren't familiar with regular expressions, it would be strange to think that [a-zA-Z]+@[a-zA-Z]+\.[a-zA-Z]+ is specifying an email address. But because of Python's ability to interpret metacharacters in regular expressions, Python has been able to interpret this search and return email addresses. Just as important, you have learned regular expressions and understand what this regular expression means too.

One important thing to remember is that there are many email addresses in the world. The regular expression in the preceding snippet will identify many email addresses, but not every possible one. For example, some domain names use characters that aren't part of the standard Roman alphabet used for the English language. The preceding regular expression wouldn't capture those email addresses. Also, email addresses can include numerals, and our regular expression wouldn't match those either. A regular expression that could reliably capture every possible combination of characters in every possible email address would be extremely complex, and going to that level of complexity is beyond the scope of this book. If you're interested in advanced regular expressions, you can look at a regular expression written by a professional that is meant to find email addresses at *https://web.archive.org/web/20220721014244/https://emailregex.com/*.

Converting Results to Usable Data

Remember that we're data scientists, not only web scrapers. After scraping web pages, we'll want to convert the results of our scraping to usable data. We can do this by importing everything we scrape into a pandas dataframe.

Let's scrape all of the (fake) email addresses listed in a paragraph at the following URL: *https://bradfordtuckfield.com/contactscrape2.html*. We can start by reading all of the text from the site, as follows:

```
import requests
urltoget = 'https://bradfordtuckfield.com/contactscrape2.html'
pagecode = requests.get(urltoget)
```

This is the same code we used before: we simply download the HTML code and store it in our `pagecode` variable. If you'd like, you can look at all the code for this page by running `print(pagecode.text)`.

Next, we can specify our regular expression to look for all email addresses in the paragraph:

```
allmatches=re.finditer('[a-zA-Z]+@[a-zA-Z]+\.[a-zA-Z]+',pagecode.text)
```

Here, we use the same characters for our regular expression. But we're using a new method: `re.finditer()` instead of `re.search()`. We do this because `re.finditer()` is able to obtain multiple matches, and we need to do this to get all of the email addresses. (By default, `re.search()` finds only the first match of any string or regular expression.)

Next, we need to compile these email addresses together:

```
alladdresses = []
for match in allmatches:
    alladdresses.append(match[0])

print(alladdresses)
```

We start with an empty list called `alladdresses`. Then we append each element of our `allmatches` object to the list. Finally, we print out the list.

We can also convert our list to a pandas dataframe:

```
import pandas as pd
alladdpd=pd.DataFrame(alladdresses)
print(alladdpd)
```

Now that our addresses are in a pandas dataframe, we can use the huge number of methods provided by the pandas library to do anything that we may have done with any other pandas dataframe. For example, we can put it in reverse alphabetical order if that's useful to us, and then export it to a *.csv* file:

```
alladdpd=alladdpd.sort_values(0,ascending=False)
alladdpd.to_csv('alladdpd20220720.csv')
```

Let's think about what we did so far. Starting with only a URL, we downloaded the full HTML code of the web page specified by the URL. We used a regular expression to find all emails listed on the page. We compiled the emails into a pandas dataframe, which can then be exported to a *.csv* or Excel file or otherwise transformed as we see fit.

Downloading HTML code and specifying regular expressions to search for certain information, as we have done, is a reasonable way to accomplish any scraping task. However, in some cases, it may be difficult or inconvenient to write a complex regular expression for a difficult-to-match pattern. In these cases, you can use other libraries that include advanced HTML parsing and scraping capabilities without requiring you to write any regular expressions. One such library is called Beautiful Soup.

Using Beautiful Soup

The *Beautiful Soup library* allows us to search for the contents of particular HTML elements without writing any regular expressions. For example, imagine that you want to collect all the hyperlinks in a page. HTML code uses an *anchor* element to specify hyperlinks. This special element is specified with a simple <a> start tag. The following is an example of what an anchor element might look like in the HTML code for a web page:

```
<a href='https://bradfordtuckfield.com'>Click here</a>
```

This snippet specifies the text Click here. When users click this text on an HTML web page, their browsers will navigate to *https://bradfordtuckfield.com*. The HTML element starts with an <a>, which indicates that it's an anchor, or hyperlink, to a web page or file. Then it has an attribute called href. In HTML code, an *attribute* is a variable that provides more information about elements. In this case, the href attribute contains the URL that a hyperlink should "point" to: when someone clicks the Click here text, their browser navigates to the URL contained in the href attribute. After the href attribute, there's an angle bracket, then the text that appears on the page. A final </a> indicates the end of the hyperlink element.

We could find all the anchor elements in a web page's code by doing a regular expression search for the <a> pattern or by specifying a regular expression to find URLs themselves. However, the Beautiful Soup module enables us to find the anchor elements more easily without worrying about regular expressions. We can find all the URLs that are linked from a website as follows:

```
import requests
from bs4 import BeautifulSoup

URL = 'https://bradfordtuckfield.com/indexarchive20210903.html'
response = requests.get(URL)
soup = BeautifulSoup(response.text, 'lxml')

all_urls = soup.find_all('a')
for each in all_urls:
    print(each['href'])
```

Here, we import the requests and BeautifulSoup modules. Just like every other third-party Python package, you will need to install BeautifulSoup before using it in a script. The BeautifulSoup module is part of a package called bs4. The bs4 package has what are called *dependencies*: other packages that need to be installed for bs4 to work correctly. One of its dependencies is a package called lxml. You will need to install lxml before you can use bs4 and `BeautifulSoup`. After importing the modules we need, we use the `requests` `.get()` method to download a web page's code, just as we've done previously in the chapter. But then we use the `BeautifulSoup()` method to parse the code and store the result in a variable called `soup`.

Having the `soup` variable enables us to use particular methods from Beautiful Soup. In particular, we can use the `find_all()` method to look for particular types of elements in the web page code. In this case, we search for all anchor elements, which are identified by the character `a`. After getting all the anchor elements, we print out the value of their `href` attributes—the URLs of the pages or files they're linking to. You can see that with Beautiful Soup, we can do useful parsing with only a few lines of code, all without using complicated regular expressions.

Parsing HTML Label Elements

The anchor element is not the only type of element in HTML code. We saw the `<title>` element earlier in the chapter. Sometimes web pages also use the `<label>` element to put labels on text or content on their page. For example, imagine that you want to scrape contact information from the *http://bradfordtuckfield.com/contactscrape.html* web page that we saw earlier. We've reproduced Figure 8-3 as Figure 8-4 here.

Demo Contact US Page

Company: Demo Company
Phone: +1 879-890-9767
Email: demo@bradfordtuckfield.com
Website: www.bradfordtuckfield.com

Figure 8-4: The content of a demo page that can be scraped easily

You may be doing a project to search web pages for email addresses, phone numbers, or websites. Again, you could try to use regular expressions to search for these items. But the phone numbers and email addresses on this page are labeled with an HTML `<label>` element, so Beautiful Soup makes it easier to get the information we need. First, let's look at how this `<label>` element is used in the HTML code for this web page. Here's a small sample of this page's code:

```
<div class="find-widget">
    Email:  <label class="email" href="#">demo@bradfordtuckfield.com</label>
</div>
```

As you saw earlier in the chapter, the `<label>` tag is used to indicate that a part of the HTML code is of a particular type. In this case, the `class` attribute identifies that this is a label for an email address. If the web page you're scraping has these <label> elements, you can search for email addresses, phone numbers, and websites as follows:

```
import requests
from bs4 import BeautifulSoup


URL = 'https://bradfordtuckfield.com/contactscrape.html'
response = requests.get(URL)
soup = BeautifulSoup(response.text, 'lxml')

email = soup.find('label',{'class':'email'}).text
mobile = soup.find('label',{'class':'mobile'}).text
website = soup.find('a',{'class':'website'}).text

print("Email : {}".format(email))
print("Mobile : {}".format(mobile))
print("Website : {}".format(website))
```

Here, we use the soup.find() method again. But instead of finding only elements labeled with a, as we did when we searched for hyperlinks, this time we also search for elements with the <label> tag. Each <label> tag in the code specifies a different class. We find the text with each kind of label (for email and mobile) and print out the text. For the website link, we search for an anchor tag with the website class. The final result is that we've been able to find every type of data we wanted: an email address, a cell phone number, and a website.

Scraping and Parsing HTML Tables

Tables are common on websites, so it's worth knowing a little about how to scrape data from website tables. You can see a simple example of an HTML table if you visit *https://bradfordtuckfield.com/user_detailsscrape.html*. This web page contains a table with information about several fictional people, shown in Figure 8-5.

Firstname	Lastname	Age
Jill	Smith	50
Eve	Jackson	44
John	Jackson	24
Kevin	Snow	34

Figure 8-5: A table that can be scraped using Beautiful Soup

Say we want to scrape information about these people from this table. Let's look at the HTML code that specifies this table:

```
<table style="width:100%">
  <tr class="user-details-header">
    <th>Firstname</th>
    <th>Lastname</th>
    <th>Age</th>
  </tr>
  <tr class="user-details">
    <td>Jill</td>
    <td>Smith</td>
    <td>50</td>
  </tr>
  <tr class="user-details">
    <td>Eve</td>
    <td>Jackson</td>
    <td>44</td>
  </tr>
  <tr class="user-details">
    <td>John</td>
    <td>Jackson</td>
    <td>24</td>
  </tr>
  <tr class="user-details">
    <td>Kevin</td>
    <td>Snow</td>
    <td>34</td>
  </tr>
</table>
```

The <table> tag specifies the beginning of the table, and </table> specifies the end of it. Between the beginning and the end are some <tr> and </tr> tags. Each <tr> tag specifies the beginning of a table row (tr is an abbreviation for *table row*). Within each table row, the <td> tags specify the content of particular table cells (td is short for *table data*). You can see that the first row is the header of the table, and it contains the names of every column. After the first row, each subsequent row specifies information about one person: their first name first, their surname second, and their age third, in three different <td> elements.

We can parse the table as follows:

```
import requests
from bs4 import BeautifulSoup


URL = 'https://bradfordtuckfield.com/user_detailsscrape.html'
response = requests.get(URL)
soup = BeautifulSoup(response.text, 'lxml')

all_user_entries = soup.find_all('tr',{'class':'user-details'})
for each_user in all_user_entries:
    user = each_user.find_all("td")
```

```
print("User Firstname : {}, Lastname : {}, Age: {}"\
.format(user[0].text, user[1].text, user[2].text))
```

Here, we use Beautiful Soup again. We create a soup variable that contains the parsed version of the website. Then we use the find_all() method to find every tr element (table row) on the page. For every table row, we use find_all() again to look for every td element (table data) in the row. After finding the contents of each row, we print them out, with formatting to label first names, last names, and ages. In addition to printing these elements, you could also consider adding them to a pandas dataframe to more easily export them, sort them, or do any other analysis you prefer.

Advanced Scraping

Scraping is a deep topic, and there is more to learn beyond the material covered in this chapter. You could start with a few areas outlined in this section.

First, consider that some web pages are dynamic; they change depending on interaction from the user, such as clicking elements or scrolling. Often the dynamic parts of web pages are rendered using JavaScript, a language with syntax that's very different from the HTML we've focused on scraping in this chapter. The requests package that we used to download HTML code, and the Beautiful Soup module that we used to parse the code, are meant to be used with static web pages. With dynamic web pages, you may want to use another tool such as the Selenium library, which is designed for scraping dynamic web pages. With Selenium, your script can do things like enter information into website forms and click CAPTCHA-type challenges without requiring direct human input.

You should also consider strategies to deal with being blocked. Many websites are hostile to all attempts to scrape their data. They have strategies to block scrapers, and if they detect that you're trying to scrape and harvest their information, they may try to block you. One response to being blocked is to give up; this will avoid any legal problems or ethical issues that may come with scraping hostile websites.

If you decide to scrape sites that are trying to block you anyway, you can take some actions to avoid being blocked. One is to set up one or more *proxy servers*. A website might block your IP address from accessing its data, so you can set up a different server with a different IP address that the website hasn't blocked. If the website continues to try to block the IP address of your proxy server as well, you can set up *rotating proxies* so that you continuously get new IP addresses that are not blocked, and scrape only with those fresh, unblocked IP addresses.

When you take this kind of approach, you should consider its ethical implications: Do you feel comfortable using strategies like these to access a site that doesn't want you to access it? Remember that in rare cases, unauthorized scraping can lead to lawsuits or even criminal prosecution. You should always be cautious and ensure that you've thought through the practical and ethical implications of everything you do.

Not all websites are averse to letting people access and scrape their data. Some websites allow scraping, and some even set up an *application programming interface (API)* to facilitate data access. An API allows you to query a website's data automatically and receive data that's in a user-friendly format. If you ever need to scrape a website, check whether it has an API that you can access. If a website has an API, the API documentation should indicate the data that the API provides and how you can access it. Many of the tools and ideas we've discussed in this chapter also apply to API usage. For example, the `requests` package can be used to interact with APIs, and after getting API data, the data can be used to populate a pandas dataframe.

Finally, timing is an important issue to consider when you set up scraping scripts. Sometimes a scraping script makes many requests to a website in quick succession, trying to download as much data as possible, as quickly as possible. This could cause a website to be overwhelmed and crash, or it may block the scraper to avoid getting overwhelmed. To prevent the target site from crashing or blocking you, you can adjust your scraper so that it works more slowly. One way to slow down your script is to deliberately add pauses. For example, after downloading one row from a table, the script can pause and do nothing (the script can *sleep*) for 1 second or 2 seconds or 10 seconds, and then download the next row from the table. Going slowly on purpose can be frustrating for those of us who like to get things done quickly, but it can often make scraping success more likely over the long term.

Summary

In this chapter, we covered web scraping. We outlined the concept of scraping, including a brief introduction to how HTML code works. We went on to build a simple scraper, one that merely downloads and prints out the code for a web page. We also searched through and parsed a website's code, including using regular expressions for advanced searches. We showed how to convert the data we scrape from websites to usable datasets. We also used Python's Beautiful Soup to easily find hyperlinks and tagged information on web pages. Finally, we briefly discussed some advanced applications of scraping skills, including API integrations and scraping dynamic websites. In the next chapter, we'll be going over recommendation systems. Let's continue!

9

RECOMMENDATION SYSTEMS

Every talented salesperson knows how to make intelligent, targeted recommendations to customers, and as online retailers have grown in size and sophistication, they have enthusiastically automated this sales tactic. But these recommendations are hard to make. For this reason, many businesses create automated *recommendation systems* that analyze data about products and customers to determine which customers would be most receptive to which products.

In this chapter, we'll go over recommendation systems in detail. We'll start with the simplest possible recommendation system: one that merely recommends the most popular items to every customer. We'll go on to discuss an important technique called *collaborative filtering* that enables us to make unique, personalized recommendations for each customer and each product. We'll go over two types of collaborative filtering: item based and user based. We'll conclude with a case study and advanced ideas related to recommendation systems.

Popularity-Based Recommendations

Before we write code for recommendation systems, we should consider how to make recommendations in general. Imagine that you're a salesperson and you want to make recommendations to a customer who walks into your store. If you're acquainted with the customer, you could make recommendations based on your knowledge of the customer's tastes and situation. If a new customer walks into your store and you want to make recommendations without knowing anything about the person, you could observe what they're browsing and make a recommendation based on that. But it's possible that you'll be asked to make a recommendation before they've browsed anything at all. The dilemma of needing to make intelligent recommendations without any specific knowledge about the customer is referred to as the *cold-start problem*.

One reasonable thing to do when faced with the cold-start problem is to recommend the most popular items. Doing this is simple and easy. It doesn't have the sophistication of knowing everything about a customer and making a personalized recommendation, but if something is popular with the general public, it's reasonable to think it could be appealing to your new customer.

Online retailers have an analogous challenge: new visitors visit their websites, and maybe those visitors don't have browsing history or are unfamiliar to the online retailers. The retailers want to make personalized recommendations based on detailed knowledge about customers, but when they face the cold-start problem, they have to fall back on something else like general popularity. The cold-start problem is especially common for online retailers, since it's easy for prospective customers to view a website anonymously without giving any personal information to the website or its sales team.

Let's think about the code that we would use to make a popularity-based recommendation. For this, or any other recommendation system, having data related to transaction history is helpful. We can download, read, and look at some fabricated transaction history data as follows:

```
import pandas as pd
import numpy as np
interaction=pd.read_csv('https://bradfordtuckfield.com/purchasehistory1.csv')
interaction.set_index("Unnamed: 0", inplace = True)
print(interaction)
```

Here, we import the pandas package to do data wrangling. We read a *.csv* file from the internet into the interaction variable, and we store it as a pandas dataframe. We specify that the first column of the data should be the index (the row name) and print the dataframe. The output we see at the end is shown in Listing 9-1.

Unnamed: 0	user1	user2	user3	user4	user5
0	item1	1	1	0	1	1
1	item2	1	0	1	1	0
2	item3	1	1	0	1	1
3	item4	1	0	1	0	1
4	item5	1	1	0	0	1

Listing 9-1: An interaction matrix, showing the history of purchases for each item

Listing 9-1 shows a matrix representing the sales history of a retailer that has five customers and five items for sale. Note we're calling the customers *users*, assuming that they're users of the retailer's website. But whatever we call them, the recommendation techniques we use will be the same.

The matrix contains a 0 if a user did not purchase a particular item and a 1 if a user did. For example, you can see that user2 purchased item3 but not item2, and user3 purchased item2 but not item3. This type of 0/1 matrix is a common format to encounter when we're building recommendation systems. We can call this matrix the *interaction matrix*; it represents information about interactions between users and items. Since nearly every company has records related to its items and their purchase histories, building recommendation systems based on interaction matrices is an extremely common practice.

Suppose that a new customer, whom we'll call user6, walks into your store (or visits your website). You face a cold start, since you know nothing about user6. If you want to make recommendations for items that user6 can purchase, you could make a list of the most popular items, as follows:

```
interaction_withcounts=interaction.copy()
interaction_withcounts.loc[:,'counts']=interaction_withcounts.sum(axis=1)
interaction_withcounts=interaction_withcounts.sort_values(by='counts',ascending=False)
print(list(interaction_withcounts.index))
```

Here we create a copy of our interaction matrix called interaction _withcounts. We'll use this copy to find the most popular items by counting the number of users who have ever purchased each item. Note that our matrix doesn't record whether a user purchased an item multiple times or only once, so our analysis will look at only whether users have purchased items at all; we won't analyze how many times each user purchased each item.

Since each row of our matrix records purchases of a unique item, we use the sum() method to take the sum of purchases in each row and store the result in a new column called counts. We then use the sort_values() method, which sorts the rows of our matrix from the highest to lowest purchase counts. By sorting from most to least purchased, it is ordering the items by popularity. Finally, we print out the index of our sorted matrix, which tells us the item names of all of our items, sorted from most to least popular:

```
['item1', 'item3', 'item2', 'item4', 'item5']
```

We can interpret this to mean that item1 is the most popular item (in fact, tied with item3), item2 is the third-most popular, and so on.

Now that you have this list, you're ready to make recommendations to unfamiliar customers. The way you present your recommendations will depend on your business strategy, your web development team's capabilities, and your marketing team's preferences. The data science portion of a recommendation system project is to create the list of prioritized recommendations and let marketers or web developers present these to users. This is one reason that recommendation system projects can be challenging: they require cooperation among several teams.

We can create a function that generates popularity-based recommendations for any interaction matrix by putting together all of our code so far:

```
def popularity_based(interaction):
    interaction_withcounts=interaction.copy()
    interaction_withcounts.loc[:,'counts']=interaction_withcounts.sum(axis=1)
    sorted = interaction_withcounts.sort_values(by='counts',ascending=False)
    most_popular=list(sorted.index)
    return(most_popular)
```

This function merely wraps up the capabilities we've written code for previously in the chapter. It takes an interaction matrix as its input. It sums up the counts of purchases for each item, sorts by number of purchases, and returns a list of item names that is sorted from most to least popular. This final sorted list can be used to make recommendations to customers, even if you're unfamiliar with the customers. You can call this function on your interaction matrix by running print(popularity_based(interaction)) in Python.

A popularity-based recommendation system is a simple, reasonable way to solve the cold-start problem and make some kind of recommendation to users. You can see popularity-based recommendations on many websites today, where *trending* content is highlighted. You can also see popularity-based recommendations in brick-and-mortar retailers, like bookstores that prominently display bestsellers.

But popularity-based recommendations are not as effective as personalized ones. Recommendation systems that can use detailed information about people and items can be more successful than generic popularity-based recommendation systems. Let's take a look at one now.

Item-Based Collaborative Filtering

Suppose that you don't face a completely cold start. Instead, you have just a little information about a sixth customer: in particular, you know that they're interested in item1. This information is all you need to make recommendations when using *collaborative filtering*.

Let's look at our interaction matrix again to get some ideas for how we should make recommendations to someone who's interested in item1:

Unnamed: 0		user1	user2	user3	user4	user5
0	item1	1	1	0	1	1
1	item2	1	0	1	1	0
2	item3	1	1	0	1	1
3	item4	1	0	1	0	1
4	item5	1	1	0	0	1

If we look at the first row of our interaction matrix, we can see the full history of customer interactions with item1. This item was purchased by user1, user2, user4, and user5, and it was not purchased by user3. If we look at item3, we can see that it has exactly the same purchase history as item1. They could be similar items, like two James Bond movies, or they could be complementary, like peanut butter and jelly. Regardless, if two items were purchased together in the past, they're likely to be purchased together in the future.

By contrast, look at the purchase histories of item1 and item2; they have less overlap in customers. These items do not have highly similar purchase histories. Since they haven't been purchased together often in the past, they won't likely be purchased together often in the future. One way to make intelligent recommendations is by using this idea: if a user is interested in an item, recommend to that customer other items whose purchase histories have the most in common with the item they're interested in. This method is called *item-based collaborative filtering*.

To recommend items with the most similar purchase histories, we need a way to quantitatively measure exactly how similar two purchase histories are. We saw that item1 and item3 have very similar (identical) purchase histories, while item1 and item2 have more different purchase histories. If we compare item1 and item5, we can see some similarity in their histories and some differences. But instead of making qualitative judgments that two purchase histories are *very similar* or *not very similar*, using numbers to precisely quantify that similarity will be useful. If we can find a metric that quantifies the similarity of two items, we can use that metric to recommend items.

Measuring Vector Similarity

Let's look more closely at one item's purchase history to get ideas for ways to quantitatively measure similarities:

```
print(list(interaction.loc['item1',:]))
```

This line of code prints out the purchase history of item1. The output looks like this:

```
[1,1,0,1,1]
```

We can think of this purchase history in several ways. It may seem like nothing more than a collection of numbers. Since the numbers are sandwiched between square brackets, Python will interpret this collection as a list. We could also think of it as a row of a matrix (our interaction matrix). Most importantly, we can think of this collection of numbers as a *vector*. You may remember from math class that a vector is a directed line segment. One way to write a vector is as a collection of coordinate numbers. For example, Figure 9-1 depicts two vectors, $\vec{A}$ and $\vec{B}$.

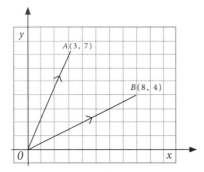

Figure 9-1: Two vectors, represented by coordinate pairs

In this example, $\vec{A}$ and $\vec{B}$ are directed line segments, or vectors. They are both two-dimensional. Just like every vector, both can be fully described by their coordinates: after we know that both vectors start at the origin, the coordinate pair (3,7) fully describes vector $\vec{A}$, and the coordinate pair (8,4) fully describes vector $\vec{B}$. The purchase history we looked at previously, [1,1,0,1,1], can be thought of as the vector representing the purchase history of item1. In fact, all the rows of our interaction matrix, or any interaction matrix, can be thought of as vectors.

Since we have vectors representing items, we may want to draw our vectors in a plot like Figure 9-1. However, in our interaction matrix, our item vectors have five coordinates each, so if we wanted to draw them, we would have to draw them in a five-dimensional plot, which is not possible to do in a way that humans can easily comprehend. Since we can't draw our item vectors, let's look at the $\vec{A}$ and $\vec{B}$ vectors in Figure 9-1 to understand how to measure vector similarity, then apply what we learn to our item vectors later.

You can see that vectors $\vec{A}$ and $\vec{B}$ are somewhat similar: both are pointing generally upward and generally toward the right. We want to find a quantitative measurement that signifies exactly how similar the two vectors are. All we need to do is measure the angle between the two vectors, as in Figure 9-2.

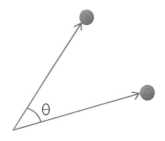

Figure 9-2: An angle between two vectors, represented by the Greek letter theta

Every pair of vectors will have an angle between them that we can measure. In two dimensions, we can get out a protractor and physically measure the angle between two vectors. In Figure 9-2, the angle is labeled with the Greek letter theta. If the angle theta is small, we conclude that the two vectors are similar. If theta is large, we conclude that the two vectors are very different. The smallest possible angle between two vectors is 0; a 0-degree angle between two vectors means that they're pointing in exactly the same direction (they overlap).

This isn't a geometry book, but try to remember just one more thing from your math and geometry classes: the *cosine*. The cosine is a function that we can measure for every angle. The cosine of a 0-degree angle is 1; that's the maximum value a cosine can be. As an angle gets larger than 0, its cosine decreases. For a 90-degree angle (also called a *perpendicular*, or *right*, angle), the cosine will be 0.

The cosine is important because we can use it to measure the similarity of two vectors. If two vectors are similar, the angle between them will be small, so the cosine of the angle between them will be large (1 or close to 1). If two vectors are perpendicular, they're quite different, and the cosine of the angle between them will be 0. Vectors like A and B in Figure 9-1 are not completely similar and not completely different, so the cosine of the angle between them will be between 0 and 1. When comparing vectors, we often refer to the *cosine similarity* of the two vectors (the cosine of the angle between the vectors). Similar vectors will have high cosine similarity, and different vectors will have low cosine similarity.

When vectors have many dimensions, like the five-dimensional vectors in our purchase histories, we don't physically measure the angles. Instead, we can use a special formula that enables us to calculate the cosine of the angle between any pair of vectors without requiring the physical use of a protractor; see Figure 9-3.

$$sim(A, B) = \cos(\theta) = \frac{A \cdot B}{\|A\|\|B\|}$$

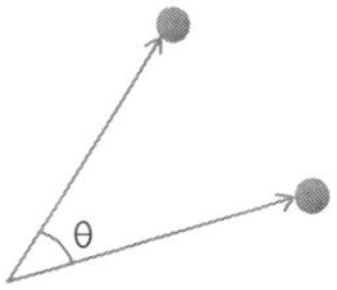

Figure 9-3: A formula for calculating the cosine of the angle between two vectors

We'll unpack this formula in the next section.

Calculating Cosine Similarity

Let's look more closely at the formula in Figure 9-3. The numerator is $A \cdot B$. In this case the dot between the vectors $\vec{A}$ and $\vec{B}$ is indicating a *dot product*, a special way to multiply vectors together. The following function calculates the dot product of any two vectors that are the same length:

```
def dot_product(vector1,vector2):
    thedotproduct=np.sum([vector1[k]*vector2[k] for k in range(0,len(vector1))])
    return(thedotproduct)
```

The denominator of the formula in Figure 9-3 shows pipe symbols ($\|$) surrounding both A and B. These pipe symbols indicate the respective sizes of vectors $\vec{A}$ and $\vec{B}$, also called their vector *norms*. The following function calculates the vector norm of any vector:

```
def vector_norm(vector):
    thenorm=np.sqrt(dot_product(vector,vector))
    return(thenorm)
```

The cosine of the angle between any two vectors (that is, the cosine similarity of the two vectors) is the dot product of the two vectors, divided by the product of the norms of the vectors. We can create a Python function that calculates the cosine similarity of any two vectors by using the two functions we just defined, combined as shown in the formula in Figure 9-3:

```
def cosine_similarity(vector1,vector2):
    thedotproduct=dot_product(vector1,vector2)
    thecosine=thedotproduct/(vector_norm(vector1)*vector_norm(vector2))
    thecosine=np.round(thecosine,4)
    return(thecosine)
```

The cosine similarity that this function calculates is a common similarity measurement that's used in many data science applications, not just for recommendation systems.

Let's try to calculate some cosine similarity measurements for our item vectors:

```
import numpy as np
item1=interaction.loc['item1',:]
item3=interaction.loc['item3',:]
print(cosine_similarity(item1,item3))
```

This snippet yields a simple output:

```
1.0
```

We can see that item1 and item3 have a cosine similarity of 1.0, meaning that the angle between these vectors is 0. Therefore, they're identical vectors, and they're as similar as it is possible to be. By contrast, you can check the cosine similarity of item2 and item5 by running the following snippet:

```
item2=list(interaction.loc['item2',:])
item5=list(interaction.loc['item5',:])
print(cosine_similarity(item2,item5))
```

These have a cosine similarity of 0.3333, meaning that the angle between these vectors is relatively large—about 71 degrees, not far from a right angle. Therefore, these two items are very different from each other. We can see that when we look at their vectors: only one user out of five purchased both items. If we follow a similar process to check the cosine similarity of item3 and item5, we find that it's 0.866, indicating that these vectors are similar but not completely identical.

Now that we can measure the similarity of any two items' histories, we're ready to use this calculation to create a recommendation system.

Implementing Item-Based Collaborative Filtering

Let's think back to our hypothetical salesperson and a hypothetical sales scenario. You have an interaction matrix that describes the purchase history of all five of your customers and all five of your items. You observe a new, unfamiliar customer entering your store (or visiting your website), and all you know about the new customer is that they are interested in item1. How should you make recommendations to them?

You can rank every item based on how similar its purchase history is to the purchase history of item1. Your recommendations will be an ordered list of items, ranked from the item whose purchase history is the most similar to item1 to the item whose purchase history is the least similar to item1.

Let's write Python code for this, using cosine similarity. We can start by defining the vectors we'll need to do our calculations:

```
ouritem='item1'
otherrows=[rowname for rowname in interaction.index if rowname!=ouritem]
otheritems=interaction.loc[otherrows,:]
theitem=interaction.loc[ouritem,:]
```

Next, we can calculate how similar each item is to our selected item and make recommendations by finding the other items that are most similar to our selected item:

```
similarities=[]
for items in otheritems.index:
    similarities.append(cosine_similarity(theitem,otheritems.loc[items,:]))

otheritems['similarities']=similarities
recommendations = list(otheritems.sort_values(by='similarities',ascending=False).index)
```

In this snippet, we create a similarities variable, which starts as an empty list. Then we create a loop that calculates the cosine similarity between our item and every other item. After that, we get our final list of recommendations: a list of all other items, sorted from most similar to least similar to our item.

You can check the recommendations by running print(recommendations), which will show you the following list:

```
['item3', 'item5', 'item2', 'item4']
```

This list is the output of your recommendation system. This final output is similar to the output of our popularity-based recommendation system: just a list of items, sorted in order of most relevant to least relevant (the highest-priority to the lowest-priority recommendations). The difference is that instead of measuring relevance in terms of overall popularity, we are measuring relevance in terms of the similarity of purchase histories: the more similar purchase histories are rated as more relevant, and therefore a higher priority to recommend to users.

We can also create a function that combines all of these capabilities together:

```
def get_item_recommendations(interaction,itemname):
    otherrows=[rowname for rowname in interaction.index if rowname!=itemname]
    otheritems=interaction.loc[otherrows,:]
    theitem=list(interaction.loc[itemname,:])
    similarities=[]
    for items in otheritems.index:
        similarities.append(cosine_similarity(theitem,list(otheritems.loc[items,:])))
    otheritems['similarities']=similarities
    return list(otheritems.sort_values(by='similarities',ascending=False).index)
```

You can run get_item_recommendations(interaction,'item1') to see the items recommended for any user who's interested in item1. You could also substitute any other item for item1 to see recommendations for users interested in other items.

The recommendation system we have created here is *item-based collaborative filtering*. It's *filtering* because instead of recommending every item to users, we filter and show only the most relevant. It's *collaborative* because we're using information related to all items and all users, so it's as if the users and items are collaborating to help us determine relevance. It's *item-based* because our recommendations are based on the similarity between items' purchase histories, rather than similarity between users or anything else.

Item-based collaborative filtering is relatively simple to implement, and it can be used to make "warm" recommendations even if we know only one fact about a potential customer (a single item that they're interested in). You can see that it can be implemented with just a few lines of code, and the only input data that's needed is an interaction matrix.

Item-based collaborative filtering has a reputation for making *obvious* recommendations. Multiple James Bond films are likely to have high overlap in their purchase histories, so using item-based collaborative filtering to make recommendations related to one James Bond film will likely yield a recommendation to view a different James Bond film. But James Bond fans are already familiar with James Bond films and don't need to get a recommendation to watch a film that they're already familiar with. Recommendation systems can be more valuable when they recommend items that are less obvious. Next, let's take a look at a method that has a reputation for generating some less obvious recommendations.

User-Based Collaborative Filtering

Suppose you want to make recommendations for a customer you're already familiar with. For example, suppose that our fifth customer, user5, walks into your store (or visits your website). Your interaction matrix already has detailed records related to user5 and everything they've purchased before. We can use this detailed information to make intelligent, "warm" recommendations for user5 with *user-based collaborative filtering*.

This approach is based on the idea that people who are similar may be interested in the same items. If we need to make recommendations for a particular customer, we find the customers who are most similar to that customer and recommend items that those similar customers purchased.

Let's start by looking at our interaction matrix yet again:

	Unnamed: 0	user1	user2	user3	user4	user5
0	item1	1	1	0	1	1
1	item2	1	0	1	1	0
2	item3	1	1	0	1	1
3	item4	1	0	1	0	1
4	item5	1	1	0	0	1

This time, instead of thinking of the *rows* as vectors related to *items*, let's think of the *columns* as vectors related to *customers*. The vector [1,0,1,1,1] (the last column of the matrix) represents the full purchase history of user5. If we look at other customer purchase history vectors, we can see that user2 has a purchase history that's similar to user5's purchase history. We can see that user3 has a purchase history that's very different from the purchase history of user5—almost no overlap. Just as we did when we were implementing item-based collaborative filtering, we can calculate the similarity of customers based on their purchase histories:

```
user2=interaction.loc[:,'user2']
user5=interaction.loc[:,'user5']
print(cosine_similarity(user2,user5))
```

The output of this snippet is 0.866, indicating that user2 and user5 have relatively high cosine similarity (remember that the closer to 1 this measurement is, the more similar two vectors are). We can change the users whose similarity we calculate by making small adjustments to this snippet:

```
user3=interaction.loc[:,'user3']
user5=interaction.loc[:,'user5']
print(cosine_similarity(user3,user5))
```

Here, we find that user3 and user5 have cosine similarity 0.3536, which is relatively low, just as expected.

We can also create a function that calculates the most similar customers to a given customer:

```
def get_similar_users(interaction,username):
    othercolumns=[columnname for columnname in interaction.columns if columnname!=username]
    otherusers=interaction[othercolumns]
    theuser=list(interaction[username])
    similarities=[]
    for users in otherusers.columns:
        similarities.append(cosine_similarity(theuser,list(otherusers.loc[:,users])))
    otherusers.loc['similarities',:]=similarities
    return list(otherusers.sort_values(by='similarities',axis=1,ascending=False).columns)
```

This function takes a customer name and an interaction matrix as its inputs. It calculates the similarity of the input customer to all other customers specified in the interaction matrix. The final output is a ranked list of customers, sorted from the most similar customer to the least similar customer.

We can use this function in several ways to get recommendations. Here's one way to get recommendations for user5:

1. Calculate how similar every user is to user5.

2. Rank customers from most similar to least similar to user5.

3. Find the most similar customer to user5.

4. Recommend everything the most similar customer has purchased that user5 has not purchased.

We can write code that implements this algorithm as follows:

```
def get_user_recommendations(interaction,username):
    similar_users=get_similar_users(interaction,username)
    purchase_history=interaction[similar_users[0]]
    purchased=list(purchase_history.loc[purchase_history==1].index)
```

```
purchased2=list(interaction.loc[interaction[username]==1,:].index)
recs=sorted(list(set(purchased) - set(purchased2)))
return(recs)
```

In this snippet, we have a function that takes an interaction matrix and a user name as its inputs. It finds the most similar user to the input user, and it stores the purchase history of that user in a variable called purchase_history. Next, it finds everything that the most similar user purchased (stored in the variable purchased) and everything that the input user purchased (stored in the variable purchased2). Then it finds everything that the most similar user purchased that was not purchased by the input user. It does this by using the set() function. The set() function creates a collection of the unique elements in a list. So when you run set(purchased) - set(purchased2), you'll get the unique elements of purchased that are not also elements of purchased2. Finally, it returns the list of these elements as the final recommendations.

You can run this function simply, by running get_user_recommendations (interaction,'user2'). You should see the following output:

```
['item4']
```

In this case, item4 is our recommendation because it was purchased by user5, the user who's most similar to user2, and it hasn't yet been purchased by user2. We've created a function that performs user-based collaborative filtering!

You could make many adjustments to this function. For example, you might want more recommendations than you get by looking at one similar customer. If so, you could look at more similar customers than just one. You could also add item-based similarity calculations so that you recommend only items that were purchased by similar users and are also similar to the items that have been purchased by the focal user.

Ensuring that you understand the similarities and differences between user-based and item-based collaborative filtering is worthwhile. Both rely on cosine similarity calculations, and both rely on an interaction matrix as input. In item-based collaborative filtering, we calculate the cosine similarity between items and recommend items that are similar to an item of interest. In user-based collaborative filtering, we calculate the cosine similarity between users and recommend items from the purchase histories of similar users. Both can lead to good recommendations.

To determine which method is right for your business, you could try both and check which one leads to better results: either more revenue, more profit, more satisfied customers, more customer engagement, or more of whatever metric you want to maximize. The best way to do this type of experimental comparison is with an A/B test, which you've already learned in Chapter 4.

User-based collaborative filtering has a reputation for giving more surprising results than item-based collaborative filtering. However, it also tends to be more computationally difficult. Most retailers have more customers than items, so user-based collaborative filtering usually requires more calculations than item-based collaborative filtering.

So far, we've been working with an unrealistically tiny and entirely fabricated dataset. Applying the ideas we've gone over so far to data that comes from a real business would be more beneficial, with real users and their real interaction histories. In the next section, we'll do just that: we'll go through a case study of generating recommendations for real users and the real items that we expect will interest them.

Case Study: Music Recommendations

We'll use data from Last.fm (*https://last.fm*). This website allows people to log in and listen to music. In this case, the "items" in our interaction matrix will be musical artists, and a 1 in the interaction matrix will indicate that a user has listened to an artist, rather than representing a purchase. Despite these minor differences, we can use all the methods we've discussed in this chapter to make recommendations about music that users should listen to next.

Let's read some data related to Last.fm users and look at it:

```
import pandas as pd
lastfm = pd.read_csv("https://bradfordtuckfield.com/lastfm-matrix-germany.csv")
print(lastfm.head())
```

As usual, we import the pandas package, read our *.csv* file, and store the data in the lastfm variable. When we print out the top few rows of the data, we see the following output:

	user	a perfect circle	abba	...	underoath	volbeat	yann tiersen
0	1	0	0	...	0	0	0
1	33	0	0	...	0	0	0
2	42	0	0	...	0	0	0
3	51	0	0	...	0	0	0
4	62	0	0	...	0	0	0

In this data, every row represents a unique (anonymous) user. Every column represents a musical artist. The entries in the matrix can be interpreted in the same way as the entries in our previous interaction matrix: every entry equal to 1 means that a particular user has listened to a particular artist, and every entry equal to 0 means that the user has not listened to that artist. In this case, we can talk about a user's or an item's listening history instead of purchase history. Regardless, the entries of this matrix show the history of interactions between users and items. We don't need the first column (the user ID number), so we can drop it:

```
lastfm.drop(['user'],axis=1,inplace=True)
```

Before we proceed, notice the difference between this interaction matrix and the previous one. In our previous interaction matrix, the rows corresponded to items, and the columns corresponded to users. This interaction matrix is reversed: the rows correspond to users, and the columns correspond to items (songs). The functions we wrote are meant to work with interaction matrices that have the former shape (rows for items, columns for users). To make sure our interaction matrix can work with our functions, we should *transpose* it, or rewrite its rows as columns and its columns as rows:

```
lastfmt=lastfm.T
```

This snippet uses our matrix's T attribute to transpose our interaction matrix, and it stores the result in the variable lastfmt. Let's check the number of rows and columns in this data:

```
print(lastfmt.shape)
```

The output here is (285,1257): the data has 285 rows and 1,257 columns. So, we're looking at information about 1,257 real users and 285 real artists whose music these users listened to. This is much more substantial than our previous, fabricated data. Let's get recommendations for these users. It's as simple as calling a function we already created earlier in the chapter:

```
get_item_recommendations(lastfmt,'abba')[0:10]
```

You'll see the following output:

```
['madonna', 'robbie williams', 'elvis presley', 'michael jackson', 'queen',
'the beatles', 'kelly clarkson', 'groove coverage', 'duffy', 'mika']
```

For people who are interested in music by ABBA, these artists are recommended via item-based collaborative filtering. They're listed in order of most relevant to least relevant. Remember, these artists were selected based on similar purchase histories: out of all artists, Madonna's listening history was the most similar to ABBA's, and Robbie Williams's listening history was the second most similar, and so on.

This is all it takes; we can call the recommendation function for any artist that interests us. Going from fabricated to real data is quite simple. We can also call our user recommendation function:

```
print(get_user_recommendations(lastfmt,0)[0:3])
```

The output shows us three recommendations for the first user (the user with index 0 in the dataset):

```
['billy talent', 'bob marley', 'die toten hosen']
```

These recommendations were obtained using user-based collaborative filtering. Remember what that means: our code found the user whose listening history is the most similar to the listening history of the first user. The final recommendations are artists that the most similar user listened to but the focal user has not yet listened to.

Generating Recommendations with Advanced Systems

Collaborative filtering is the most common way to build recommendation systems, but it's not the only one. Several other techniques allow generation of intelligent recommendations. One approach, called *singular value decomposition*, relies on matrix algebra to *decompose* the interaction matrix into several smaller matrices. These smaller matrices can be multiplied in various ways to predict which products will appeal to which customers. Singular-value decomposition is one of several methods that use linear algebra to predict customer preferences. Another such linear algebra method is called *alternating least squares*.

The clustering methods we discussed in Chapter 7 can also be used to generate recommendation systems. These clustering-based recommendation systems use an approach like the following:

1. Generate clusters of users.
2. Find the most popular items in each cluster of users.
3. Recommend those popular items, but only within each cluster.

This method is the same as the popularity-based recommendation system we discussed at the beginning of the chapter, with one improvement: we look at popularity within clusters of similar customers, instead of global popularity.

Other recommendation systems rely on the analysis of content. For example, to make recommendations about songs on a music-streaming service, you might download a database of song lyrics. You could use some NLP tools to measure the similarity between distinct songs' lyrics. If a user listened to Song X, you could recommend that they listen to the songs whose lyrics have the highest similarity to Song X's lyrics. This is an item-based recommendation system, but instead of using purchase histories, it uses item attributes to find relevant recommendations. *Attribute-based systems* (also called *content-based recommender systems*) like this can work effectively in some situations. Many corporations that implement recommendation systems today collect a wide variety of data to use as inputs, and a wide variety of prediction methods, including neural networks, to predict what each user will like. The problem with a content-based approach is that it can be difficult to get attribute data that's reliable and comparable across items.

Attribute data is not the only kind of data that can be added to recommendation systems. Using dates in your recommendation systems could also be valuable. In a popularity-based system, dates or timestamps can enable you to replace *all-time most popular* lists with *today's most popular* lists, or lists that show trending content across the most recent hour, week, or any other time frame.

You may also need to build recommendation systems with interaction matrices that are not 0/1 matrices. For example, you could have an interaction matrix whose entries indicate the number of times a song has been played, rather than a 0/1 indicator of whether a song has been played. You might also find an interaction matrix that contains ratings rather than interactions. The same methods you implemented in this chapter can be applied to these alternative types of interaction matrices: you can still calculate cosine similarities and make recommendations based on the most similar items and users.

The world of recommendation systems is big. There's room for creativity and new approaches, and you can open your mind while trying to discover new ways to improve the field.

Summary

In this chapter, we discussed recommendation systems. We started with popularity-based systems to show how to recommend trending items and bestsellers. We continued with collaborative filtering, including how to measure the similarity of items and customers and how to use similarity to make item-based and user-based recommendations. We presented a case study in which we used our collaborative-filtering code to get recommendations related to a music-streaming service. We concluded with some advanced considerations, including other approaches that could be used and other data that can be leveraged.

Next, we'll go over some advanced natural language processing methods for analysis of text.

10

NATURAL LANGUAGE PROCESSING

 Finding ways to mathematically analyze textual data is the main goal of the field known as *natural language processing (NLP)*. In this chapter, we'll go over some important ideas from the world of NLP and talk about how to use NLP tools in data science projects.

We'll start the chapter by introducing a business scenario and thinking through how NLP can help with it. We'll use the word2vec model, which can convert individual words to numbers in a way that enables all kinds of powerful analyses. We'll walk through the Python code for this conversion and then explore some applications of it. Next, we'll discuss the Universal Sentence Encoder (USE), a tool that can convert entire sentences to numeric vectors. We'll go over the Python code for setting up and using the USE. Along the way, we'll find ways to use ideas from previous chapters. Let's begin!

Using NLP to Detect Plagiarism

Suppose that you're the president of a literary agency. Your agency receives hundreds of emails every day, each containing book chapters from aspiring authors. Chapters can be quite long, consisting of thousands or tens of thousands of words each, and your agency needs to carefully sift through these long chapters, trying to find a small number to accept. The longer it takes agents to filter through these submitted emails, the less time they'll have to spend on their other important tasks, like selling books to publishers. It's difficult, but possible, to automate some of the filtering that literary agencies have to do. For example, you could write a Python script that could automatically detect plagiarism.

Literary agencies are not the only businesses that could be interested in plagiarism detection. Suppose that you're the president of a large university. Every year, your students submit thousands of long papers, which you want to make sure are not plagiarized. Plagiarism is not only a moral and educational matter but also a business concern. If your university gains a reputation for allowing plagiarism, graduates will face worse job prospects, alumni donations will go down, fewer students will want to enroll, and the revenue and profits your university makes will surely take a nosedive. Your university's professors and graders are overworked already, so you want to save them time and find an automated approach to plagiarism detection.

A simple plagiarism detector might look for exact matches of text. For example, one of your university's students may have submitted the following sentences in one of their papers:

> People's whole lives do pass in front of their eyes before they die.
> The process is called "Living."

Maybe you read this paper and the idea sounds familiar to you, so you ask your librarians to search for this text in their book databases. They find an exact match of every character of this sentence in Terry Pratchett's classic *The Last Continent*, indicating plagiarism; the student is punished accordingly.

Other students may be more wily. Instead of directly copying text from published books, they learn to paraphrase so they can copy ideas with minor, insignificant changes to phrasing. For example, one student may wish to plagiarize the following text (also by Pratchett):

> The trouble with having an open mind, of course, is that people
> will insist on coming along and trying to put things in it.

The student rephrases the sentence slightly, changing it to the following:

> The problem with having an open mind is that people will insist
> on approaching and trying to insert things into your mind.

If your librarians do a search for exact matches of this student's sentence, they won't find any, since the student rephrased the sentence slightly. To catch clever plagiarists like this one, you will need to rely on

NLP tools that can detect not only exact text matches but also "loose" or "fuzzy" matches based on the meanings of similar words and sentences. For example, we'll need a method that can identify that *trouble* and *problem* are similar words used roughly as synonyms in the student's paraphrase. By identifying synonyms and near-synonyms, we'll be able to determine which non-identical sentences are similar enough to each other to constitute evidence for plagiarism. We'll use an NLP model called word2vec to accomplish this.

Understanding the word2vec NLP Model

We need a method that can take any two words and quantify exactly how similar they are. Let's think about what it means for two words to be similar. Consider the words *sword* and *knife*. The alphabetic letters in these words are totally different, with no overlaps, but the words refer to things that are similar to each other: both are words for sharp, metallic objects used to cut things. These words are not exact synonyms, but their meanings are fairly similar. We humans have a lifetime of experience that has given us an intuitive sense for how similar these words are, but our computer programs can't rely on intuition, so we have to find a way to quantify the similarity of these words based on data.

We'll use data that comes from a large collection of natural language text, also called a *corpus*. A corpus may be a collection of books, newspaper articles, research papers, theatrical plays, or blog posts or a mix of these. The important point is that it consists of *natural language*—phrases and sentences that were put together by humans and reflect the way humans speak and write. Once we have our natural language corpus, we can look at how to use it to quantify the meanings of words.

Quantifying Similarities Between Words

Let's start by looking at some natural language sentences and thinking about the words in them. Imagine two possible sentences that might contain the words *sword* and *knife*:

Westley attacked me with a sword and cut my skin.

Westley attacked me with a knife and cut my skin.

You can see that these sentences are identical, except for the detail of whether the attacker used a sword or a knife. With one word substituted for the other, they still have rather similar meanings. This is one indication that the words *sword* and *knife* are similar: they can be substituted for each other in many sentences without drastically changing the sentence's meaning or implications. Of course, it's possible that something other than a sword or knife could be used in an attack, so a sentence like the following could also be in the corpus:

Westley attacked me with a herring and cut my skin.

Though a sentence about a skin-puncturing attack with a herring is technically possible, it's less likely to appear in any natural language corpus than a sentence about a sword or knife attack. Someone who doesn't know any English, or a Python script, could find evidence for this by looking at our corpus and noticing that the word *attack* frequently appears near the word *sword*, but doesn't frequently appear near the word *herring*.

Noticing which words tend to appear near which other words will be very useful to us, because we can use a word's neighbors to better understand the word itself. Take a look at Table 10-1, which shows words that often appear near the words *sword*, *knife*, and *herring*.

Table 10-1: Words That Tend to Appear Near Each Other in Natural Language

Word	Words that often appear nearby in a natural language corpus
sword	cut, attack, sheath, fight, sharp, steel
knife	cut, attack, pie, fight, sharp, steel
herring	pickled, ocean, fillet, pie, silver, cut

Swords and knives both tend to be *sharp*, made of *steel*, used to *attack*, and used to *cut* things and to *fight*, so we see in Table 10-1 that all of these words often appear near both *sword* and *knife* in a natural language corpus. However, we can also see differences between the lists of nearby words. For example, *sword* appears often near *sheath*, but *knife* doesn't often appear near *sheath*. Also, *knife* often appears near *pie*, but *sword* usually doesn't. For its part, *herring* appears near *pie* sometimes (since people sometimes eat herring pie) and also appears near *cut* sometimes (since people sometimes cut herring when preparing meals). But the other words that tend to appear near *herring* have no overlap with the words that tend to appear near *sword* and *knife*.

Table 10-1 is useful because we can use it to understand and express the similarity of two words, using data rather than gut reactions. We can say that *sword* and *knife* are similar, not just because we have a gut feeling that they mean similar things, but because they tend to appear near the same neighbors in natural language texts. By contrast, *sword* and *herring* are quite different, because little overlap exists between their common neighbors in natural language texts. Table 10-1 gives us a data-centric way to determine whether words are similar, rather than a way based on vague intuition, and importantly, Table 10-1 can be created and interpreted even by someone who doesn't know a single word of English, since even a non-English speaker can look at a text and find which words tend to be neighbors. The table can also be created by a Python script that reads any corpus and finds common neighbors.

Our goal is to convert words to numbers, so our next step is to create a version of Table 10-1 that has numeric measurements of how likely words are to be each other's neighbors, as in Table 10-2.

Table 10-2: Probabilities of Words Appearing Near Each Other in a Natural Language Corpus

Word	Neighbor word	Probability that the neighbor appears near the word in a natural language corpus
sword	cut	61%
knife	cut	69%
herring	cut	12%
sword	pie	1%
knife	pie	49%
herring	pie	16%
sword	sheath	56%
knife	sheath	16%
herring	sheath	2%

Table 10-2 gives us much of the same information as Table 10-1; it shows which words are likely to appear near other words in a natural language corpus. But Table 10-2 is more precise; it gives us numeric measurements of the likelihood of words appearing together, instead of just a list of neighbor words. Again, you can see that the percentages in Table 10-2 seem plausible: *sword* and *knife* frequently have *cut* as a neighbor, *knife* and *herring* are more likely than *sword* to have *pie* as a neighbor, and *herring* doesn't often have *sheath* as a neighbor. Again, Table 10-2 could be created by someone who doesn't speak English, and it could also be created by a Python script that had a collection of books or English language texts to analyze. Similarly, even someone who doesn't know a word of English, or a Python script, could look at Table 10-2 and have a good idea about the similarities and differences between various words.

Creating a System of Equations

We're almost ready to represent words purely as numbers. The next step is to create something even more numeric than Table 10-2. Instead of representing these percentage likelihoods in a table, let's try to represent them in a system of equations. We will need only a few equations to succinctly represent all the information in Table 10-2.

Let's start with a fact from arithmetic. This arithmetic fact may seem useless, but you'll see later why it's useful:

$$61 = 5 \cdot 10 - 5 \cdot 1 + 3 \cdot 5 + 1 \cdot 1$$

You can see that this is an equation for the number 61—that's exactly the probability that the word *cut* appears near the word *sword* according to Table 10-2. We can also rewrite the right side of the equation by using different notation:

$$61 = (5, -5, 3, 1) \cdot (10, 1, 5, 1)$$

Here, the dot is meant to represent the dot product, which we introduced in Chapter 9. When calculating the dot product, we multiply the first elements of both vectors together, multiply the second elements of both vectors together, and so on, summing up the results. We can write out this dot product as a more standard equation using only multiplication and addition as follows:

$$61 = 5 \cdot 10 + (-5) \cdot 1 + 3 \cdot 5 + 1 \cdot 1$$

You can see that this is just the same equation we started with. The 5 and 10 are multiplied together, since they're the first element of the first and second vectors, respectively. The numbers -5 and 1 are also multiplied together, because they're the second elements of the first and second vectors, respectively. When we take a dot product, we multiply all of these corresponding elements together and sum up the results. Let's write one more fact of arithmetic in this same dot product style:

$$12 = (5, -5, 3, 1) \cdot (2, 2, 2, 6)$$

This is just another fact of arithmetic, using dot product notation. But notice, this is an equation for 12—exactly the probability that the word *cut* appears near the word *herring* according to Table 10-2. We can also notice that the first vector in the equation, $(5,-5, 3, 1)$, is exactly the same as the first vector in the previous equation. Now that we have both of these arithmetic facts, we can rewrite them yet again as a simple system of equations:

$$\text{sword} = (10, 1, 5, 1)$$
$$\text{herring} = (2, 2, 2, 6)$$
$$\text{Probability that } cut \text{ appears near a word} = (5, -5, 3, 1) \cdot \text{the word's vector}$$

Here, we've taken a leap: instead of just writing down arithmetic facts, we're claiming that we have numeric vectors that represent the words *sword* and *herring*, and we're claiming that we can use these vectors to calculate the probability that the word *cut* is near any word. This may seem like a bold leap, but soon you're going to see why it's justified. For now, we can keep going and write more arithmetic facts as follows:

$$60 = (5, -5, 3, 1) \cdot (10, 1, 5, 9)$$
$$1 = (1, -10, -1, 6) \cdot (10, 1, 5, 1)$$
$$49 = (1, -10, -1, 6) \cdot (2, 2, 2, 6)$$
$$16 = (1, -10, -1, 6) \cdot (10, 1, 5, 9)$$
$$56 = (1, 6, 9, -5) \cdot (10, 1, 5, 1)$$
$$16 = (1, 6, 9, -5) \cdot (2, 2, 2, 6)$$
$$2 = (1, 6, 9, -5) \cdot (10, 1, 5, 9)$$

You can look at these as just arbitrary arithmetic facts. But we can also connect them to Table 10-2. In fact, we can rewrite all of our arithmetic facts so far as the system shown in Equation 10-1.

$$sword = (10, 1, 5, 1)$$
$$knife = (10, 1, 5, 9)$$
$$herring = (2, 2, 2, 6)$$

Probability that *cut* appears near a word = $(5, -5, 3, 1) \cdot$ the word's vector
Probability that *pie* appears near a word = $(1, -10, -1, 6) \cdot$ the word's vector
Probability that *sheath* appears near a word = $(1, 6, 9, -5) \cdot$ the word's vector

Equation 10-1: A system of equations containing vector representations of words

Mathematically, you can verify that all the equations in Equation 10-1 are correct: by plugging the word vectors into the equations, we're able to calculate all the probabilities in Table 10-2. You may wonder why we created this system of equations. It seems to be doing nothing more than repeating the probabilities that we already have in Table 10-2, but in a more complicated way with more vectors. The important leap we've taken here is that by creating these vectors and this system of equations instead of using Table 10-2, we've found numeric representations of each of our words. The vector $(10, 1, 5, 1)$ in some sense "captures the meaning" of *sword*, and the same goes for $(10, 1, 5, 9)$ and *knife* and $(2, 2, 2, 6)$ and *herring*.

Even though we have vectors for each of our words, you may not feel convinced that these vectors really represent the meanings of English words. To help convince you, let's do some simple calculations with our vectors and see what we can learn. First, let's define these vectors in a Python session:

```
sword = [10,1,5,1]
knife = [10,1,5,9]
herring = [2,2,2,6]
```

Here, we define each of our word vectors as a Python list, a standard way to work with vectors in Python. We're interested in knowing how similar our words are to each other, so let's define a function that can calculate the distance between any two vectors:

```
import numpy as np
def euclidean(vec1,vec2):
    distance=np.array(vec1)-np.array(vec2)
    squared_sum=np.sum(distance**2)
    return np.sqrt(squared_sum)
```

This function is called euclidean(), because it's technically calculating a Euclidean distance between any two vectors. In two dimensions, a *Euclidean distance* is the length of the hypotenuse of a right triangle, which we can calculate with the Pythagorean theorem. More informally, we often refer to the Euclidean distance as just *distance*. In more than two dimensions, we use the same Pythagorean theorem formula to calculate a Euclidean distance, and the only difference is that it's harder to draw. Calculating Euclidean distances between vectors is a reasonable way to calculate the similarity of two vectors: the closer the Euclidean distance between the vectors, the more similar they are. Let's calculate the Euclidean distances between our word vectors:

```
print(euclidean(sword,knife))
print(euclidean(sword,herring))
print(euclidean(knife,herring))
```

You should see that *sword* and *knife* have a distance of 8 from each other. By contrast, *sword* and *herring* have a distance of 9.9 from each other. These distance measurements reflect our understandings of these words: *sword* and *knife* are similar to each other, so their vectors are close to each other, while *sword* and *herring* are less similar to each other, so their vectors are further apart. This is evidence that our method for converting words to numeric vectors has worked: it's enabling us to quantify word similarities successfully.

If we want to detect plagiarism, we'll have to find numeric vectors that represent more than just these three words. We'll want to find vectors for every word in the English language, or at least the majority of the words that tend to appear in student papers. We can imagine what some of these vectors might be. For example, the word *haddock* refers to a type of fish, not too different from a herring. So, we'll expect to find that *haddock* has similar neighbors to *herring* and similar probabilities in Table 10-2 (a similar probability of having *cut* or *pie* or anything else as a neighbor).

Anytime two words have similar probabilities in Table 10-2, we expect that they'll have similar vectors, since we'll be multiplying those vectors according to the system of equations in Equation 10-1 to get those probabilities. For example, we might find that the numeric vector for *haddock* is something like (2.1, 1.9, 2.3, 6.5). This vector will be close in Euclidean distance to the vector for *herring* (2, 2, 2, 6), and if we multiply the *haddock* vector by the other vectors in Equation 10-1, we'll find that *haddock* should have probabilities of being near each neighbor word that are similar to the probabilities for *herring* in Table 10-2. We'll similarly need to find vectors for thousands of other words in English, and we'll expect that words that have similar meanings should have similar vectors.

It's easy to say that we need vectors for every English word, but then the question becomes: How should we determine each of these vectors? To understand how we can determine the vectors for every word, consider a diagram of the system of equations in Figure 10-1.

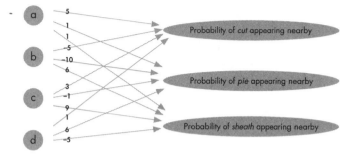

Figure 10-1: A visual representation of the probabilities of words appearing near each other

This diagram looks complex, but it's meant to illustrate nothing more and nothing less than our system of equations. In Equation 10-1, we represent every word as a vector with four elements, like this: (a, b, c, d). The a, b, c, and d on the left of Figure 10-1 represent these elements. Each arrow extending from those elements represents a multiplication. For example, the arrow marked with a 5 that extends from the circle labeled a to the oval labeled *probability of cut appearing nearby* means that we should multiply every a value by 5, and add it to the estimated probability of *cut* appearing near a word. If we consider all the multiplications indicated by all of these arrows, you can see from Figure 10-1 that the probability of *cut* appearing near a word is $5 \cdot a - 5 \cdot b + 3 \cdot c + 1 \cdot d$, just as described in Equation 10-1. Figure 10-1 is just another way to represent Equation 10-1. If we can find the right a, b, c, and d values for every word in English, we'll have the word vectors we need to check for plagiarism.

The reason we drew Figure 10-1 is to point out that it has exactly the form of a neural network, the type of supervised learning model we already discussed in Chapter 6. Since it constitutes a neural network, we can use advanced software (including several free Python packages) to train the neural network and find out exactly what a, b, c, and d should be for every word in English. The whole point of creating Tables 10-1 and 10-2, and the system of equations in Equation 10-1, is to create a neural network like the hypothetical one shown in Figure 10-1. As long as we have data like that in Table 10-2, we can use this neural network software to train the neural network shown in Figure 10-1 and find all the word vectors we need.

The most important output of this neural network training will be values of *a*, *b*, *c*, and *d* for every word in our data. In other words, the output of the neural network training will be (*a*, *b*, *c*, *d*) vectors for every word. This process is called the *word2vec* model: create a table of probabilities like Table 10-2 for every word in a corpus, use that table to set up a neural network like the one shown in Figure 10-1, and then train that neural network to find numeric vectors that represent every word.

The word2vec model is popular because it can create numeric vectors for any words, and those vectors can be used for many useful applications. One reason that word2vec is popular is that we can train a word2vec model by using only raw text as input; we don't need to annotate or label any words before training the model and getting our word vectors. So, even someone who doesn't speak English can create word vectors and reason about them by using the word2vec approach.

If this sounds complex, don't worry. Next, we'll go through code for working with these kinds of vectors, and you'll see that although the ideas and theory of word2vec are complex, the code and applications can be straightforward and simple. For now, try to feel comfortable with the basic overall idea of what we've discussed so far: if we create data about which words appear near each other in natural language, we can use that data to create vectors that allow us to quantify the similarity of any pair of words. Let's continue with some code, where we can see how to use these numeric vectors for detecting plagiarism.

Analyzing Numeric Vectors in word2vec

Not only has someone already created the word2vec model, but they've also already done all its hard work for us: written the code, calculated the vectors, and published all of it online for us to download anytime for free. In Python, we can use the Gensim package to access word vectors for many English words:

```
import gensim.downloader as api
```

The Gensim package has a `downloader` that allows us to access many NLP models and tools just by using the `load()` method. You can load one such collection of vectors in one line as follows:

```
vectors = api.load('word2vec-google-news-300')
```

This code loads a collection of word vectors that was created from a corpus of news texts containing about 100 billion words. Essentially, someone got the information that would be in a table like our Table 10-2, but with thousands more words in it. They obtained these words and probabilities from real news sources written by humans. Then they used that information to create a neural network like the one in Figure 10-1—again, with thousands more words in it. They trained this neural network and found vectors for every word in their corpus.

We've just downloaded the vectors they calculated. One reason we expect these vectors to be useful is that the text corpus used to create these vectors was large and diverse, and large, diverse text data sources tend to lead to higher accuracy in NLP models. We can look at the vector corresponding to any word as follows:

```
print(vectors['sword'])
```

Here, we print out the vector for the word *sword*. The output you'll see is a vector with 512 numeric elements. Word vectors like this one, which represents the word *sword* according to the model we downloaded, are also called *embeddings*, because we've successfully *embedded* a word in a *vector space*. In short, we've converted a word to a vector of numbers.

You'll notice that this 512-element vector for *sword* is not the same as the vector we used for *sword* previously in the chapter, which was (10, 1, 5, 1). This vector is different from our vector for a few reasons. First, this vector uses a different corpus than the one we used, so it will have different probabilities listed in its version of Table 10-2. Second, the creators of this model decided to find vectors with 512 elements instead of 4 elements as we did, so they get more vector elements. Third, their vectors were adjusted to have values close to 0, while ours were not. Every corpus and every neural network will lead to slightly different results, but if we're using a good corpus and a good neural network, we expect the same qualitative result: vectors that represent words and enable us to detect plagiarism (and do many other things).

After downloading these vectors, we can work with them just like any other Python object. For example, we can calculate distances between our word vectors, as follows:

```
print(euclidean(vectors['sword'],vectors['knife']))
print(euclidean(vectors['sword'],vectors['herring']))
print(euclidean(vectors['car'],vectors['van']))
```

Here, we're doing the same Euclidean distance calculations that we did before, but instead of calculating distances with the vectors in Equation 10-1, we're doing calculations with the vectors we downloaded. When you run these comparisons, you'll see the following outputs:

```
>>> print(euclidean(vectors['sword'],vectors['knife']))
3.2766972
>>> print(euclidean(vectors['sword'],vectors['herring']))
4.9384727
>>> print(euclidean(vectors['car'],vectors['van']))
2.608656
```

You can see that these distances make sense: the vector for *sword* is similar to the vector for *knife* (they have distance about 3.28 from each other), but it's different from the vector for *herring* (they have distance about 4.94 from each other, much larger than the difference between *sword* and *knife*). You can try the same calculation for any other pairs words that are in the corpus, like *car* and *van* as well. You can compare differences between pairs of words to find out which pairs have the most and the least similar meanings.

Euclidean distance is not the only distance metric people use to compare word vectors. Using cosine similarity measurements is also common, just as we did in Chapter 9. Remember that we used this code to calculate cosine similarities:

```python
def dot_product(vector1,vector2):
    thedotproduct=np.sum([vector1[k]*vector2[k] for k in range(0,len(vector1))])
    return(thedotproduct)

def vector_norm(vector):
    thenorm=np.sqrt(dot_product(vector,vector))
    return(thenorm)

def cosine_similarity(vector1,vector2):
    thecosine=0
    thedotproduct=dot_product(vector1,vector2)
    thecosine=thedotproduct/(vector_norm(vector1)*vector_norm(vector2))
    thecosine=np.round(thecosine,4)
    return(thecosine)
```

Here we define a function called cosine_similarity() to check the cosine of the angle between any two vectors. We can check some cosine similarities between vectors as follows:

```python
print(cosine_similarity(vectors['sword'],vectors['knife']))
print(cosine_similarity(vectors['sword'],vectors['herring']))
print(cosine_similarity(vectors['car'],vectors['van']))
```

When you run this snippet, you'll see the following results:

```
>>> print(cosine_similarity(vectors['sword'],vectors['knife']))
0.5576
>>> print(cosine_similarity(vectors['sword'],vectors['herring']))
0.0529
>>> print(cosine_similarity(vectors['car'],vectors['van']))
0.6116
```

You can see that these metrics are doing exactly what we want: they give us lower values for words that we perceive as different and higher values for words that we perceive as similar. Even though your laptop doesn't "speak English," just by analyzing a corpus of natural language text, it's able to quantify exactly how similar and exactly how different distinct words are.

Manipulating Vectors with Mathematical Calculations

One famous illustration of the power of word2vec comes from an analysis of the words *king* and *queen*. To see this illustration, let's start by getting the vectors associated with some English words:

```
king = vectors['king']
queen = vectors['queen']
man = vectors['man']
woman = vectors['woman']
```

Here, we define some vectors associated with several words. As humans, we know that a king is a male head of a monarchy and a queen is a female head of a monarchy. We might even express the relationship between the words *king* and *queen* as follows:

$$king - man + woman = queen$$

Starting with the idea of a *king*, and taking away from that the idea of a *man*, then adding to that the idea of a *woman*, we end up with the idea of a *queen*. If we're thinking about just the world of words, this equation might seem ridiculous, since it's typically not possible to add and subtract words or ideas in this way. However, remember that we have vector versions of each of these words, so we can add and subtract vectors from each other and see what we get. Let's try to add and subtract the vectors corresponding to each of these words in Python:

```
newvector = king-man+woman
```

Here, we take our king vector, subtract our man vector, add our woman vector, and define the result as a new variable called newvector. If our additions and subtractions do what we want them to, our newvector should capture a specific meaning: the idea of a king without any attributes of a *man*, but with the added attributes of a *woman*. In other words, even though the newvector is a sum of three vectors, none of which are the vector for *queen*, we expect their sum to be close to, or equal to, the vector for *queen*. Let's check the difference between our newvector and our queen vector to see whether this is the case:

```
print(cosine_similarity(newvector,queen))
print(euclidean(newvector,queen))
```

We can see that our newvector is similar to our queen vector: their cosine similarity is 0.76, and their Euclidean distance is 2.5. We can compare this to the differences between other familiar pairs of words:

```
print(cosine_similarity(vectors['fish'],vectors['herring']))
print(euclidean(vectors['fish'],vectors['herring']))
```

You should see that *king* – *man* + *woman* is more similar to *queen* than *fish* is to *herring*. Our mathematical calculations with the words' vectors lead to exactly the results we expect based on what we know about the words' linguistic meanings. This demonstrates the usefulness of these vectors: we can not only compare them to find similarities between pairs of words but also manipulate them through addition and subtraction to add and subtract concepts. The ability to add and subtract these vectors, and get results that make sense, is more evidence that these vectors are reliably capturing the meanings of their associated words.

Detecting Plagiarism with word2vec

Let's go back to the plagiarism scenario from earlier in the chapter. Remember that we introduced the following two sentences as an example of plagiarism:

> The trouble with having an open mind, of course, is that people will insist on coming along and trying to put things in it. [original sentence]

> The problem with having an open mind is that people will insist on approaching and trying to insert things into your mind. [plagiarized sentence]

Since these two sentences differ in a few places, a naive plagiarism checker that looks for exact matches won't detect plagiarism here. Instead of checking for exact matches for every character of both sentences, we want to check for close matches between the meanings of each word. For words that are identical, we'll find that they have 0 distance between them:

```
print(cosine_similarity(vectors['the'],vectors['the']))
print(euclidean(vectors['having'],vectors['having']))
```

The results of this are not surprising. We find that a word's vector has perfect (1.0) cosine similarity with itself and a word's vector has 0 Euclidean distance from itself. Every word is equal to itself. But remember, wily plagiarists are paraphrasing, not using the exact same words as published texts. If we compare words that are paraphrased, we expect that they'll be similar to the words of the original, but not exactly the same. We can measure the similarity of potentially paraphrased words as follows:

```
print(cosine_similarity(vectors['trouble'],vectors['problem']))
print(euclidean(vectors['come'],vectors['approach']))
print(cosine_similarity(vectors['put'],vectors['insert']))
```

You'll see the following results from this code snippet:

```
>>> print(cosine_similarity(vectors['trouble'],vectors['problem']))
0.5327
>>> print(euclidean(vectors['come'],vectors['approach']))
2.9844923
>>> print(cosine_similarity(vectors['put'],vectors['insert']))
0.3435
```

This snippet compares the words of the plagiarized text and the words of the original text. The results show close matches in almost every case: either a relatively small Euclidean distance or a relatively high cosine similarity. If the individual words of a student's sentence are all close matches to the individual words of a published sentence, that's good evidence of plagiarism, even if there are few or no exact matches. Importantly, we can check for these close matches automatically, not based on slow, costly human judgment, but based on data and quick Python scripts.

Checking for close matches for all the individual words in sentences is a reasonable way to start detecting plagiarism. However, it's not perfect. The main problem is that so far, we've learned to evaluate only individual words instead of full sentences. We can think of sentences as collections or sequences of individual words. But in many cases, it will be better to have a technique that can evaluate meanings and similarities for entire sentences simultaneously, treating sentences as individual units instead of only as collections of words. For that, we'll turn to a powerful new approach.

Using Skip-Thoughts

The *skip-thoughts* model is an NLP model that uses data and neural networks to convert entire sentences to numeric vectors. It's quite similar to word2vec, but instead of converting individual words one at a time to vectors, we convert entire sentences to vectors as units.

The theory behind skip-thoughts is similar to the theory behind word2vec: you take a natural language corpus, find which sentences tend to appear near each other, and train a neural network that can predict which sentences are expected to appear before or after any other sentence. For word2vec, we saw an illustration of a neural network model in Figure 10-1. For skip-thoughts, a similar illustration is shown in Figure 10-2.

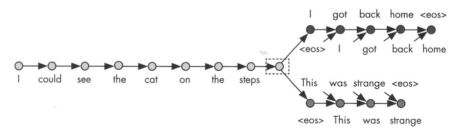

Figure 10-2: We use the skip-thoughts model to predict which sentences appear near each other.

Figure 10-2 is based on the model from the 2015 paper titled "Skip-Thought Vectors" by Ryan Kiros and colleagues (*https://arxiv.org/pdf/1506 .06726.pdf*). You can see that the sentence on the left of the figure is taken as the input. This sentence is a sequence of individual words, but all the words are considered together as a single unit. The skip-thoughts model attempts to find a vector representation of this sentence that, when used as an input in a neural network, can predict sentences that are most likely to come before and after it (including the sentences on the right of Figure 10-2). Just as word2vec is based on which individual words are expected to be near other words, skip-thoughts is based on predicting the full sentences that are near other sentences. You don't need to worry about the theory too much; just try to remember that skip-thoughts is a way to encode natural language sentences as vectors by calculating probabilities of other sentences appearing nearby.

Just as with word2vec, writing code for any of this ourselves is not necessary. Instead, we'll turn to the *Universal Sentence Encoder (USE)*. This tool converts sentences into vectors, using the idea of skip-thoughts to find the vectors (plus other advanced technical methods). We're going to use the vector outputs of the USE for plagiarism detection, but USE vectors can also be used for chatbot implementations, image tagging, and much more.

The code for the USE is not hard to work with, because someone else has written it for us. We can start by defining sentences that we want to analyze:

```
Sentences = [
    "The trouble with having an open mind, of course, is that people will insist on coming
along and trying to put things in it.",\
    "The problem with having an open mind is that people will insist on approaching and trying
to insert things into your mind.",\
    "To be or not to be, that is the question",\
    "Call me Ishmael"
]
```

Here we have a list of sentences, and we want to convert each into a numeric vector. We can import code someone else has written to do this conversion:

```
import tensorflow_hub as hub
embed = hub.load("https://tfhub.dev/google/universal-sentence-encoder-large/5")
```

The `tensorfow_hub` module allows us to load the USE from an online repository. The USE is a big model, so don't panic if loading it into your Python session takes a few minutes or more. When we load it, we save it as a variable called `embed`. Now that we have the USE in our Python session, we can create word embeddings (vectors) with one simple line of code:

```
embeddings = embed(Sentences)
```

Our `embeddings` variable contains vectors that represent each of the sentences in our `Sentences` list. You can look at the vector for the first sentence by checking the first element of the `embeddings` variable as follows:

```
print(embeddings[0])
```

When you run this snippet, you'll see a numeric vector with 512 elements, the first 16 of which are shown here:

```
>>> print(embeddings[0])
tf.Tensor(
[ 9.70209017e-04 -5.99743128e-02 -2.84200953e-03  7.49062840e-03
  7.74949566e-02 -1.00521010e-03 -7.75496066e-02  4.12207991e-02
 -1.55476958e-03 -1.11693323e-01  2.58275736e-02 -1.15299867e-02
 -3.84882478e-05 -4.07184102e-02  3.69430222e-02  6.66357949e-02
```

This is the vector representation of the first sentence in your list—not the individual words in the sentence, but the sentence itself. Just as we did with our word2vec vectors, we can calculate the distance between any two of our sentence vectors. In this case, the distances between vectors will represent the degree of difference between the overall meanings of two sentences. Let's check the distance between our first two sentences as follows:

```
print(cosine_similarity(embeddings[0],embeddings[1]))
```

We can see that the cosine similarity is about 0.85—indicating that the first two sentences in our Sentences list are quite similar to each other. This is evidence that the student's sentence (the second one in our Sentences list) is plagiarized from Pratchett's sentence (the first one in our Sentences list). By contrast, we can check distances between other vectors and see that they're not quite so similar. For example, if you run print(cosine_similarity(embeddings[0],embeddings[2])), you can see that the cosine similarity of these two sentences is about 0.02, indicating that these sentences are almost as different as it's possible for two sentences to be. This is evidence that Pratchett didn't plagiarize *Hamlet*. If you run print(cosine_similarity(embeddings[0],embeddings[3])), you can see that the cosine similarity of these two sentences is about −0.07, another low similarity score, indicating that Pratchett also didn't plagiarize *Moby Dick*.

You can see that checking the distances between the meanings of any two sentences is straightforward. Your plagiarism detector can simply check for the cosine similarity (or Euclidean distance) between a student's work and previously published sentences, and if the similarities appear to be large (or the Euclidean distances appear to be too small), you can take it as evidence that the student is guilty of plagiarism.

Topic Modeling

To finish the chapter, let's introduce one final business scenario and talk about how we can combine NLP tools with tools from previous chapters to deal with it. In this scenario, imagine that you run a forum website. Your site has become so successful that you can no longer read all the threads and conversations yourself, but you still want to understand the topics people are writing about on your site so you can understand who your users are and what they care about. You want to find a reliable, automated way to analyze all the text on your site and discover the main topics being discussed. This goal, called *topic modeling*, is common in NLP.

To start, let's take a collection of sentences that might have appeared on your site. A successful forum website could receive thousands of comments every second, but we'll start by looking at a small sample of the full data, just eight sentences:

```
Sentences = [
    "The corn and cheese are delicious when they're roasted together",
    "Several of the scenes have rich settings but weak characterization",
    "Consider adding extra seasoning to the pork",
    "The prose was overwrought and pretentious",
    "There are some nice brisket slices on the menu",
    "It would be better to have a chapter to introduce your main plot ideas",
    "Everything was cold when the waiter brought it to the table",
    "You can probably find it at a cheaper price in bookstores"
]
```

Just as you did before, you can calculate the vectors, or embeddings, for all these sentences:

```
embeddings = embed(Sentences)
```

Next, we can create a matrix of all our sentence embeddings:

```
arrays=[]
for i in range(len(Sentences)):
    arrays.append(np.array(embeddings[i]))

sentencematrix = np.empty((len(Sentences),512,), order = "F")

for i in range(len(Sentences)):
    sentencematrix[i]=arrays[i]

import pandas as pd
pandasmatrix=pd.DataFrame(sentencematrix)
```

This snippet starts by creating a list called arrays and adding all the sentence vectors to the list. Next, it creates a matrix called sentencematrix. This matrix is just your sentence vectors stacked on top of each other, with one row for each sentence vector. Finally, we convert this matrix into a pandas dataframe, so it's easier to work with. The final result, called pandasmatrix, has eight rows; each row is a sentence vector for one of our eight sentences.

Now we have a matrix that contains our sentence vectors. But getting our vectors isn't enough; we need to decide what to do with them. Remember that our goal is topic modeling. We want to understand the topics that people are writing about and which sentences relate to which topics. We have several ways to accomplish this. One natural way to accomplish topic modeling is by using clustering, something we already discussed in Chapter 7.

Our clustering approach is simple: we'll take our matrix of sentence vectors as our input data. We'll apply clustering to determine the natural groups that exist in the data. We'll interpret the groups (clusters) that we find as the distinct topics being discussed on your forum website. We can do this clustering as follows:

```
from sklearn.cluster import KMeans
m = KMeans(2)
m.fit(pandasmatrix)

pandasmatrix['topic'] = m.labels_

pandasmatrix['sentences']=Sentences
```

You can see that the clustering requires only a few lines of code. We import the KMeans code from the sklearn module. We create a variable called m and then use its fit() method to find two clusters for our matrix (the pandasmatrix). The fit() method uses Euclidean distance measurements with our sentence vectors to find two clusters of documents. The two clusters it finds are what we will take to be the two main topics of our collection of sentences. After we find these clusters, we add two new columns to our pandasmatrix: first, we add the labels that are the result of our clustering (in the topic variable), and second, we add the actual sentences that we're trying to cluster. Let's look at the results:

```
print(pandasmatrix.loc[pandasmatrix['topic']==0,'sentences'])
print(pandasmatrix.loc[pandasmatrix['topic']==1,'sentences'])
```

This snippet prints out two sets of sentences: first, sentences that are labeled as belonging to cluster 0 (sentences on rows with the topic variable equal to 0) and second, sentences that are labeled as belonging to cluster 1 (sentences on rows with the topic variable equal to 1). You should see the following results:

```
>>> print(pandasmatrix.loc[pandasmatrix['topic']==0,'sentences'])
0    The corn and cheese are delicious when they're...
2          Consider adding extra seasoning to the pork
4       There are some nice brisket slices on the menu
6     Everything was cold when the waiter brought it...
Name: sentences, dtype: object
>>> print(pandasmatrix.loc[pandasmatrix['topic']==1,'sentences'])
1     Several of the scenes have rich settings but w...
3            The prose was overwrought and pretentious
5     It would be better to have a chapter to introd...
7     You can probably find it at a cheaper price in...
Name: sentences, dtype: object
```

You can see that this method has identified two clusters in our data, and they've been labeled as cluster 0 and cluster 1. When you look at the sentences that have been classified as cluster 0, you can see that many seem to be discussions about food and restaurants. When you look at cluster 1, you can see that it seems to consist of critiques of books. At least according to this sample of eight sentences, these are the main topics being discussed on your forum, and they've been identified and organized automatically.

We've accomplished topic modeling, using a numeric method (clustering) on non-numeric data (natural language text). You can see that USE, and word embeddings in general, can be useful in many applications.

Other Applications of NLP

One useful application of NLP is in the world of recommendation systems. Imagine that you run a movie website and want to recommend movies to your users. In Chapter 9, we discussed how to use interaction matrices to make recommendations based on comparisons of transaction histories. However, you could also make a recommendation system based on comparisons of content. For example, you could take plot summaries of individual movies and use the USE to get sentence embeddings for each plot summary. Then you could calculate distances between plot summaries to determine the similarity of various movies and, anytime a user watches a move, recommend that that user also watch movies with the most similar plots. This is a *content-based recommendation system.*

Another interesting application of NLP is *sentiment analysis.* We encountered sentiment analysis a little already in Chapter 6. Certain tools can determine whether any given sentence is positive, negative, or neutral in its tone or the sentiment it expresses. Some of these tools rely on word embeddings like those we've covered in this chapter, and others don't. Sentiment analysis could be useful for a business that receives thousands of emails and messages every day. By running automatic sentiment analysis on all of its incoming emails, a business could determine which customers were the most happy or unhappy, and potentially prioritize responses based on customer sentiment.

Many businesses today deploy *chatbots* on their websites—computer programs that can understand text inputs and answer questions. Chatbots have varying levels of sophistication, but many rely on some kind of word embeddings like the word2vec and skip-thought methods described in this chapter.

NLP has many other possible applications in business. Today, law firms are trying to use NLP to automatically analyze documents and even automatically generate or at least organize contracts. News websites have tried to use NLP to automatically generate certain kinds of formulaic articles, like recaps of sports games. There's no end to the possibilities of NLP as the field itself continues to develop. If you know some powerful methods like word2vec and skip-thoughts as a starting point, there's no limit to the useful applications you can create.

Summary

In this chapter, we went over natural language processing. All of the applications of NLP that we discussed relied on embeddings: numeric vectors that accurately represent words and sentences. If you can represent a word numerically, you can do math with it, including calculating similarities (which we did for plagiarism detection) and clustering (which we did for topic modeling). NLP tools might be difficult to use and master, but they can be astonishing in their capabilities.

In the next chapter, we'll shift gears and wrap up the book by going over some simple ideas about working with other programming languages that are important for data science.

11

DATA SCIENCE IN OTHER LANGUAGES

All of our business solutions so far have had one thing in common: they've used only Python. Python is standard in the world of data science, but it's not the only language out there. The best data scientists are versatile and capable of writing code in multiple languages. This chapter contains a short introduction to both Structured Query Language (SQL) and R, two common languages that every good data scientist should know. This chapter isn't a comprehensive overview of either language. It's only a basic introduction that will enable you to recognize and write a few lines of SQL or R code.

We'll start the chapter by introducing a business scenario. Then we'll go over some simple SQL code to set up a database and manipulate data within it. We'll go on to discuss R and how to use it to perform simple operations and linear regressions. Instead of spending a lot of effort setting up environments for running SQL and R commands, you'll learn how to run SQL and R commands from within a Python session.

Winning Soccer Games with SQL

Imagine that you receive a job offer to be the manager of a European soccer team. This may seem like more of a sports scenario than a business scenario, but remember that sports is a business, one with billions of dollars of revenues worldwide every year. Teams hire managers to maximize their revenues and profits and make sure everything runs well.

One of the most important things every team needs to do from a business perspective is win games—teams that win often earn higher profits than teams that tend to lose. As a good data scientist, you know exactly what to do first to set yourself up for success in your new job: you start diving into and exploring data, and trying to learn what it takes to win soccer games.

Reading and Analyzing Data

You can download several files that contain data related to European soccer from the following URLs: *https://bradfordtuckfield.com/players.csv*, *https://bradfordtuckfield.com/games.csv*, and *https://bradfordtuckfield.com/shots.csv*. The first file, *players.csv*, contains a list of professional soccer players, including their names and unique ID numbers. The next file, *games.csv*, contains detailed statistics related to thousands of individual soccer games, including which teams played, the number of goals scored, and much more. The third file, *shots.csv*, is the largest. It contains information about hundreds of thousands of individual shots taken during games, including who took the shot, which foot the player used, where the shot was taken, and the result of the shot (whether it was blocked, missed, or a goal).

If you can do rigorous analysis of this data, you can get a deep understanding of European soccer and have much of the most important knowledge you'll need to succeed as a manager. (The original sources of this public domain data include *https://www.kaggle.com/technika148/football-database*, *https://understat.com*, and *https://www.football-data.co.uk*.)

Let's start by reading these files. We'll use Python here, but don't worry, we'll be using SQL soon:

```
import pandas as pd
players=pd.read_csv('players.csv', encoding = 'ISO-8859-1')
games=pd.read_csv('games.csv', encoding = 'ISO-8859-1')
shots=pd.read_csv('shots.csv', encoding = 'ISO-8859-1')
```

So far, this should look familiar. It's standard Python code for reading *.csv* files. After importing pandas, we read in datasets that have information about European soccer. You can see that we read all three datasets that we'll be working with here: players, which contains data about individual players; games, which contains data about individual games; and shots, which contains data about shots that players took during games.

Let's look at the first few rows of each of these datasets:

```
print(players.head())
print(games.head())
print(shots.head())
```

The players table has only two columns, and when you run print(players.head()), you should see the top five rows of both of them:

	playerID	name
0	560	Sergio Romero
1	557	Matteo Darmian
2	548	Daley Blind
3	628	Chris Smalling
4	1006	Luke Shaw

The shots data is more detailed. When you run print(shots.head()), you should see its top five rows:

	gameID	shooterID	assisterID	...	xGoal	positionX	positionY
0	81	554	NaN	...	0.104347	0.794	0.421
1	81	555	631.0	...	0.064342	0.860	0.627
2	81	554	629.0	...	0.057157	0.843	0.333
3	81	554	NaN	...	0.092141	0.848	0.533
4	81	555	654.0	...	0.035742	0.812	0.707

You can see that by default, the pandas package has omitted some columns that don't fit in the output console. You can see a list of all the columns in the dataset by running print(shots.columns), which will show you the following list:

```
Index(['gameID', 'shooterID', 'assisterID', 'minute', 'situation',
       'lastAction', 'shotType', 'shotResult', 'xGoal', 'positionX',
       'positionY'],
      dtype='object')
```

We have detailed data about each shot. We know the foot that was used to shoot (in the shotType column), the results of the shot (in the shotResult column), and the position at which it was taken (in the positionX and positionY columns). But one thing that's not stated explicitly in this data is the name of the player who took the shot. All we have is the shooterID, a number. If we want to find out the name of the person who took the shot, we have to look it up: find the shooterID number in the shots data, then look at the players dataset to find the name of the player whose ID matches that shooterID number.

The first shot, for example, was taken by the player with `shooterID` 554. If we want to know the name of that player, we need to look at the `players` dataset. If you scroll through the `players` data, or if you run `print(players.loc[7,'name'])` in Python, you can see that this player is Juan Mata.

Getting Familiar with SQL

Let's go over some SQL code that will enable you to do these kinds of lookups. We'll start by looking at SQL code, and we'll discuss how to run the code later. Individual SQL commands are usually called SQL *queries*. The following code is a SQL query that will show you the entire `players` dataset:

```
SELECT * FROM playertable;
```

Often, short SQL queries are simple to interpret as long as you know English. In this snippet, `SELECT` tells us that we're selecting data. The `FROM playertable` text at the end of the query means that we'll be selecting data from the table called `playertable`. Between `SELECT` and `FROM playertable` is where we're supposed to specify the columns we want to select from the `playertable` data. The asterisk (*) is a shortcut that means that we want to select all the columns of the `playertable` table. The semicolon (;) tells SQL that we've finished this particular query.

So, this SQL query selects our entire `players` table. If you don't want to select all the columns of the data, you can replace the * with the names of one or more columns. For example, both of the following are also valid SQL queries:

```
SELECT playerID FROM playertable
SELECT playerID, name FROM playertable
```

The first query will select only the `playerID` column from the `playertable`. The second will select both the `playerID` and the `name` columns from the `playertable` table—the output we get from specifying that we want both columns by name is the same as the output we get from writing an asterisk.

You may have noticed that our SQL queries use all caps for their keywords. This is a common practice when writing SQL queries, though it's not technically required in most environments. We'll do it to follow convention.

Setting Up a SQL Database

If you paste the preceding SQL queries directly into a Python session, they won't run correctly; they're not Python code. If you're running SQL frequently, you will probably want to set up an environment that's designed for editing and running SQL queries. However, this is a Python book, and we don't want to get you bogged down in the details of setting up a SQL environment. Instead, let's go over a few steps that will allow you to run SQL queries directly in Python. You can start by running the following commands in Python:

```
import sqlite3
conn = sqlite3.connect("soccer.db")
curr = conn.cursor()
```

Here, we import the SQLite3 package, which allows us to run SQL queries in Python. SQL is a language that's designed to work with databases, so we need to use SQLite3 to connect to a database. On the second line, we tell SQLite3 to connect to a database called soccer.db. You probably don't have a database on your computer called soccer.db, so there may be nothing for SQLite3 to connect to. That's all right, because the SQLite3 module is very helpful: when we specify a database we want to connect to, it will connect to the database if it exists, and if we try to connect to a database that doesn't exist, it will create the database for us and then connect to it.

Now that we're connected to our database, we need to define a *cursor* to access this database. You can think of this cursor as similar to the cursor you use on your computer; it helps you select and manipulate objects. If that's not clear to you now, don't worry. The way we use this cursor will become clearer later.

Now that we have a database, we want to fill it up. Usually, a database contains a collection of tables, but our soccer.db database is currently empty. The three pandas dataframes we've worked with so far can all be saved to our database as tables. We can add the players dataframe to our database with one line:

```
players.to_sql('playertable', conn, if_exists='replace', index = False)
```

Here, we use the to_sql() method to push our players dataframe to the database's playertable table. We use the connection we created before, called conn, which ensures that the table gets pushed to our soccer.db database. Now the players data is stored in our database instead of being accessible only as a pandas dataframe in our Python session.

Running SQL Queries

We're finally ready to run our SQL query on our data. This is Python code that will run our SQL query:

```
curr.execute('''
SELECT * FROM playertable
        ''')
```

You can see that the cursor we created, curr, is finally useful. The cursor is the object we'll use to execute SQL queries on our data. In this case, we execute a simple query that selects the entire table called playertable. It's important to note that this has selected the data, but it hasn't displayed it. If we want to actually see the data that we selected, we need to print it to our console:

```
for row in curr.fetchall():
    print(row)
```

The cursor has selected the data and pushed it to your Python session's memory, but we need to use the fetchall() method to access this data. When you run fetchall(), it selects a list of rows. That's why we print each row individually in a for loop. The playertable table has thousands of rows, and you may not want to print all of them to your screen at once. You can limit the number of rows returned by your query by adding a LIMIT clause:

```
curr.execute('''
SELECT * FROM playertable LIMIT 5
        ''')
for row in curr.fetchall():
    print (row)
```

Here, we run the same code as before, adding only seven characters: LIMIT 5. By adding LIMIT 5 to the SQL query, we limit the rows that are returned to only the first five. Since we get only the top five rows in the table, printing them to the screen becomes easier. This shows us the same data as we see when we run print(players.head()) when we're using pandas in Python. But be careful: in this case, LIMIT 5 will give us the top five rows, but in other database environments, it will give you a random five rows. You can depend on getting five rows from the LIMIT 5 clause, but you can't always be sure which five you'll get.

We often want only particular subsets of our data. For example, what if we want to find the player with a particular ID:

```
curr.execute('''
SELECT * FROM playertable WHERE playerID=554
        ''')
for row in curr.fetchall():
    print (row)
```

Here, we run much of the same code, but we add a WHERE clause. Instead of selecting the whole table, we select only rows for which a particular condition is true. The condition we're interested in is playerID=554. The output shows us one row, and that row tells us that the player with playerID equal to 554 is named Juan Mata. This tells us what we wanted to know, that Juan Mata is the person who took the first shot recorded in the data. You should be starting to notice a pattern here: when creating SQL queries, we start with a short query that selects a whole table, and then we add *clauses* to the query (like the LIMIT clause or WHERE clause we added here) to refine the results we get. SQL queries consist of many clauses, each of which has an effect on the data the query selects.

We can use WHERE clauses to select all sorts of conditions. For example, we can use a WHERE clause to select the ID of a player with a particular name:

```
curr.execute('''
SELECT playerID FROM playertable WHERE name="Juan Mata"
        ''')
for row in curr.fetchall():
    print (row)
```

We can also use the AND operator to specify multiple conditions:

```
curr.execute('''
SELECT * FROM playertable WHERE playerID>100 AND playerID<200
        ''')
for row in curr.fetchall():
    print (row)
```

In this case, we select the rows of the playertable that satisfy two conditions simultaneously: both playerID>100 and playerID <200.

You may want to look up a name in a table, but feel uncertain about the spelling. In that case, you can use the LIKE operator:

```
curr.execute('''
SELECT * FROM playertable WHERE name LIKE "Juan M%"
        ''')
for row in curr.fetchall():
    print (row)
```

In this case, we're using the percent character (%) as a *wildcard*, meaning that it stands for any collection of characters. You may notice that this is similar to the way we used the asterisk earlier in the query (SELECT *). We use * to mean all columns and % to mean any possible character. But though these uses are similar (both representing unknown values), they're not interchangeable, and there are two important differences. First, the * can be used as part of a query itself, while the % can be used only as part of a string of characters. Second, the * is used to refer to columns, and the % is used to refer to other characters.

When you look at the results of this code, you can see that we've found several players whose names start with *Juan M*:

```
(554, 'Juan Mata')
(2067, 'Juan Muñoz')
(4820, 'Juan Manuel Falcón')
(7095, 'Juan Musso')
(2585, 'Juan Muñiz')
(5009, 'Juan Manuel Valencia')
(7286, 'Juan Miranda')
```

If what we've done so far feels familiar, it should. The string we searched for, Juan M%, is a regular expression, just like the regular expressions we covered in Chapter 8. You can see that every programming language has its own rules and syntax, but huge overlaps occur across these languages. Most languages allow the use of regular expressions to search for text. Many languages allow you to create tables and select their top five rows. Often, when you learn a new programming language, you're not learning totally new capabilities, but rather learning to do things you've already done in new ways.

You can create and work with tables by using Python and pandas, as well as SQL. The advantage of using SQL is that in many cases, SQL can be faster, more reliable, and more secure than pandas. It also may have compatibility with some programs that do not allow you to use Python and pandas.

Combining Data by Joining Tables

So far, we've worked with our players table. But we can also work with our other tables. Let's read in our games table, push it to our soccer database, and then select its top five rows:

```
games=pd.read_csv('games.csv', encoding = 'ISO-8859-1')

games.to_sql('gamestable', conn, if_exists='replace', index = False)

curr.execute('''
SELECT * FROM gamestable limit 5
        ''')

for row in curr.fetchall():
    print (row)
```

This snippet does everything we did previously with the players table: reads it, converts it to a SQL database table, and selects rows from it. We can do the same thing yet again, for our shots table:

```
shots=pd.read_csv('shots.csv', encoding = 'ISO-8859-1')

shots.to_sql('shotstable', conn, if_exists='replace', index = False)

curr.execute('''
SELECT * FROM shotstable limit 5
        ''')

for row in curr.fetchall():
    print (row)
```

Now, our database has three tables: one for players, one for shots, and one for games. This situation is a little new to us. Throughout most of this book, we've had data conveniently gathered into a single table in each of our chapters. However, the data you're interested in could be spread across several tables. In this case, we already noticed that our shots table has detailed information about individual shots, but it doesn't have the name of the player who took each shot. To find out the name of the player who took a shot, we have to find the shooterID in the shots table and then look up this ID number in the players table.

We have to do matching and lookups across multiple tables. If we have to do this only once or twice, manually scrolling through tables is probably not a big deal. But if we have to get the names of players who took thousands of shots, using manual lookups over and over again will become extremely time-consuming.

Instead, imagine if we could automatically combine the information in these two tables. This is a natural specialty of SQL. We can see what we need to do in Figure 11-1.

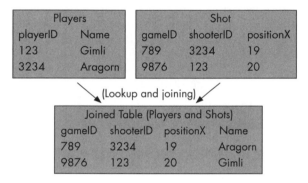

Figure 11-1: Joining two tables together, so lookups become easier and faster

You can see that if we join two tables together, we no longer have to look at multiple tables to find all the information we need. Each row contains not only the information from the shots table but also the shooter name from the players table. We're going to accomplish the joining illustrated in Figure 11-1 by using a SQL query:

```
SELECT * FROM shotstable JOIN playertable ON
shotstable.shooterID=playertable.playerID limit 5
```

Let's look at this snippet, one piece at a time. We start with SELECT *, just like our previous SQL queries. Next, we have FROM shotstable, indicating that we'll be selecting from the table called shotstable. However, that's where the difference starts. We see shotstable JOIN playertable, indicating that we're not going to select only from the shotstable, but instead want to join these two tables and select from the combined table.

But how should they be joined? We need to specify the way to join these two tables. Specifically, we're going to join these tables by looking up where the IDs match. Every place where the shotstable column called shooterID is the same as the playertable column called playerID, we know that our rows match, and we can join them together. Finally, we add LIMIT 5, indicating that we want to see only the top five rows so the quantity of output rows isn't overwhelming.

We can run this SQL query in Python as follows:

```
curr.execute('''
SELECT * FROM shotstable JOIN playertable ON shotstable.shooterID=playertable.playerID limit 5
    ''')

for row in curr.fetchall():
    print(row)
```

Here, we run the SQL query explained previously on the tables in our database. Our SQL query joins our tables together in the way shown in Figure 11-1. In that figure, you can see that for every shooter ID, we found the player with a matching player ID and added that player's name to the matching row of the joined table. Our query does the same thing: since we specify WHERE shotstable.shooterID=playertable.playerID, it will find all matches between shooterID values (from the shotstable) and playerID values (from the playertable). After finding those matches, it will combine information from rows that match, and the final result will be a joined table with more complete information.

After we run our query, we print out the rows that the query has returned. Overall, we've followed the same process we followed before: executing a query with the cursor, then fetching what we selected and printing it to the console.

The output looks like this:

```
(81, 554, None, 27, 'DirectFreekick', 'Standard', 'LeftFoot', 'BlockedShot', 0.104346722364426,
0.794000015258789, 0.420999984741211, 554, 'Juan Mata')
(81, 555, 631.0, 27, 'SetPiece', 'Pass', 'RightFoot', 'BlockedShot', 0.064342200756073, 0.86,
0.627000007629395, 555, 'Memphis Depay')
(81, 554, 629.0, 35, 'OpenPlay', 'Pass', 'LeftFoot', 'BlockedShot', 0.0571568161249161,
0.843000030517578, 0.332999992370605, 554, 'Juan Mata')
(81, 554, None, 35, 'OpenPlay', 'Tackle', 'LeftFoot', 'MissedShots', 0.0921413898468018,
0.848000030517578, 0.532999992370605, 554, 'Juan Mata')
(81, 555, 654.0, 40, 'OpenPlay', 'BallRecovery', 'RightFoot', 'BlockedShot',
0.0357420146465302, 0.811999969482422, 0.706999969482422, 555, 'Memphis Depay')
```

You can see that this output shows the data we want: shots, combined with information about the players who made the shots (their names are the last element of each row). Joining tables in this way can be valuable to enable advanced analyses like the ones we've done in previous chapters.

Joining tables may seem simple, but the process has many subtleties that you should learn about if you want to become great at SQL. For example, what happens if you have a shot with an ID that doesn't appear in the players table? Or, what if two players have the same ID—how will we know which player took a shot that had their ID assigned to it? By default,

SQL performs joining with INNER JOIN. An inner join will return nothing if no player ID matches a particular shooter ID; it will give you only rows where it knows exactly which player took a shot. But SQL provides other types of joins, and each uses different logic and follows different rules.

This is not a SQL book, so we won't go into every detail of the language and every type of join. When you study SQL more deeply, you'll learn that advanced SQL capabilities usually consist of more and more sophisticated ways to select data and join tables. For now, you can feel proud that you're able to do basic SQL queries. You're able to put data in a database, select data from tables, and even join tables together.

Winning Soccer Games with R

R is another language that can be useful for a data science career. Let's go over how to run R commands that will help you with your soccer management career. Just as we did with SQL, we can run our R commands from within a Python session instead of worrying about setting up an R environment. In many ways, R is similar to Python, so after gaining Python skills for data science, you may find that picking up R skills is less challenging.

Getting Familiar with R

Let's start by looking at some R code. Just as we did with SQL queries, we'll start by looking at the R code before running it:

```
my_variable<-512
print(my_variable+12)
```

The first line defines a variable called my_variable. If we were writing Python, the equivalent statement would be my_variable=512. In R, we use <- instead of =, because in R, <- is the *assignment operator*—the collection of characters used to define the values of variables. The <- characters are meant to resemble an arrow pointing from right to left, indicating that the number 512 is being pushed from the right to be assigned as the value of my_variable. After we assign the variable, we can add to it, or print it out, or do anything else we want with it. In our snippet, we print out the value of our variable plus 12 by writing print(my_variable+12).

Just like when we were running SQL queries, you may wonder: How can we run this R code? If you'd like, you can download R and set up an R environment where this code can be run. But instead, we can run it from within the comfort of our Python session, after some straightforward preparation. Let's start by importing a module we need:

```
from rpy2 import robjects
```

In this case, the rpy2 package will be helpful for running R commands within a Python session. Now that we've imported our package, running R code is a breeze:

```
robjects.r('''
my_variable<-512
print(my_variable+12)
''')
```

This is similar to what we did to run SQL code. We can use the robjects.r() function to run any R code within a Python session. You can see that the output shows 524, the result of the addition we did in the code.

So far, we've run simple R code, but nothing related to your soccer management job. Let's run R code related to our soccer data, as follows:

```
robjects.r('''
players<-read.csv('players.csv')
print(head(players))
''')
```

Here, the first line reads our *players.csv* file, using the read.csv() command. We store the data in the players variable by using the same assignment operator as before (<-). In the second line, we print the top few rows of the data.

By looking at this R code, you can see some differences between R and Python. In Python, we use pd.read_csv(), and in R, we use read.csv(). Both are functions for reading *.csv* files, but there are small differences in the way they're written. Similarly, in Python, we need to use players.head() to get the top rows of the data. In R, we use head(players). When we're working with pandas datasets, the head() method gives us the top five rows. But in R, the head() function gives the top six rows. R and Python have many similarities, but they are not identical.

We can read our other tables in the same way:

```
robjects.r('''
shots<-read.csv('shots.csv')
print(head(shots))
''')
```

This time, we read and print the top few rows of the shots data. We can also print out the top few elements of particular columns of our data:

```
robjects.r('''
print(head(shots$minute))
print(head(shots$positionX))
''')
```

In R, the dollar sign ($) is used to refer to columns by name. This snippet prints out the head (top six elements) of the minute and positionX columns in our shots data. The `minute` column has the following top six elements:

```
[1] 27 27 35 35 40 49
```

These are the minutes at which the first six shots (in our data) were taken. The first six elements of `positionX` are these:

```
[1] 0.794 0.860 0.843 0.848 0.812 0.725
```

These are the x-positions at which these first six shots (in our data) were taken. Here, we use the term *x-position* to mean how far "down the field" each shot was taken. One team's goal has an x-position of 0, and the other team's goal has an x-position of 1, so the x-position tells us how close to the opposing team's goal a particular shot was taken.

Applying Linear Regression in R

Whenever we look at data, we can try to learn from it. One thing we might want to learn is how shots from the beginning of the game are different from shots at the end of the game. How does the time during the game influence the position from which shots are being taken? Several hypotheses could be true:

- Offensive players could get more tired and desperate as a game progresses, so they start to take shots from farther away from the goal (a lower x-position).

- Defensive players could get more tired and careless as a game progresses, so players are able to take shots from closer to the goal (a higher x-position).

- Maybe neither of the first two hypotheses is true, or another pattern exists in the relationship between the minutes of a game and the x-position of shots.

To decide which of these hypotheses is true, we can try linear regression in R:

```
robjects.r('''
shot_location_model <- lm(positionX~minute,data=shots)
print(summary(shot_location_model))
''')
```

Here, we use the `lm()` command to run a linear regression. This regression attempts to find the relationship between the `minute` variable and the `positionX` variable in our shots data. Just as we did in Chapter 2, we want to look at the coefficients that are part of the output of every linear regression. Remember that the coefficient can be interpreted as the slope of a line. If we find a positive coefficient from this regression, we interpret that to mean that people take shots that are closer to the goal later in the game. If we find a negative coefficient, we interpret that to mean that people take shots that are farther from the goal later in the game. When we look at the output of our linear regression code, we see that it looks like this:

```
Call:
lm(formula = positionX ~ minute, data = shots)

Residuals:
    Min      1Q   Median      3Q      Max
-0.84262 -0.06312  0.01885  0.06443  0.15716

Coefficients:
             Estimate Std. Error  t value Pr(>|t|)
(Intercept) 8.414e-01  3.291e-04 2556.513   <2e-16 ***
minute      5.251e-05  5.944e-06    8.835   <2e-16 ***
---
Signif. codes:  0 '***' 0.001 '**' 0.01 '*' 0.05 '.' 0.1 ' ' 1

Residual standard error: 0.09 on 324541 degrees of freedom
Multiple R-squared:  0.0002404,   Adjusted R-squared:  0.0002374
F-statistic: 78.05 on 1 and 324541 DF,  p-value: < 2.2e-16
```

If you look in the Estimate column of this output, you can see that the estimated coefficient for the minute variable is 5.251e-05. This is a positive coefficient, so as games progress through time, we expect to see shots that are (slightly) closer to the goal.

Using R to Plot Data

Now that we've performed our regression, we can draw a plot of our data, together with the regression results:

```
robjects.r('''
png(filename='the_plot_chapter11.png')
plot(shots$minute,shots$positionX)
abline(shot_location_model)
dev.off()
''')
```

In the first line, we use the png() command. This tells R to open a file to draw a plot on. We also have to specify a filename where we'll write the file. Next, we use the plot() command. We specify what we'll put on the x-axis first, and then we specify the y-axis. The abline() command is used to draw a line for our regression output. Finally, we run dev.off(). This command turns off the graphics device, meaning it tells R that we've finished the plotting, and the file should be written to your computer's memory. After you run this snippet, you should be able to see the file saved to your laptop; it should look like Figure 11-2.

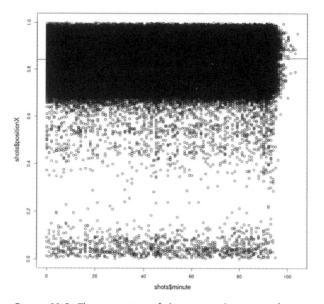

Figure 11-2: The x-position of shots at each minute of thousands of soccer games, with a regression line

If you have trouble finding the output file on your laptop, you can change the filename argument in the preceding snippet. For example, you can write png(filename='*/home/Yossarian/Documents/*plotoutput.png') to save it to any specific location on your computer.

You can see a huge number of shots on this plot, and many are being plotted right on top of one another. The regression line is barely visible—you can see it poking out at the left and right of the plot close to where *y* is about 0.85. It has a positive slope, but it's only slightly positive; very little pattern can be discerned in the shot locations by minute of soccer games. This is something that you could have done with Python, using the code and ideas from Chapter 2, but now you're able to do it in another language as well.

This one plot and one regression won't make you a perfect soccer manager yet, but it will give you information and context that will be helpful as you study what it takes to win soccer games and help your team succeed. Instead of relying on theories or hearsay, you have the skills of a data scientist, so you can determine what works well in soccer games by examining the data directly. After reading this chapter, you can examine data and learn from it not only with Python but also with SQL and R.

We can do so much more with R; anything we've done with Python in this book can also be done with R. In addition to plots and linear regression, you could do supervised learning, k-means clustering, and much more. But already, you know how to do a lot: you can read data, calculate a regression, and draw a plot.

Gaining Other Valuable Skills

After you finish this book and close it, you'll have some strong data science skills. But you can always learn more. One thing you should consider is gaining proficiency in even more programming languages. In addition to Python, SQL, and R, there are many other programming languages that you might want to learn, at least at a beginner or intermediate level. Here are some other languages that you might consider learning:

C++

C++ is a high-performance language; code written in C++ is powerful and fast. It tends to be harder to work with than Python.

Scala

Scala is used for working with big data—that is, datasets that have millions or billions of rows.

Julia

Julia has been growing in popularity in recent years, gaining a reputation for efficiency and the speed of mathematical calculations.

JavaScript

JavaScript is extremely common in web programming. It enables you to create dynamic, interactive websites.

MATLAB

Short for *matrix laboratory*, MATLAB was designed for precision in mathematical calculations, including matrix manipulation. It's often used for scientific computing, but only by people or institutions that can afford its hefty price tag.

SAS, Stata, SPSS

These are proprietary statistics packages. Stata is in common use among professional economists. SPSS, owned by IBM, is commonly used by some social scientists. SAS is used by some businesses. Just like MATLAB, all of these languages also have hefty price tags that often persuade people to use free alternatives like Python, SQL, and R.

Besides these, many others exist. Some data scientists say that a data scientist should be a better programmer than any statistician, and a better statistician than any programmer. Speaking of statistics, you may want to study the following topics in advanced statistics further:

Linear algebra

Many statistical methods like linear regression are, at heart, linear algebra methods. When you read textbooks related to advanced data science or advanced machine learning, you will see notation from linear algebra, and linear algebra ideas like matrix inversion. If you can gain deep knowledge of linear algebra, you'll be better able to master these advanced topics.

Bayesian statistics

In recent decades, a set of statistical techniques known as *Bayesian statistics* have become popular. Bayesian techniques allow us to reason effectively about our levels of confidence about different ideas and how we update our beliefs in the face of new information. They also allow us to use our prior beliefs in our statistical inferences and reason carefully about the uncertainty we have about statistical models.

Nonparametric statistics

Like Bayesian statistics, nonparametric methods allow us to reason about data in new ways. Nonparametric methods are powerful because they require us to make very few assumptions about data, so they're robust and applicable to all kinds of data, even data that isn't "well behaved."

Data science is about more than statistical theory. It's also about deploying technology. Here are some technical skills related to technology deployment you will want to gain:

Data engineering

In most of the chapters of this book, we provided you clean data for analysis. However, in many real-life scenarios, you'll receive data that's messy, incomplete, badly labeled, constantly changing, or otherwise in need of careful management. Data engineering is a set of skills for working with big, unruly datasets in a careful and effective way. You may find yourself working at a company that has data engineers on staff to clean and prepare data for you, but you'll likely find yourself in many situations where you need to do these tasks yourself.

DevOps

After a data scientist performs some analysis, more steps are often required before the analysis is useful. For example, if you use linear regression to do forecasting, you may want to install the regression on a server and have it performed regularly. How and where will you install it? Do you need to update it regularly? How will you monitor it? How and when will you redeploy it? These kinds of questions are related to machine learning DevOps, also called *MLOps,* and if you can gain some DevOps and MLOps skills, you can have more success in your data science career.

Advanced/fluent/efficient programming

A beginner data scientist can write code that works. A talented data scientist, by contrast, can write code that's efficient. It will run fast, and will be readable and concise.

Besides these skills, you will want to gain expertise in applied fields related to the work you do (or the work you want to do). If you're interested in working as a data scientist in the world of finance, you should study mathematical finance and the types of quantitative models that top finance companies use. If you're interested in working for a pharmaceutical or medical company, you should consider biostatistics or even just pure biology as fields to dive into. The more you know, the more effective you'll be in your data science career.

Summary

In this chapter, we discussed other languages besides Python that can be useful for data scientists. We started with SQL, a powerful language used to work with tables. We used SQL to select data from tables as well as to join tables together. We continued with a discussion of R, a language designed by statisticians that can be used for many powerful data analyses. Now you've completed the book, and you have excellent data science skills. Congratulations, good luck, and all the best!

INDEX

V

Varian, Hal, xix
variance, 145
vector
    degree, 196–197, 199, 225
    similarity, measuring, 195
    space, 219

W

\w, 180
web scraping, 169, 171–172, 189. *See also* scraping
    converting results to data, 182–184
    warning, 173
websites, 170–171
    predicting traffic, 118–119

X

x-position, 243

Y

y-intercept, 38
Yum, xxiii

Z

zero-based indexing, 10

Welch's t-test, 68. *See also* t-test
Wilcoxon rank-sum test, 68
wildcard (.), 180
Williams, Robbie, 205
word2vec, 211, 218, 221–224

Dive Into Data Science is set in New Baskerville, Futura, Dogma, and The Sans Mono Condensed.

RESORCES

Visit *https://nostarch.com/dive-data-science* for errata and more information.

More *no-nonsense books from*  **NO STARCH PRESS**

DIVE INTO ALGORITHMS
A Pythonic Adventure for the Intrepid Beginner
BY BRADFORD TUCKFIELD
248 PP., $39.95
ISBN 978-1-7185-0068-6

PYTHON TOOLS FOR SCIENTISTS
An Introduction to Using Anaconda, JupyterLab, and Python's Scientific Libraries
BY LEE VAUGHAN
744 PP., $49.99
ISBN 978-1-7185-0266-6

PRACTICAL DEEP LEARNING
A Python-Based Introduction
BY RONALD T. KNEUSEL
464 PP., $59.95
ISBN 978-1-7185-0074-7

MINING SOCIAL MEDIA
Finding Stories in Internet Data
BY LAM THUY VO
208 PP., $29.95
ISBN 978-1-59327-916-5

BAYESIAN STATISTICS THE FUN WAY
Understanding Statistics and Probability with Star Wars, LEGO, and Rubber Ducks
BY WILL KURT
256 PP., $34.95
ISBN 978-1-59327-956-1

STATISTICS DONE WRONG
The Woefully Complete Guide
BY ALEX REINHART
176 PP., $24.95
ISBN 978-1-59327-620-1

PHONE:
800.420.7240 or
415.863.9900

EMAIL:
SALES@NOSTARCH.COM
WEB:
WWW.NOSTARCH.COM

Never before has the world relied so heavily on the Internet to stay connected and informed. That makes the Electronic Frontier Foundation's mission—to ensure that technology supports freedom, justice, and innovation for all people—more urgent than ever.

For over 30 years, EFF has fought for tech users through activism, in the courts, and by developing software to overcome obstacles to your privacy, security, and free expression. This dedication empowers all of us through darkness. With your help we can navigate toward a brighter digital future.

ELECTRONIC FRONTIER FOUNDATION EFF